INTERNATIONAL HUMAN RESOURCE MANAGEMENT

D1495449

Dennis R. Briscoe
University of San Diego

Library of Congress Cataloging-in-Publication Data

Briscoe, Dennis R.
    International human resource management / Dennis Briscoe.
        p.   cm.
    Includes index.
    ISBN 0-13-191008-6 (pbk.)
    1. International business enterprises--Personnel management.
    2. International business enterprises--United States--Personnel
managment.   I. Title.
    HF5549.5.E45B74 1995
    658.3--dc20   94-47505
                                                           CIP

©1995 by Dennis R. Briscoe
15 Pawnee Dr.
Boulder, CO 80303
Originally published by Prentice-Hall, Inc.

ISBN 0-13-191008-6

Contents

Preface

My primary motivation for writing this book was to develop a comprehensive reference on international human resource management (IHRM) because no such book existed. I needed such a book, and, as it turns out, so do a lot of other people. I wanted it to be as up-to-date and comprehensive as possible and to reflect both empirical research and the state of practice in industry.

The seeds for this book were planted in a number of places. The first seed was probably planted in my overseas work and travel experiences, fertilized by my experience and academic training in human resource management (HRM). These led me throughout my academic and HRM careers overseas to seek assignments and constant learning about the ever-expanding world of international business.

The second seed was planted in my writing of a chapter on international HRM for a text on human resource management. This was the beginning of my awareness that most HRM textbooks did not include much internationalization and my realization that not much information was published anywhere about international aspects of HRM. The only limited exception to this was the scarce literature on the selection, preparation, and compensation of expatriates. Early on I thought it would be fun to expand this chapter into a full text. (Little did I realize at that time how difficult such a task would be!)

The third seed was planted when I was asked to teach a short course on IHRM at Bocconi University in Milan, Italy. My search for materials for this course reinforced my already formed concern about the lack of published articles and books. At that time there were only two books of readings available and a few narrowly focused articles.

The fourth seed that was planted came from my experiences in trying to put together with colleagues from the United States and Italy (and authors from many other countries) a book of readings on the practice of labor relations in twenty-five countries. This also reinforced the realization that there are only limited materials available from traditional journal and magazine sources (or books) with international information about even this area of HRM.

But the last seed that was planted probably was the one that led to this attempt to plant a complete field of information about the discipline of international HRM in a comprehensive text. I was asked to teach a certificate course on IHRM to practitioners and businesspeople interested in IHRM. This course, full of HR managers with international responsibilities and HR managers being assigned such responsibilities for the first time, led me to realize that not only was there a need for better and more comprehensive literature on IHRM for the students (practitioners) but also I needed such literature myself. That is, I didn't know as much about the international aspects of HRM as I thought.

Thus my primary motivation to write this book stemmed from a sense of frustration that such a book didn't already exist. And I wanted and needed to know more about this topic that I found so interesting (as did other professors who wanted to teach full or partial courses on IHRM, researchers who wanted to examine practical and theoretical questions about IHRM, and practitioners who were being given increasing responsibilities for IHRM).

The end result of these experiences was my desire to develop the information and to write the first comprehensive text on IHRM. It was not easy. As the field matures, more research and experience will become available. But this book represents most of what is currently known or experienced. Much of the information in this book was developed from "private" sources; for example, consulting firms, seminars at national and global HRM conferences, and interviews with HRM managers in multinational and global firms. Clearly, increasing numbers of academics and corporate researchers are examining aspects of IHRM and increasing numbers of HR managers are practicing IHRM, with the result that knowledge about what is happening and what should be happening is rapidly developing. I hope this book provides a good resource for researchers, professors, and practitioners as they all confront the types of experiences I had that led me to want just such a book.

I thank all the individuals and firms that helped me in the research for this book; and for their helpful critical comments, Mark Mendenhall, University of Tennessee—Chattanooga; Allan Bird, New York University; Sheila Puffer, Northeastern University; Janet Henquinet, Metropolitan State University; Paula Ann Hughes, University of Dallas; Gary Oddou, San Jose State University; Charles M. Vance, Loyola Marymount University; and Randall S. Schuler, New York University. You are recognized throughout the book for your contributions. But I also must primarily thank my wife, Georgia, our son, Forrest, and the School of Business at the University of San Diego for constantly feeding and supporting my interests in and pursuit of international experience and knowledge. Without them, this book would not have been possible or practicable.

1

Introduction to International HRM

The conduct of business is increasingly global. Markets for most goods and services are now global. At least one in six of all products sold anywhere in the world crosses international boundaries on its way to market.[1] It is estimated that between one fifth and one fourth of the American economy is involved with international trade.[2] In some countries—for example, Germany—this figure approaches one half.[3] One sixth of all American manufacturing jobs depend directly on exports, and over 70 percent of U.S. goods are exposed to foreign competition.[4]

Resources of all types (raw materials, capital, manufactured goods, people, and services—such as insurance, communication systems, information) flow relatively freely across national borders. Thousands of American firms operate abroad, and thousands of foreign companies operate in the United States (as well as in other countries "foreign" to them). It is estimated that at least 2 million Americans live abroad working for their American firms (often with their families). Of course, millions of employees and their families from *other* countries also live "overseas"—in the United States and elsewhere—working for firms from *their* home countries. And millions of people live "abroad" (in foreign countries) working for firms in those countries, as guest workers or as permanent "alien" residents. For example, it was estimated in 1991 that there were 2 million European Community (EC) citizens (and with their families about 5.5 million people) working and living in EC countries other than their home countries. There were another approximately 8 million "guest workers" from outside the EC who worked within the EC.[5] And the volume of international business continues to expand dramatically from year to year within this context.

1

Earlier in this century, it was estimated that much of the total volume of international business was conducted by American firms (although this estimate may not have included much of the trade—particularly of raw materials—from colonies or former colonies to their colonizing countries, such as within the British Commonwealth or with the French, Spanish, Dutch, or Japanese colonial empires). But this is no longer the case. Commerce has truly become global. As recently as 1959, for example, only six of the fifty largest international industrial firms were non-American.[6] But by 1993, thirty-six of the fifty largest—ranked by sales—industrial multinational enterprises (MNEs or, as often referred to, multinational corporations, MNCs) were other than American, with nine different countries represented.[7] In the next fifty, thirty-four of the fifty were non-American, with an additional six countries represented. In the largest global businesses ranked by market value, only twenty-three of the top fifty are American firms and six countries are represented.[8] In the top 500 global service businesses, twenty-five countries are represented.[9]

Because most early international business was conducted by firms involved in extraction (oil, mining) or manufacturing for export (often with imported raw materials), much of the writing about international business is from the perspective of industrial enterprises. But today the reality is that every type of firm is conducting or can conduct international business.

To illustrate this point, the following is a representative list of American multinational firms, compiled to show the incredible diversity of firms conducting business in other countries. These businesses range from the familiar IBM and Coca-Cola to the more surprising Century 21 (real estate offices), Manpower (temporary help offices), and Amway (multilevel marketing of home products). All of these are large firms, which is not meant to suggest that only large firms are active overseas. The diversity of smaller firms operating in foreign countries is, if anything, even greater.

Indeed, the concept of the "national" identity of firms itself is becoming obsolete. When this list was originally developed, the author did not realize (until reminded by others) that at least one of these firms—Holiday Inn, a very traditionally American firm—is now owned by the British firm Bass. As multinational firms acquire, merge with, and carry out joint ventures and alliances with firms in other countries, it becomes increasingly problematic to identify any large firm as purely American or Japanese or British or French. Honda

IBM	Ford Motor Co.	Citicorp
Proctor & Gamble	Dow Chemical	AMOCO
American Express	McDonald's	Holiday Inn
Merck	Fluor	Stanley Tools
Century 21 (real estate)	Universal Studios (films)	Marlboro (RJ Reynolds)
Nike (shoes, clothing)	Nabisco	Avis Car Rental
CNN (TV)	Mattel Toys	Toys "Я" Us
Midas Mufflers (shops)	Haagen Dazs (ice cream)	Levi Strauss
Disneyland	*The Wall Street Journal*	Max Factor
Manpower (temporary help)	AIG (insurance)	U.P.S.
United Airlines	Monroe (auto parts)	Amway

builds cars in plants in the United States and exports them back to Japan; IBM builds computers in France; Whirlpool owns the appliance division of Philips; Firestone is owned by Bridgestone, a Japanese firm; and RCA is owned by Thomson, a French firm. The economy of the world is becoming thoroughly interconnected and global.

The tremendous increase in the volume and nature of international business has occurred for many reasons. These include:

- Increased pressure on costs (so firms move to where labor and other resources are cheapest);
- Search for new markets (for growth and to be able to compete more effectively with global competitors);
- Government policy (that encourages foreign investment for local development, or that may open up markets such as telecommunications, health care, and mass media when public sector firms are privatized, and that encourages local firms to export to develop better trade balances and to earn hard currency);
- Technological development (multinational firms must be willing to search the globe for the best technology because no country now has a corner on it, and new technology has allowed smaller, more flexible manufacturing plants that can be placed closer to the new segmented markets);
- Worldwide communication and information flow, which at least partially creates global knowledge of and demand for products and services;
- The interdependence of nations in trading blocs, such as the European Community, the Association of South East Asian Nations (ASEAN), and the North American Free Trade Agreement (NAFTA) countries; and
- The integration of cultures and values through the impact of global communication and the spread of products and services such as music, food, and clothing, which has led to common consumer demands around the world.[10]

In many industries, purely domestic markets are too small. Even the biggest companies in the biggest countries cannot survive on their domestic markets if they are in global industries. They have to be in all major markets—that means at least North America, Europe, and the Pacific Rim. For example, in the pharmaceutical business, in the 1970s it cost about $16 million and took four to five years to develop a new drug.[11] The drug could be produced in Great Britain or the United States and eventually exported. But development costs would be recovered through domestic sales. Today, though, it costs about $250 million and takes as long as twelve years to develop a new drug. Only sales to a global market can support that much risk.

At least 136 industries—from accounting to zippers—have been identified as global, in which firms have to play "world chess."[12] These industries include autos, banking, consumer electronics, entertainment, pharmaceuticals, publishing, travel services, and washing machines.

The feature IHRM in Action 1.1 describes the experience of Cummins Engine as it moved from being only minimally involved in international trade to becoming a truly global firm. Its reasons for making this move echo the above comments about the causes of increased worldwide commerce, including the need for new sales growth, the search for lower-cost sources of materials, and the need to apply global pressure on its new foreign competitors.

IHRM IN ACTION 1.1
CUMMINS ENGINE GOES
GLOBAL

The emergence of the global marketplace as a center-ring business occurred for Cummins in the latter part of the 1970s. There were four key reasons for this.

1. It began to look in earnest for major new market opportunities outside the United States. Growth in the developed world began to slow and there began to be a battle for market share for diesel engines and related products and services that Cummins Engine was determined to win. But with the development of the Newly Industrializing Countries and their large needs for infrastructure and transportation needs (powered by diesel engines), Cummins felt it was imperative to establish a strong presence in this marketplace as well.
2. The constant search for high-quality, low-cost sources for forgings, castings, and machined components has led Cummins to the purchase of material from a growing list of countries. Product cost reduction is one of Cummins Engine's highest priorities.
3. The worldwide diesel engine industry is rationalizing. There is overcapacity on a worldwide basis. So now that the market has become global, many firms and countries are having to cut back their capacities. Cummins wants to make sure that it emerges as the dominant supplier of diesel engines when this process finishes.
4. In the early 1980s, Cummins Engine and its U.S. original equipment manufacturer (OEM) customers felt for the first time the "hot breath" of foreign competition in the U.S. market—the U.S. heavy truck and equipment market. This competition came first from European truck manufacturers like Volvo and Mercedes Benz, then from Japanese manufacturers like Komatsu and Hino, who offered both complete vehicles and pieces of equipment, or loose engines.

These four conditions—new markets, new sources of supply, rationalization, and new competition—thrust upon Cummins Engine the need to manage with a far more global perspective and with much greater international activity than ever before in its history.

This book is about the implications of this global business activity on the management function labeled personnel management or human resource management (HRM). Thus the focus of this text is International HRM (IHRM).

INTERNATIONALIZATION OF HRM

As more and more firms operate "off-shore," the impact on various business functions becomes more pronounced. Practitioners in each business function must develop the skills, knowledge, and experience in the international arena which will help their companies succeed in this new environment. This is just as true (if not more so) for the human resource management (HRM) function as it is for other functions. The purpose of this book is to describe those skills and that knowledge and experience for IHRM.

Forms of International HRM

In the case of human resource management, potential internationalization can take many forms. From the perspective of HRM practice within any particular company in any particular country, such as the United States, HR managers can find themselves involved in—and therefore must understand—IHRM issues in any of the following possible situations (which include most HRM positions at firms within a local economy, as referred to in Figure 1.1).

The operation of parent-country firms overseas

This situation involves working in the headquarters of the traditional multinational enterprise (MNE), such as Firm X in Figure 1.1. This is the best-known of the international business situations and includes, for example, the operation of firms like Coca-Cola, Ford, IBM, Bechtel, and Citibank that have extensive foreign business activity. Typical HRM responsibilities include transferring of parent-

Figure 1.1 International Human Resource Management

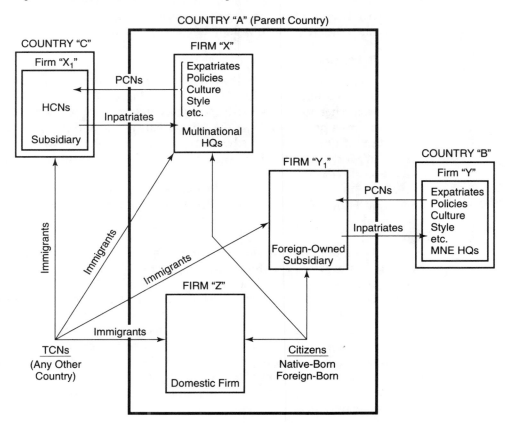

company personnel abroad as well as establishing HRM policies and practices for the foreign operations. Usually the parent firm either applies its parent-country HRM practices directly to its foreign subsidiaries, or it tries to merge its personnel practices with those that are common in the host countries.

As a matter of practice, and probably necessity, local human resource managers are almost always host-country nationals (HCNs). This practice makes sense because the workforce is normally hired locally and work rules and practices must fit local laws and customs. HCNs are more likely to be effective than are expatriate HR managers from the parent firm. But it does create problems with interface for host-country (subsidiary) managers—including HRM managers—who will differ in their orientations from the parent-company HRM managers.

Government agencies and not-for profit organizations

Even though this text primarily discusses IHRM in the business context, many other types of organizations are also international. The U.S. military, the United Nations, the Roman Catholic Church, and Habitat for Humanity International all send hundreds of people from their "headquarters" operations to their overseas operations. Many international human resource activities for these organizations are similar to those faced by their commercial counterparts. For example, the problems associated with locating and compensating employees in multiple countries are not much different for IBM than they are for the International Red Cross.

The operation of foreign firms in the home country

This situation involves the HR manager who works at home in the foreign subsidiary of a foreign MNE, such as Firm Y in Figure 1.1. This includes working with a foreign headquarters and typically involves having to integrate into the local operations a philosophy and organizational culture and practices that are different and/or unfamiliar. Thus human resource management as practiced by the American working in the U.S. subsidiaries of foreign firms such as Sumitomo Bank, Sony, Asea Brown Boveri, or Volkswagen would be included in this category. These firms often want to retain many of their parent-company management styles and HRM practices. Thus HR managers in this situation confront most of the same issues as do HR managers in the first situation, but from the receiving end.

From the point of view of American executives working in these types of firms in the United States, the impact on the American-based but foreign-owned business is generally seen as positive. And yet these executives find the different communication, corporate, and business-practice styles, motivations, and organizational structures, to say nothing of the frequent lack of understanding by the foreign partners of American culture, markets, and employment practices, as generally negative.[13] These negative perceptions by the American executives working for foreign-owned firms in the United States even get worse over time. In one survey *no* U.S. executives who had worked for firms with foreign ownership for at least fifteen years expressed overall positive attitudes about the experience.[14]

The employment of foreign citizens (or recent immigrants)

In the situation of Firm Z in Figure 1.1, the HR manager works in a domestic organization, such as a hospital, a farm, or a restaurant (or the purely domestic operations of an MNE, such as working for a McDonald's fast-food restaurant in any city in the United States), and employs foreign citizens or recently naturalized U.S. citizens to meet job needs. Sometimes this is done because the employer cannot find an adequate number of "traditional" citizens to fill positions. Or it is done simply because these individuals make up a large percentage of the available local labor force. This will include needing knowledge of local laws that govern such employees (such as visa requirements) as well as integrating these employees with different language and cultural backgrounds into the local (domestic) firm. This situation includes the McDonald's that hires recent immigrants from El Salvador, Russia, and Vietnam who barely speak English (as was the situation recently for a McDonald's restaurant in Boulder, Colorado) to the community hospital that hires nurses from the Philippines and doctors from Europe and Asia to universities that employ professors from other countries. The hiring of recent permanent immigrants (or, even, the first generation since immigration) can lead to many of the same concerns as faced by an MNE, such as the merger of cultures, languages, and general work expectations.

The feature IHRM in Action 1.2 illustrates how the firm Barden of Danbury, Connecticut, has dealt with the challenge of hiring recent immigrants and the payoffs for the firm in terms of improved employee commitment and performance and easier recruiting. Barden's experience with recent immigrants from many different countries shows that through creative efforts to integrate these types of new employees, a firm can reap unforeseen yet significant benefits. But it also illustrates that in some (maybe many) communities employers must rely on the hiring of recent foreign immigrants to fill job openings.

In addition, an HR manager could be employed in a situation that might include a combination of these situations, such as being employed by Sony in Southern California and needing to fill many assembly-worker positions with recent Vietnamese and Latin American immigrants.

IHRM IN ACTION 1.2
COPING WITH LABOR FORCE
AND JOB SKILL CHANGES

According to Donald Brush, vice-president and general manager of Barden, a precision ball-bearing manufacturer located in Danbury, Connecticut:

> By mid-1988 it had become evident that we had an opportunity to significantly increase our business. In order to achieve otherwise unattainable goals, we would need to increase our hourly workforce by a net of about 125 employees (that is, in addition to normal turnover, retirements, etc.) in one year. I asked Personnel to test the waters, recognizing that unemployment in the Danbury market had reached an unprecedented low of about 2.5%. The answer that came back to me was a qualified yes. That is, we could do so by using our imagination (e.g., bounties to em-

ployees for successful referrals, imaginative publicity such as an open house) and, importantly, by recruiting workers whose English was very poor.

It was the latter that enabled us to achieve our goal in about six months' time—twice as fast as our original target. In recent years we had come to realize that Portuguese immigrants, for example, became very reliable, long-term Barden employees. We had used a buddy system to help them learn their jobs and to acquire a modest "Barden" vocabulary.

During this recruiting push, we became aware of a significant pool of bright potential employees who spoke little or no English. Our buddy system was wholly inadequate to deal with this veritable United Nations from such diverse countries as Cambodia, Laos, Colombia, Brazil, the Dominican Republic, Guatemala, Chile, Lebanon, Pakistan, Thailand, and Yemen.

To begin to be functioning, qualified Barden employees, newcomers not only must master the basic "Barden" vocabulary and be able to look up standard operating procedures as well as material safety data sheets, they also must master basic shop mathematics, measurement processes, and blueprint reading. This is a tall order for the immigrants (many of whom, we discovered, had received surprisingly good educations in their home countries).

We asked Personnel to investigate how we might teach these people enough English to pay their way. The upshot: We retained Berlitz. A special, intensive course was developed in cooperation with our training unit. We have now educated [1990] four groups of eight, and two more groups are being taught at this writing. All students are on our payroll; they meet with a Berlitz instructor for 4 hours a day for 15 consecutive workdays during work hours. The effect has been electric. The confidence level of the students has soared as they have tried out their new language ability. Supervisors are impressed. And the word is getting out in the community with positive results.

Source: Randall S. Schuler and J. W. Walker, "Human Resources Strategy: Focusing on Issues and Actions." Reprinted by permission of publisher, from ORGANIZATION DYNAMICS, Summer, 1990, © 1990. American Management Association, New York. All rights reserved.

Similar to these situations—and also involving the employment of foreign citizens—is the situation that exists in the parent-country operations of an MNE when it brings "inpatriates," that is, employees from its foreign subsidiaries, to its headquarters or other home-country operations. These could be local-country hires or third-country hires from the firm's foreign operations who are either being developed by the firm for further management responsibilities or who have special skills or experiences that the firm needs in the home country. This type of situation is likely to become more common as firms truly globalize their management ranks (these types of situations will be described in more detail later in the text).

Each of these situations creates special concerns for HRM. One of the fundamental problems is to identify or train HR managers who, although they were raised and experienced in one culture, can effectively interact with and manage people raised in one or more different cultures, and who can develop effective HRM practices and policies in each of the various business environments in which the employer operates. Decisions have to be made concerning issues such as (1) the numbers and proportions of host-country nationals, third-country nationals, and expatriates (parent-company nationals) to staff plants and offices around the world;

(2) where and how to recruit these individuals and how to compensate them for their performance; and (3) whether personnel practices will be uniform across all locations or will be tailored to each location.[15] Whether the local HR manager is a host-country national (HCN), a third-country national (TCN), or an expatriate (parent-country or parent-company, national—PCN), he or she is sandwiched between his or her own culture and the "foreign" cultures. Human resource managers at the local, regional, and headquarters levels must integrate and coordinate activities taking place in diverse environments with people of diverse backgrounds. The reality today is that most firms experience one or more aspects of international HR management, and the successes or failures of these firms are often a function of how well they handle these IHRM concerns.

The Development of IHRM

Some authors argue that there have not been many major developments in the practice of IHRM over the last twenty or thirty years. International HRM has been described as more fact than fiction.[16] Some have suggested that "International HRM is still at the infancy stage."[17] Yet others believe that there is definitely an identifiable "body of knowledge and practice" that provides an important starting point for studying IHRM.[18] However, even though increasing numbers of firms are "going international," the number of published articles in either the academic or HRM practitioner press has not increased much in recent years,[19] which continues to make this body of knowledge and practice more private than public.

One of the reasons for the apparent lack of development in IHRM may be the problems inherent in studying international organization issues. International and comparative management research in general and IHRM research in particular have been criticized as lacking in analytical rigor, relying too heavily on description of organizational practices, being expedient in research design and planning, and lacking the sustained effort needed to develop case material and other types of longitudinal studies.[20]

There are numerous reasons for this. Multinational research is expensive, takes more time, typically involves more travel, and often requires skills in multiple languages, sensitivity to multiple cultures, and cooperation among numerous companies, countries, and governments. All of this conspires to make such research quite difficult. Throw in problems with cultural differences, translation problems, interpretation variances among multinational research teams, and difficulties with research designs such as the use of control groups and the creation of equivalent groups, and one can see some of the reasons for the lack of rigorous research in international HRM in particular and, to a lesser extent, international management in general.[21]

Comparative management researchers have specifically reported frustration with four particular problems:

- Inconsistent and vague definitions of terms like *culture*;
- Inaccurate translation of key terminology (for example, see IHRM in Action 1.3);
- Difficulty in obtaining representative samples; and
- Difficulty in isolating cultural differences—versus those which might be common across varying cultures—amid national economic and political realities.[22]

IHRM IN ACTION 1.3
SOME CONCEPTS DO NOT
TRANSLATE WELL FROM ONE
CULTURE TO ANOTHER

The concept most difficult to translate to different cultures [is] . . . the multidimensional concept of achievement. In most work outside of America, Great Britain, and other Anglo-American societies, this word has been refined to mean autonomy and/or creativity. Similarly, the value-laden concept of "success," which in American literature appears to mean individual success, is not readily transferable to Japanese or Asian cultures. The successful man in Thailand may be one who looks after his extended family. The successful person in North American writings achieves through education, the accumulation of assets, and corporate ladder climbing. The "high achiever" (if such translation were possible) in parts of Asia succeeds primarily in his relationships and in disowning attachment to possessions; corporate ladder climbing has much lower significance. Further, for the Hindu manager in India, uncertainty is not an issue, simply because his whole life is predetermined and certain. By contrast, one's lot is clearly uncertain in Christian societies.

Source: J. W. Hunt, "Applying American Behavioral Science: Some Cross-Cultural Problems," ORGANIZATIONAL DYNAMICS, Summer 1981, p. 58.

Differences Between International and Domestic HRM

Nevertheless, surveys in multinational firms suggest that IHRM differs from its domestic counterpart in terms of a number of factors. These include the following:[23]

Being responsible for a greater number of functions and activities

The HRM department in a multinational firm must engage in a number of activities that are not present in the typical domestic HRM department. These include relocation and orientation of personnel (and their families) transferred to and from other countries, taxation counseling for employees posted to countries other than their home country, assistance with services such as housing in foreign assignments, building close relationships with host-country governments (for example, in order to acquire work visas for expatriates), and provision of language translation services (for business documents as well as for personal affairs, such as housing contracts, personal banking, etc.).

Requiring a broader perspective

International HR managers must expand their areas of expertise to include knowledge of multiple foreign cultures, HR practices, and legal frameworks, as well as global business, economic, and political issues that will impact their HR decisions and practices. In terms of purely HRM issues and of political, cultural, and economic concerns, HR practitioners must have a much broader perspective in order to make effective decisions in this international arena.

Greater involvement in employees' lives

At least initially, as an MNE's international business increases, it tends to use increasing numbers of expatriates from the parent firm (PCNs). Because of the very visible role that PCNs (and their families) usually play in foreign subsidiaries in representing the parent company to the local firm and its workforce, to the local culture, and to the local government, the selection, preparation, and monitoring of these expatriates is very important. This often requires maintaining close involvement in the expatriates' and their families' lives. In many countries, the personal lives and habits of foreigners are as important as are their professional lives and behaviors. In addition, ensuring successful adaptation to the foreign assignment requires helping with travel arrangements, housing problems (both the old and the new), education options for children, obtaining visas, health and safety concerns and so forth.

Having to change its emphasis as the employee mix of parent- and host-country nationals varies at different locations and over time

The next chapter discusses the development of the typical firm's international operations. One of the factors that such development illustrates is the change that occurs in HRM activities as foreign operations mature. Earlier in that development firms tend to rely more heavily on the use of PCNs in key managerial, technical, and sales positions. As foreign activity increases, firms tend to rely more heavily on HCNs. Thus the emphasis will change from managing the expatriation process (for example, with moves from headquarters to subsidiaries) to one of locating and/or training local nationals to take over these key positions.

Experiencing greater exposure to problems and difficulties

The problems associated with purely domestic HRM are great enough. But the IHRM manager's exposure to problems includes all of the typical domestic problems (but in multiple countries) plus the additional difficulty of dealing with the high expense and risk of sending managers and technical people abroad. When these assignments don't work out, the cost to the firm can be quite substantial. To the extent that the selection and preparation of expatriates and key local nationals is an HRM responsibility, HRM is held accountable for favorable results and for holding down the costs involved.

Coping with more external influences

Multinational firms typically keep very closely involved with their foreign subsidiaries. This is also true for parent-company human resource managers. IHRM managers need to maintain close relationships with local governmental authorities, to understand local political and legal systems as they impact employment practices, and to understand local cultures and how they impact the success or failure of PCN expatriates and interaction of HCNs with the parent firm. Issues such as union relations, government regulations, benefit and taxation practices, and health and safety rules will vary from country to country and directly influence how IHRM manages its activities. In addition, the IHR manager is likely to also be involved with administering company-provided or -financed housing, education, and possibly other facilities or services, such as recreational and medical, that may not be readily available in the overseas location. All of these add considerably to the number of outside influences with which the IHR manager must learn to deal.

Having to consider greater overall complexities in decision making

All of the above factors contribute to much greater overall complexity in decision making for the international HR manager. Having to consider the requirements of multiple cultures, of multiple legal and regulatory systems, and of multiple educational and social systems often makes it difficult for IHR managers to determine policy and practice for the multiple operations of their firms throughout the world.

HRM PROBLEMS FOR THE MULTINATIONAL/GLOBAL FIRM

Many of the problems encountered by the multinational or global firm are associated with the responsibilities of the HRM department. Learning to manage workforces in multiple countries is a major challenge. Many such challenges stem from the differences encountered in various countries' cultures. The next few paragraphs provide a short introduction to some of the ways in which cultural differences can impact the selection, training, and management of human resources.

Cultural Constraints

One of the biggest challenges to IHRM, as well as to successful international business, in general, is coping with the significant constraints imposed by cultural differences between countries. Indeed, dealing with these cultural differences may well provide the most important variable in whether or not international ventures succeed or fail. The following is only a short introduction to the nature of this problem.

In terms of sociological and educational issues, constraints such as those listed in Table 1.1 illustrate the variety of concerns with which international HR managers must contend. In particular, varying attitudes about the role of business and management and related values as well as the level of development of and attitudes about education can either facilitate or hinder the transfer of products, services, and business practices to overseas locations. The farther away from the values of the parent country and company are those found in the foreign location, the more difficult it may be to transfer products, technology, and management systems.

A few studies have tried to assess whether or not the wide variety of cultures around the world can be reduced to a limited number of similar categories. If so, it might greatly reduce the number of problems associated with determining management and HRM practices in various countries. The best-known of these studies was performed in the subsidiaries (in fifty-three countries) of one of the major multinational corporations.[24] In particular, this study focused on identifying coun-

Table 1.1 Cultural Constraints That Have an Impact on Management Practices

SOCIOLOGICAL

View toward business and its managers
View toward authority and subordinates
Interorganizational cooperation—between business, unions, government, education
View of "achievement"
Class structure and individual mobility
View toward wealth and material gain
View toward scientific method
View toward risk taking
View toward change

EDUCATIONAL

Literacy level and extent of primary education
Specialized vocational and technical training and general secondary education
Higher and advanced education
Special management training programs (not run by firms)
Attitude toward education and training in general
Education match with requirements of firms
Availability of business education

try differences and regional similarities on the basis of a series of work-related values, including power distance between bosses and subordinates, degree of individualism or collectivism, degree of masculinity or femininity, and degree of uncertainty avoidance or tolerance for ambiguity. Geert Hofstede, the author of this study, found not only that certain countries consistently show similar characteristics based on these factors but also there are clearly major differences between these various groupings of countries. The significant conclusion was that the idea that managerial and organizational systems as developed and practiced in the parent country and parent company should be imposed upon the MNE's foreign subsidiaries is clearly wrong.[25] As discussed earlier, such large-scale research is difficult and expensive. And, not surprisingly, such research has been very difficult to replicate.

Just as this text was being completed, Fons Trompenaars, another researcher from Holland (The Netherlands), published a study similar in scope and size to that of Hofstede (cultural values as identified by over 15,000 workers from over 50 countries).[26] Even though Trompenaars focused on different aspects of culture—such as how different cultures accord status to members of their cultures, the varying attitudes toward time and nature, and differing attitudes toward individuals and groups and resulting relationships between members of society—his overall conclusions are very similar to Hofstede's, ultimately identifying four distinct types of culture into which the countries in his studies can be categorized.

Management Processes

One significant sub-component of cultural differences is encountered when looking at the variations in management practices around the world. There clearly is more than "one best way" to manage successful enterprises. This reality makes it necessary for multinational firms to understand the major differences in management style practiced in different countries and to find ways to accommodate those differences while holding on to the aspects of their own managerial and corporate structures that are necessary for worldwide coordination. The inability to merge corporate and management styles in joint ventures or mergers and acquisitions and the resistance encountered when trying to impose a parent-company style or culture on a foreign subsidiary demonstrate how important this problem can become. Indeed, a survey conducted by the *International Herald Tribune* of firms involved with cross-border acquisitions found that ". . . cultural differences among senior managers are one of the major obstacles to making an acquisition work."[27] Only slightly over half of cross-border acquisitions (52 percent) succeeded with 35 percent of executives in the survey ranking cultural differences as the most important problem and an additional 20 percent ranking unrealistic expectations as the most important.[28]

In terms of particular management processes, there are a number of issues and concerns that are impacted directly by the type of cultural constraints discussed in the previous section. Table 1.2 illustrates a number of these, showing that many activities of management can be influenced by variances in cultural values and practices. Many of these specific problems are of importance to the development of human resource practices in a multinational environment, including issues such as methods and criteria for selecting employees, nature of benefits provided employees, importance of family linkages in employee selection and placement, and the nature of education and job preparation for host-country nationals.

Table 1.3 shows the responses to three of the questions in a survey conducted to determine just how great some of these differences are. These three questions illustrate significant concerns for determining how best to manage. If, for example, an American MNE maintained an ethnocentric attitude (one that holds that how things are done in America and in that company is best, e.g., using a high degree of participation and shared decision making) in managing its overseas operations in the countries illustrated, it would surely have difficulty in Italy and Indonesia, where attitudes in favor of the authority of managers higher up in the hierarchy are quite different than those held in the United States.

A report which synthesizes the few (eight) studies to that time which had tried to determine geographic regions for the purposes of facilitating international management, produced the following synthesis:[29]

MNC Regional Divisions Based on Employee Attitudes

---

1. Anglo: Australia, Canada, Ireland, New Zealand, South Africa, United Kingdom, United States;
2. Arab: Abu-Dhabi, Bahrain, Kuwait, Oman, Saudi Arabia, United Arab Emirates;
3. Far Eastern: Hong Kong, Indonesia, Malaysia, Philippines, Singapore, South Vietnam, Taiwan, Thailand;
4. Germanic: Austria, Germany, Switzerland;
5. Latin American: Argentina, Chile, Colombia, Mexico, Peru, Venezuela;
6. Latin European: Belgium, France, Italy, Portugal, Spain;
7. Near Eastern: Greece, Iran, Turkey;
8. Nordic: Denmark, Finland, Norway, Sweden; and
9. Independent: Brazil, India, Israel, Japan.

Table 1.2 Management Practices Impacted by Cultural Constraints

Planning methods, tools
Time horizon of plans
Degree to which organization is "mechanistic"
Types of performance and control standards used
Degrees of specialization
Degree of centralization or decentralization
Spans of control
Grouping of activities and departmentation
Extent and use of committees
Selection and promotion criteria used
Nature and extent of training programs
Degree of participative versus authoritarian management
Communication structure and techniques
Techniques for motivating personnel
Nature and extent of employee benefits, welfare services, facilities
The ease or difficulty of obtaining employees with the desired skills and abilities
The ease or difficulty of motivating employees—both managers and workers—to perform their jobs efficiently and effectively, and to improve performance
The degree to which individuals identify with their departments and the overall firm
The degree of frustration, high morale, absenteeism, and turnover among employees
The degree of cooperation and conflict common among employees
The degree of information distortion and ineffective communication in the organization
The degree of unproductive time spent in unmeaningful bargaining, restrictive practices, and socializing
The ease or difficulty of introducing changes
The degree to which the "scientific method" is used to deal with problems, both in terms of understanding causation and in decision making
The degree of organizational flexibility to cause or adapt to changing conditions.

These kinds of studies—even if they only confirm managers' assumptions about certain country characteristics—can provide some guidance to general managers and HR managers as they structure policies and practices in foreign operations. At a minimum, these studies provide support for decentralizing many aspects of organizational structure and management and offer a suggestion for creating regional divisions for managing the multinational firm.

Organizational Problems

The next chapter focuses on organizational issues that a firm may confront as its international operations mature from basic export activity to becoming a truly global firm with multiple activities and alliances around the world. The amount of international activity (as a percent of the firm's revenues) as well as the nature of the industry in which the firm is engaged all can influence the nature of the organizational problems that an MNE will confront.[30] The above discussion illustrates many of the issues created by the variety of national, social, cultural, educational, and governmental systems with which MNEs must interact.

In terms of the HRM function, the impact of international activity will vary according to these same considerations.[31] At times there may be considerable demand for international services from the IHRM function (for example, when the need for increased numbers of expatriates arises), but these activities may not be

Table 1.3 Managerial Differences Related to Culture

(PERCENTAGE OF EXECUTIVES FROM EACH COUNTRY THAT AGREE WITH THE STATEMENT.)

1. In order to have efficient work relationships, it is necessary to bypass the hierarchy.

AGREE		
SWEDEN	*U.S.*	*ITALY*
22%	32%	75%

2. The main reason for hierarchy is so everyone knows who has authority over them.

AGREE		
U.S.	*ITALY*	*INDONESIA*
18%	50%	86%

3. It is important for the manger to have at hand precise answers to most questions that subordinates might ask about their work.

AGREE				
SWEDEN	*U.S.*	*ITALY*	*INDONESIA*	*JAPAN*
10%	18%	66%	73%	78%

Source: Adapted from A. Laurent, "The Cultural Diversity of Western Conceptions of Management," INTERNATIONAL STUDIES OF MANAGEMENT AND ORGANIZATION, 13 (1/2), 1983, 75–96.

the essential core of the HR function—partially because many of these services can be provided by consultants or through other forms of temporary assistance. The main role for HRM at the typical MNE is to support the activities of the firm (and the local HR function) in each domestic market in which the parent company is engaged. That is, the HRM function is likely to be fairly well decentralized. However, when the firm is involved with a global industry and is pursuing a worldwide business strategy, the need for coordination and centralization for worldwide consistency of HR policy and practice will become more important. This tension between decentralization/localization and centralization/consistency often becomes the major conflict within the multinational enterprise's strategic management planning and, specifically, within IHRM's support of those plans.[32]

> In order to build, maintain, and develop their corporate identity, multinational organizations need to strive for consistency in their ways of managing people on a worldwide basis. Yet, in order to be effective locally, they also need to adapt those ways to the specific cultural requirements of different societies. While the global nature of the business may call for increased consistency, the variety of cultural environments may be calling for differentiation.[33]

The end result of trying to cope with this problem is to leave HRM with a number of related problems to resolve in the international arena. These problems and their resolutions provide the focus for the rest of this book. A short summary of these key issues include the following:[34]

- How does HRM fit into an international strategy?
- Which HRM practices are *designed* at headquarters? Which locally? By whom? When are international teams to be used?

- How does the firm reach agreement on company objectives while allowing variable (national, local) paths to achieving them?
- How much *consistency* in HRM policies should be insisted on? Which policies should be global and which local? If global, whose laws and cultural practices take precedence? Which are best (for organizational results)?
- Which *nationalities* should be represented by key managers at headquarters and in the main subsidiaries?
- How much and which *expatriation* should occur? Parent country to foreign subsidiary? Foreign subsidiary to parent company? Third-country nationals? Foreign subsidiary to foreign subsidiary?
- How should the whole expatriation process be managed? How are management potential and performance judged when criteria differ from country to country?
- How should the management of careers be orchestrated internationally?

In addition, these issues must be addressed in the midst of trying to manage the day-to-day HRM and IHRM problems of staffing, training and development, compensation, employee relations, and health and safety. In the end, the IHR manager, in order to develop a truly international view, must:[35]

1. Explicitly recognize how home-country ways of managing human resources are a function of cultural values and assumptions;
2. Recognize that these ways are neither better nor worse than others around the world;
3. Take action to make cultural differences discussable, and therefore, usable; and
4. Develop a genuine belief that more creative and effective ways of managing come from cross-cultural learnings.

The value of this sort of comparative awareness lies in the comparison of the various systems, the analysis of the causes that have produced those differences, and then the study of the different solutions found to similar problems.[36] Then this diversity of solutions can be applied to the more effective management of the global enterprise.

The extent to which corporate cultures can or should override national cultures will be at the forefront of the discussion throughout this text. MNEs and global firms have a need for worldwide integration and coordination while retaining responsiveness to local customers and employees.[37] At the local level this means determining what needs to be done differently in the context of requirements for integration. The push from headquarters to conform to a global corporate culture often is met with an equal push at the local level to preserve uniqueness (this issue is discussed in more detail in the next chapter in the context of fitting IHRM practices to the strategic plans of the firm). As discussed earlier, research demonstrates that even within large MNEs, famous for their strong cultures and socializing efforts, national cultures continue to play a major role in differentiating work values. These issues are at the forefront of discussions within the IHRM function, as it helps employers to develop the balance between localization and globalization, and as it tries to figure out how to do that within its own areas of responsibility. This text describes IHRM practices and polices in managing expatriates, repatriates, inpatriates, local workforces, and global managers in the context of trying to find a balance between these pressures for localization and centralization.

Sensitivity to local conditions can be quite complementary to strong corporate loyalty, rather than these being mutually exclusive orientations.[38] Each corresponds to important but fundamentally different strategic requirements in the running of various businesses. As a result, most businesses require that their managers (and their IHRM) provide a blending of sensitivity to local interests *and* loyalty to overall corporate (i.e., global) interests.

> The ideal, then, is to differentiate in such a way as to make integration more effective, or to decentralize activities in such a way that an ever broader diversity gets coordinated by the "central nervous system" of [the] corporation. In matters of cultural diversity, there is always a challenge, but, where this challenge is met, valuable connections result.[39]

THE GLOBAL ROLE OF THE IHR PROFESSIONAL

In order to enhance the competitive advantages of a global firm, its human resource activities need to focus on developing their own international competences.[40] At the same time, the IHRM function needs to shift from an administrative orientation to one that places primary attention on the processes of internationalization so that it can help reconcile the types of organizational paradoxes described above that are inherent in the activities of global firms. This not only creates new demands on how specific HR activities are performed but also sets a new agenda for HR professionals and their global role.

First, HR executives need to learn about the fundamentals of global business. They cannot assume a global strategic role without understanding global strategy. Second, a solid knowledge of strategy must be complemented by the globalization of their individual professional expertises. This rests primarily on the acceptance and understanding of the cultural relativity of many HR practices. And this is in turn complemented by an understanding of how their firms' principle global competitors plan and execute their global HR strategies, what tools and methods they use to build their organizational competences, and what implications for competitiveness arise from their actions.

This understanding of global strategy, cultural differences, and HR capabilities requires a thorough globalization of the HR function by developing a cadre of HR professionals with an international perspective. Presently, however, the number of HR executives with multicountry experience or who are on an international promotion and development track is quite limited.

The lack of international experience among HR professionals is not surprising, but this must change if IHRM is to be recognized as a strategic partner in the management of global firms. Global firms will need not only to set up regional HR positions and assign global responsibilities to corporate HR managers but also select, develop, and motivate HR professionals with very much the same intensity and approach that is currently used for global executives in other areas of management.

Firms that have successfully globalized their human resource activities share several important characteristics:[41]

- The global HR role has the strong support of top management in terms of high expectations about the contributions the IHRM function can make to the formulation and implementation of effective global strategies and the readiness of the IHRM function to step up to its responsibilities.
- The expectations and support of top management for the IHRM role are usually derived from a longstanding commitment to dedicate management energy and resources to human resource issues as a reflection of a people-oriented corporate culture.
- Cultural diversity (including national diversity) is encouraged as a natural way of life.
- Ambiguity as a way of dealing with the many paradoxes imbedded in global HR issues is also accepted as normal. Not much is seen or accepted as "black or white."
- The final condition for a successful implementation of IHRM strategies is the competence and credibility of the IHRM staff. To earn that credibility, IHR managers must accept the risk and responsibility for putting forward policies and practices that make a difference in the achievement of corporate global strategies.

These characteristics are described, explained, and discussed throughout this text. They essentially provide the framework and orientation within which this text presents the current state of international human resource management.

ORGANIZATION OF THE TEXT

The majority of this text discusses the IHRM issues faced by a multinational firm, from the perspective of the parent company or headquarters, mostly from a U.S. perspective (although, to some extent, an attempt has been made to make the discussion relevant to any MNE). That is, the focus will be placed on IHRM problems created by performing business operations in more than one country, rather than those posed by working for a foreign firm at home or by employing foreign employees in the local firm. These latter two issues, however, will be addressed as they become important for particular IHRM responsibilities.

The core functions of human resource management in firms active in global marketplaces remain the same ones managed by domestic firms. These include:

- staffing (discussed in Chapter 3);
- training, development, and performance appraisal (Chapter 4);
- compensation and benefits (Chapter 5); and
- union and employee relations and health and safety (Chapter 6).

Each of these core responsibilities, however, involves additional and more complex activities in the international arena. These additional activities are the primary foci of this book.

The typical activities that support the core IHRM responsibilities, such as HR planning, information systems, and job analysis and evaluation, are also affected by involvement in IHRM. MNE practices in these activities will be examined in Chapter 7. As with domestic HRM, IHRM has also been given responsibility for certain additional support activities that are unique to the international setting, such as providing translation services or handling travel arrangements for expatriates. These responsibilities are also discussed in Chapter 7.

The last individual topic to be examined in this text involves summary discussions of the HRM practices of other countries, especially those of particular interest to U.S. multinational firms—because of their differences from U.S. practices, or because they are found in the major countries in which they operate. These concerns are addressed in Chapter 8.

Lastly, Chapter 9 provides a discussion of future trends in international business, specifically as they affect IHRM.

SUMMARY

This chapter has shown how economic activity around the world has become increasingly integrated. Business interaction has become truly global in most industries. This internationalization of the American (and world) economy impacts every area of business. One of the most difficult challenges to international operations is the management of human resources. An effective and informed HRM function is vital to the success of all firms with multinational operations. Conducting business successfully in more than one country—at any level of activity above import–export—requires the development of culturally sensitive HRM programs. The purpose of this book is to describe and explain the scope and practice of the emerging field of international human resource management (IHRM).

IHRM encompasses many different management issues. There are a certain number of HRM activities in all firms involved in international business that occur purely because of the multinational nature of their businesses. There are other aspects of international business that primarily impact the day-to-day operations of the core personnel functions of selection, training and development, compensation, employee relations, and health and safety. And the activities such as HR planning, HR information systems, job analysis, performance measurement and appraisal, and HR research that normally support the core HRM responsibilities, are also impacted by the conducting of international business. The international nature of all of these HRM responsibilities are described in this book.

ENDNOTES

1. Hodgson, J. D., "Personnel Can Lead the Way in Improving Productivity," *Personnel Administrator*, August 1981, p. 23.
2. U.S. Department of Commerce; and Krugman, P. *Peddling Prosperity: Economic Sense & Nonsense in the Age of Diminished Expectations* (New York: W. W. Norton, 1994).
3. See, for example, Templeman, J., with G. E. Schares, S. Toy, and W. Glasgall, "Germany Takes Charge," *Business Week*, February 17, 1992, pp. 50–58.
4. Central Intelligence Agency, *Handbook of Economic Statistics, 1983*, February 1984; Bergsten, C. F., "International Economic Relations," *Trans Atlantic Perspectives*, February 1982;

Maginer, I. C., and R. B. Reich, *Minding America's Business* (New York: Random House, 1983).

5. "Europeans Resist Open Job Market," *The European,* June 25–July 1, 1993, pp. 1–2; and Rubin, B. L., "Europeans Value Diversity," *HR Magazine,* January 1991, pp. 38–41, 78.

6. "The Fortune Directory: The 500 Largest U.S. Industrial Companies," *Fortune,* July 1959, pp. 125–135; "The Fortune Directory: Part II: The 100 Largest Foreign Industrial Companies," *Fortune,* August 1959, pp. 125–140.

7. "The Global 500: The World's Largest Industrial Corporations," *Fortune,* July 26, 1993, pp. 188–231. (These rankings are published every year in July.)

8. "The Global 1000: A Topsy-Turvy Year for Giants," *Business Week,* July 12, 1993, pp. 52–109.

9. "The Global Service 500: The World's Largest Service Corporations," *Fortune,* August 23, 1993, pp. 159–196.

10. See, for example, Naisbitt, J., and P. Aburdene, *Megatrends 2000* (New York: William Morrow, 1990).

11. Main, J., "How to Go Global—and Why," *Fortune,* August 28, 1989, pp. 70–76.

12. Ibid.

13. Johnson, J. F., "Squeeze Play," *Across the Board,* December 1991, pp. 57–58.

14. Ibid.

15. Dowling, P. J., and R. S. Schuler, *International Dimensions of Human Resource Management* (Boston: PWS-Kent, 1990), p. vii.

16. Morgan, P. V., "International HRM: Fact or Fiction?" *Personnel Administrator,* 31(9), 1986, 43–47.

17. Laurent, A., "The Cross-Cultural Puzzle of International Human Resource Management," *Human Resource Management,* 25(1), 1986, 91–102.

18. See, for example, Adler, N. J., and F. Ghadar, "Strategic Human Resource Management: A Global Perspective," in *Human Resource Management: An International Comparison,* ed. R. Pieper (Berlin: Walter de Gruyter, 1990); Briscoe, D. R. "International Human Resources Management: What Does It Look Like?" paper presented to the Annual Conference of the Association of Human Resources Management and Organizational Behavior, Boston, November 1–4, 1989; Dowling and Schuler, *International Dimensions of Human Resource Management*; Dulfer, E., "Human Resource Management in Multinational and Internationally Operating Companies," in Pieper, ed., *Human Resource Management.*

19. McEvoy, G. M., and P. F. Buller, "International Human Resource Management Publications: Even in the Eighties and Needs for the Nineties," paper presented at the Western Academy of Management International Conference, Leuven, Belgium, June 21–24, 1992.

20. Dowling, P. J., "International HRM," in *Human Resource Management: Evolving Roles and Responsibilities,* ed. L. Dyer, (Washington, DC: Bureau of National Affairs, 1988); McEvoy, G. M., and P. F. Buller, "New Directions in International Human Resource Management Research," paper presented at the Academy of International Business Annual Meeting, Maui, Hawaii, October 21–24, 1993; and Scholhammer, H., "Current Research on International and Comparative Management Issues," *Management International Review,* 15(2/3), 1975, 29–40.

21. See also the appendix in Dowling and Schuler, *International Dimensions of Human Resource Management.*

22. Kreitner, R., *Management,* 4th ed (Boston: Houghton Mifflin, 1989).

23. Adapted from Dowling, P. J., "International and Domestic Personnel/Human Resource Management: Similarities and Differences," in *Readings in Personnel and Human Resource Management,* 3rd ed, eds. R. S. Schuler, S. A. Youngblood, and V. L. Huber (St. Paul, MN: West, 1988).

24. Hofstede, G., *Culture's Consequences: International Differences in Work-Related Values* (Beverly Hills, CA, and London: Sage, 1980); Hofstede, G., *Cultures and Organizations: Software of the Mind* (London: McGraw-Hill, 1991).

25. See, for example, Hofstede, G., "The Cultural Relativity of the Quality of Life Concept," *Academy of Management Review,* 9(3), 1984, 389–398; and Hofstede, G., "The Cultural Relativity of Organizational Theories," *Journal of International Business Studies,* 14(2), 1983, 75–90.

26. Trompenaars, F., *Riding the Waves of Culture: Understanding Diversity in Global Business* (New York: Richard D. Irwin, 1993 and 1994).

27. *International Herald Tribune,* December 1, 1989.

28. Ibid.

29. Ronen, S., and O. Shenkar, "Clustering Countries on Attitudinal Dimensions: A Review and Synthesis," *Academy of Management Review,* 10(3), 1985, 435–454; and Ronen, S., and O. Shenkar, "Using Employee Attitudes to Establish MNC Regional Divisions," *Personnel,* August 1988, pp. 32–39.

30. Porter, M. E., *Competitive Advantage: Creating and Sustaining Superior Performance* (New York: Free Press, 1985); Porter, M. E., *The Competitive Advantage of Nations* (New York: Free Press, 1990).

31. For example, see Dowling and Schuler, *International Dimensions of Human Resource Management.*

32. See, for example, Doz, Y., and C. K. Prahalad, "Controlled Variety: A Challenge for Human Resource Management in the MNC," *Human Resource Management,* 25(1), 1986, 55–71; Evans, P. A. L., "Human Resource Management and Globalization," keynote paper presented at the Third Conference on International Personnel and Human Resources Management, Ashridge Management College, Berkhamsted, Hertfordshire, England, July 2–4, 1992; Evans, P. A. L., E. Lank, and A. Farquhar, "Managing Human Resources in the International Firm: Lessons from Practice," in *Human Resource Management in International Firms,* P. A. L. Evans, Y. Doz, and A. Laurent, eds. (London: Macmillan, 1989); Evans, P. A. L. and P. Lorange, "The Two Logics Behind Human Resource Management," in Evans, Doz, and Laurent, eds., *Human Resource Management in International Firms;* and Evans, P. A. L., and Y. Doz, "The Dualistic Organization," in Evans, Doz, and Laurent, eds., *Human Resource Management in International Firms.*

33. Laurent, "The Cross-Cultural Puzzle of International Human Resource Management," p. 97.

34. Adapted from Laurent, A., "The Cross-Cultural Puzzle of International Human Resource Management," pp. 91–102.

35. Laurent, "The Cross-Cultural Puzzle of International Human Resource Management."

36. Neghandi, A. R., *International Management* (Newton, MA: Allyn & Bacon, 1987).

37. Many authors have discussed this issue. This section is adapted from Schneider, S. C., "National vs. Corporate Culture: Implications for Human Resource Management," *Human Resource Management,* 27(1), 1988, 133–148.

38. Doz and Prahalad, "Controlled Variety."

39. Trompenaars, *Riding the Waves of Culture,* p. 185.

40. Pucik, V., "Globalization and Human Resource Management," in *Globalizing Management: Creating and Leading the Competitive Organization,* eds. V. Pucik, N. M. Tichy, and C. K. Barnett (New York: John Wiley, 1992).

41. Ibid.

2

Development of International Business and Strategic IHRM

The first chapter introduced international human resource management. The human resource department's role is not the same in all firms. Firms differ in their stages of development and in the extent of their international operations. This chapter provides an overview of how these variances in the nature and activities of firms influence IHRM.

EVOLUTION OF THE MULTINATIONAL ENTERPRISE

In order to place IHRM in context, it is necessary to have an appreciation for the development of the international firm. There have been a number of approaches to this issue.[1] The following, therefore, is only a simplified synthesis of these various models.

Businesses pass through a number of stages as they increase their internationalization.[2] Not all businesses pass through all of these stages as they progress from being purely domestic firms to global ones. In general, however, most companies experience all of these stages. These stages are important to the discussion of IHRM because each stage makes distinct demands on the HR department. The HRM function in a firm just beginning to internationalize faces very different responsibilities than does the IHRM department in a multinational, global, or transnational firm (these terms are described in the following paragraphs).

As firms increase their levels of international activity, their organizational structures and HRM responsibilities become increasingly complex. Most large multinational (manufacturing) firms that now have numerous subsidiaries all over the world began their foreign activities by exporting (See Figure 2.1). As this stage became successful for them, they typically proceeded to establish sales companies overseas to market their exports. Where and when the sales companies were able to develop sufficiently large markets, plants to assemble imported parts were established, and, finally, the complete product was manufactured locally. In recent years, additional patterns have developed. Some firms have used complete manufacturing plants as their means of initial entry to certain countries, and others have employed all of these methods simultaneously to reach their worldwide markets.

Obviously the pattern of development experienced in different industries varies widely. A bank, such as Citibank, or an insurance company, such as Lloyds, may initially locate in a foreign country in order to provide services to home-country clients who are active in the foreign country. A firm such as McDonald's has to prepare an infrastructure in foreign locations in order to provide its foreign restaurants with the quality and types of foods such as beef, potatoes, and catsup, and products such as hamburger buns and wrappers, needed before it establishes its traditional fast-food outlets. And department or grocery store chains, such as Kmart,

Figure 2.1.   Evolution of the Multinational Enterprise

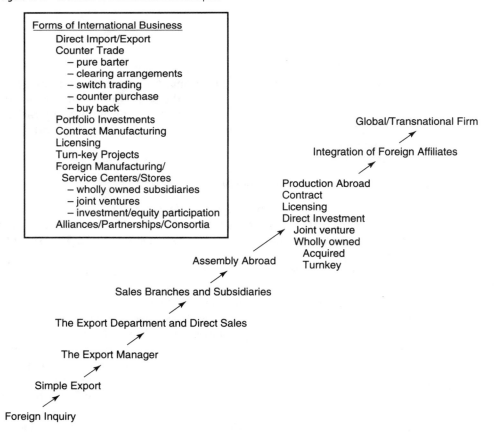

Toys "Я" Us, or Safeway, may acquire existing similar businesses or enter foreign markets by building new stores similar to those in their home countries. Keeping that in mind, however, much of the following discussion is drawn from the experiences of multinational organizations that manufacture their products for either commercial or retail sale. Frequent comments and examples tie the discussion to the experiences of service organizations.

Stage 1: Export

This is the initial stage of internationalization for most firms and usually occurs while the firm is relatively small. Due to a foreign inquiry as to the possibility of buying or selling the firm's product(s) or the desire by the firm to expand beyond its domestic markets, many firms begin to export their products or services to foreign markets through the use of direct sales to foreign customers, or they sell through import/export firms or through foreign distributors. Franchise-based businesses, such as McDonald's, Midas Mufflers, or Century 21, will establish franchises to export their services. Retail establishments, such as banks or department stores, often merge with, acquire, or set up joint ventures with local enterprises to begin their foreign sales.

At this stage, the firm has very few people (if any) from the parent company involved extensively with the foreign sales. Foreign sales will be a small fraction of total sales and they are typically handled by domestic salespeople. Because of this, the HRM department—if there is one (because the firm is typically pretty small)—will have very little if any international responsibility. As foreign sales increase in importance, the firm will assign a sales manager responsibility for international sales. This individual may travel to foreign countries in which the firm has sales but is likely to be chosen purely for reasons of sales experience and competence. Indeed, often employees with little experience or competence are chosen to handle the foreign sales because at this stage the foreign sales are not considered important nor does anyone in the firm yet perceive that they might become important.

Stage 2: Sales Subsidiary

When the sales in any particular country become significantly large, the firm is likely to establish its own sales office there. At least initially, this office is probably staffed by personnel from the home office. The HRM department will become primarily involved in compensation and relocation issues for the parent-company nationals (PCNs) assigned to the sales subsidiary. Selection of salespeople for these offices will probably remain with the sales or marketing function, and little preparation is likely to be provided for the foreign assignments. In addition, the HRM department may be asked to help with selection and compensation for any host-country nationals (HCNs) hired to staff these sales offices. These subsidiaries will initially report directly to sales managers, either domestic (with secondary international responsibilities) or international (if one is created to handle these newly significant foreign sales).

Stage 3: International Division

When foreign sales reach over 10 to 20 percent of total revenues, the firm may choose to form an international division which will be responsible for all international operations. Many service-oriented businesses may begin at this stage, with a significant number of stores or service centers established in one or more foreign countries. At this stage, the industrial organization will begin to consider local assembly and then complete manufacturing of its products and/or services. This division may initially be located within the marketing division, and as sales and involvement increase, it will become an independent division, equivalent to domestic product or regional divisions.

At this level of development, the international responsibilities of the HRM department expand dramatically and become much more complex. Not only will the number of PCN expatriates (people sent from the parent company to work for an extended period in a foreign assignment) increase dramatically but now the HRM department will also become involved with development of HRM policies, practices, and decisions in the foreign operations.

Stage 4: Multinational Enterprise (MNE)

In this stage, the organization's operations in a number of countries reach such size and importance that there is increased need for integration at corporate headquarters. Typically, the MNE has operations in a number of nations with each viewed and treated as a relatively separate enterprise (sometimes this stage is referred to as a multidomestic strategy). The firm may develop global product divisions with global coordination of finance, HRM, marketing, and research and development. Or the MNE may organize into major country subsidiaries with regional headquarters to coordinate operations on a regional basis. Nevertheless, at this stage, the company will have significant operations (assembly, manufacturing, service centers, R&D, branch offices) in many countries and may well reach the condition where half or more of its sales and employment is in foreign countries.

Key personnel in the subsidiaries and regional offices are usually from the company's home offices with many decisions still being made at corporate headquarters. Thus, although the subsidiaries are largely staffed by people from the countries in which they are located, managers from the home office retain much authority. The MNE at this level of development generally views each national market as a specialized market for its particular subsidiaries' products. Each subsidiary concentrates its efforts on the nation in which it is located.

The HR department's role at this stage becomes much more complex and difficult. Now HRM must not only provide services—such as relocation, compensation, and benefits—for typically hundreds of employees (expatriates) working in foreign (to them) subsidiaries or at the parent-company headquarters (inpatriates, or foreign employees transferred for typically two to three years to headquarters), but also coordinate the HRM activities and practices of the many subsidiaries, seeking both consistency with policies of the parent company and accommodation of local values and practices. In addition, training for expatriates, local nationals, and parent-company employees to handle foreign assignments and interaction with foreign counterparts will increase dramatically. Most of the examples in this text describe firms at this level of development.

Stage 5: Globalization

In recent years, many MNEs have reached the state of internationalization where their operations essentially become blind to national borders.[3] Products or services are designed for and marketed to customers all over the world. The best technology and innovative ideas are sought everywhere and applied to individual markets throughout the world. Production and services are created where costs are the lowest, quality is the highest, and time to delivery is the shortest, and delivered wherever demand is sufficient. And resources (money, material and parts, insurance, even people) are sought from wherever the best quality for cost can be found.

These firms are increasingly being referred to as "global" or "transnational" businesses.[4] Reaching this stage of development is not purely a matter of size or maturity in internationalization. IHRM in Action 2.1 describes one moderately sized firm which is making this shift, the Ferro Corporation of Cleveland.

> Running a global company is an order of magnitude more complicated than managing a multinational or international firm. The global corporation—or transnational corporation . . . —looks at the whole world as *one market*. It manufactures, conducts research, raises capital, and buys supplies wherever it can do the job best. It keeps in touch with technology and market trends all around the world. National boundaries and regulations tend to be irrelevant, or a mere hindrance. Corporate headquarters might be anywhere.[5]

At this level of development, the role of the HR department must again shift. Now personnel are hired everywhere in the world, wherever the necessary skills, training, and experience can be found. Worldwide policies are developed for many aspects of HRM responsibility, possibly based on practices followed in numerous places around the world. Management development will require international experience and managers and executives will be developed from all major countries or regions of operation. At the same time, increased sophistication in locating certain HRM practices will become even more important, as the firm tries to be a global enterprise by being seen as a local firm in the many countries and marketplaces in which it conducts business.

This usually means fewer expatriates in local subsidiaries, an increased use of third-country nationals, and broader-based multinational composition of corporate boards and top-management teams. And in many firms this means trying to develop an international corporate culture that transcends national boundaries and national cultures. Key employees must be multilingual, experienced in a number of countries, and culturally sensitive, and their country of origin makes no difference.

The Bechtel Corporation of San Francisco provides a good example of this globalizing of a firm's workforce. In the aftermath of the Gulf War, the Bechtel Corporation was given a major part of the contract to squelch the fires in the oil fields of Kuwait.[6] The HR staff in San Francisco had to sift through 30,000 employee files and 105,000 phone inquiries to mobilize 16,000 Americans, Britons, Filipinos, Australians—people from 37 countries in all— to rectify the Kuwaiti disaster. "We're almost nationality-blind," says Patrick Morgan, human resource manager for special projects at Bechtel. "A person's passport is about as meaningful to us as the name of the bank on their savings-account passbooks."[7] When human resource managers of a firm reach this level of globalization, they too have truly become global.

IHRM IN ACTION 2.1
THE SHIFT TO BEING A GLOBAL
COMPANY

By many yardsticks, Cleveland-based Ferro Corporation, a $1-billion manufacturer of coatings, plastics, specialty chemicals and ceramics, has been a successful international enterprise for almost three quarters of a century. Several of its foreign operations, particularly those in Europe and Latin America, have existed for fifty, sixty, even seventy years. The company currently operates in twenty-two countries on six continents. About two thirds of its employees are non-U.S. nationals, and over 60 percent of its revenues and profits are derived from foreign operations.

Despite its impressive international record, only recently has Ferro become a global company, admits David B. Woodbury, Ferro's vice-president of human resources. "There was quite a bit of sharing of information and technology among our operations in various countries, but each foreign division or subsidiary operated highly independently, formulating much of its own strategy for manufacturing, marketing, finance and human resources," says Woodbury.

Since then Ferro has reorganized its corporate structure to focus on products and business lines across international borders. "Each business thinks of the world as its marketplace now," says Woodbury. "We're developing broad-based global strategies, with increased communications and a greater sharing of assets throughout the world."

High on that list of "shared assets" is human resources. "We realize there is a strong need for global managers," says Woodbury. "We have to identify, train and develop people with an international outlook, skills and experience. Like all other facets of the corporation, human resources has to evolve into a global operation."

Source: E. Brandt, "Global HR." Reprinted with permission of PERSONNEL JOURNAL, March, 1991, © 1991, ACC Communications, Inc., Costa Mesa, CA. All rights reserved.

At this stage, which is sometimes touted as the direction in which all international commerce is headed, the salient management (and HRM) question may become how to manage the cultural diversity that this level of business activity necessarily experiences.[8] When integration is needed (as in joint ventures and in development of global workforces), cultural diversity needs to be valued but to have its impacts minimized; but when cultural diversity is needed to differentiate products and services to meet local markets, other corporate practices are required.

As discussed at the end of the last chapter, this tension between integration and differentiation is becoming a major problem for IHRM and large global firms.[9] Firms must become simultaneously more highly differentiated and more integrated or coordinated. Local nationals may feel that they can run operations in their own countries, even though their firms now require a global perspective and global qualifications. And local laws and practices may dictate certain HR practices and yet an international perspective may require different approaches to routine HR responsibilities.

As Percy Barnevik, president and CEO of ABB Asea Brown Boveri, puts this issue:

> You want to be able to optimize a business globally—to specialize in the production of components, to drive economies of scale as far as you can, to rotate managers and technologists around the world to share expertise and solve problems. But you also want to have deep local roots everywhere you operate—building products in the countries where you sell them, recruiting the best local talent from the universities, working with the local government to increase exports. If you build such an organization, you create a business advantage that's damn difficult to copy.[10]

Most of the discussion in this book will be focused on IHRM practices as they apply to traditional MNEs and the newly emerging global or transnational enterprises. However, this difference between multinational and transnational firms is significant.[11] In the traditional multinational company, free-standing subsidiaries or stand-alone foreign operations may be so loosely affiliated that valuable opportunities for economies of scale, joint marketing efforts, or shared technology may be lost.

In HRM, the MNE philosophy of staffing with locals sounds reasonable. But if only Frenchmen work in France, only Chinese in China, and only Americans in the United States, the firm loses the input of talented individuals with different backgrounds and perspectives on products, services, markets, and international needs. And this may limit the firm's awareness of new technologies and product ideas enough so as to create a definite competitive disadvantage relative to more global competitors. And such diverse perspective is also important to IHRM, bringing multiple viewpoints and experiences to bear on human resource problems in the parent company as well as in subsidiaries.

Stage 6: Alliances, Partnerships, and Consortia

Firms at this stage of international development do not necessarily replace the MNE or global/transnational firm.[12] But it is the next step in internationalization. Increasingly global firms are developing alliances, partnerships, joint ventures, and other kinds of linkages to draw upon resources (technology, research, laboratories, personnel, materials, parts and supplies, etc.) that can give the firm advantages it would not have access to any other way.

For example, MCI Corporation, a $6-billion, 18,000-employee firm with annual growth of 22 to 25 percent, gets its technology from fifty-three major subcontractors located all over the world, including its major competitor, AT&T.[13] MCI owns a \$65-million R&D complex but doesn't develop new technology there. Instead, this is where MCI takes leading-edge technologies developed by the independent contractors and tests, perfects, and integrates them into the MCI telecommunications network. In an industry where new products routinely become obsolete in about thirteen months, MCI finds it more efficient to spend time looking for innovative subcontractors than developing its own technology. MCI's executive vice-president explains, "I have access to the intellectual assets of [other firms'] 9,000 engineers. If I did my own development, what would I have? 500 engineers?"[14]

Other examples of recent cross-border linkages include IBM and Siemens pooling resources to develop and produce advanced computer chips and FORD linking with Mazda for minivan design and development. Such alliances are becoming more common, yet the human resource problems associated with coordinating workforces and managements from firms in different countries remain the primary stumbling blocks to gaining the desired benefits.

In summary, the two basic means for going overseas are exporting products or services to foreign markets or manufacturing or producing those products or services in the local markets. Many different forms of business structure can be used to expand into international commerce which is conducted in foreign countries. These include (1) wholly owned subsidiaries (acquired or built from the ground up, i.e., turn-key operations); (2) partial ownership of—investment in—existing operations (an option being actively encouraged by the newly opened Central and Eastern European countries); (3) joint ventures (two partners—usually one foreign and one local—creating a new entity in which each has some equity participation); (4) licensing (of local manufacturing in which the local firm handles promotion and sales); (5) contract manufacturing (in which the foreign firm continues to handle promotion and sales); and (6) franchising (local ownership).

Each of these levels of involvement and types of organizational structure creates different requirements for HRM policies and practices. In the simplest form of international business, that is, *export*, few employees are sent on international business trips and none on expatriate (longer-term) assignments. The overall impact on the HRM department is very limited. But as a firm moves to larger sales offices overseas and even to *assembly* and *production* (in the case of manufacturing) or *complete offices* or *stores* (in the case of service businesses), the HRM implications increase steadily. Such a firm will send parent-country sales representatives to market products overseas, technical experts to transfer technology to overseas production sites, and managing directors and financial officers to control overseas operations. At this stage, foreign operations are typically viewed as sites for replicating what has already been done at home. Thus parent-company management style, corporate culture, and HRM practices are usually transferred to the foreign locations. The international operations are still viewed as secondary to the success of the firm.

Further development, however, brings the international operations to greater responsibility for revenue and profit generation and thus for the success of the firm. The best employees will be utilized in foreign assignments, and firms will begin to develop an international management pool with a common language and culture. Often these more "advanced" stages of international involvement are achieved through acquisition of existing foreign operations or merger with such. International mergers and acquisitions present even more complex problems for IHRM and will be discussed in some detail later in the chapter.

The Organizational "Chart"

The basic configurations of international organizations are similar to those of purely domestic firms. The larger the firm, and the more complicated in terms of multiple locations, products, services, and functions, the more complex the organizational structure.[15] The types of structures that firms use to manage their foreign activities can generally be divided into three categories based on the degree of internationalization:

> 1. *Little or no formal organizational recognition of the international activities of the firm.* This category ranges from domestic operations handling an occasional international transaction on an *ad hoc* basis to the establishment of a separate export department, usually within the existing marketing structure.
>
> 2. *International division.* Firms in this category recognize the ever-growing importance of their international sales by establishing what is essentially a marketing division for international sales. Sometimes this division reports to the vice-president of sales and sometimes it is an independent division reporting directly to the senior operating officer.
>
> 3. *Global organizations.* The most complex international firms structure their complete firms on a global basis. This may initially mimic their domestic structure, with the firm organized by one of the following: product line, geographic region, traditional functional responsibility, processes peculiar to the firm's industry (e.g., exploration and mining operations for a mining firm), or customer (when the firm serves very different types of customers, such as commercial versus government customers). And, of course, many firms have developed organizational structures that use more than one of these possibilities. As multinational firms have grown and become more complex, their structures have also grown and become more complex, such that now many of the largest truly global firms, such as Asea Brown Boveri, Unilever Corporation, IBM, Ford Motor Company, Coca-Cola, Motorola, Whirlpool-Philips, General Electric, and Ciba-Geigy, now have very complicated organizations that combine local companies with regional, functional, and product line reporting and committee structures.[16]

Indeed, the typical (if there is such) global firm today is dissatisfied with its organizational structure and is searching for new ways to provide the necessary coordination to take advantage of worldwide innovations and resources while ensuring that local customer demands are met effectively. All of the traditional sources of organizational differentiation (as mentioned above) have something to contribute; yet each must be ready and willing to interact with the other interests of the firm in ways that lead to achievement of truly global objectives. IHRM becomes a major player in this milieu, not only in terms of advice pertaining to the strategic use of human resources but also as a consultant on the actual organizational processes themselves (this is described in more detail later in the chapter).

IHRM in Action 2.2 describes the reorganizing efforts of Fluor Corp., one of the world's largest engineering and construction services firms. Fluor provides an example of how to more effectively use a global workforce that can result in higher profits for the company.

IHRM IN ACTION 2.2
FLUOR: HOW TO MINE HUMAN
RESOURCES

It's the corporate conundrum of the nineties: how to do more work with fewer people, while improving quality and customer service. Fluor Corp., the engineering and construction services giant, has an answer. Since 1990, Fluor's mining and metals unit has seen its quarry of engineering projects grow 230 percent—from $300 million to over $1 billion—with only a 25 percent increase in its workforce.

What's the trick? Three years ago the mining and metals operation took enough time off from designing steel mills and copper smelters to reengineer itself. Investing heavily in training and technology, it has learned to stretch its management talent in ways that many a wide-ranging multinational could emulate.

Before the reorganization, each local office operated autonomously, with its own team of engineering, procurement, marketing, and operations managers responsible for the bottom line at its site. Besides adding overhead, this setup kept the offices from cooperating and sharing talent.

Today one team of mobile managers, who communicate constantly via fax, phone, and E-mail, preside over all the offices, moving work and technical talent among sites as needed. Says Victor Medina, general manager of the mining and metals division, "We are conscious of the fact that we're in the business to run projects. We're not in the business to run offices." Through electronic work sharing, engineers in New Orleans are preparing drawings for a copper mine expansion on the Indonesian island of Irian Jaya. Similarly, the Vancouver office has done structural engineering work for Fluor's Quebrada Blanca project—a challenging copper mine being built 14,000 feet up in the Andes. The Vancouver engineers used to be fully utilized about 40 percent of the time; now its 90 percent.

INTERNATIONAL HRM STRATEGY

In the ideal world, a firm conducting international business will be actively engaged in strategic planning and strategic management. The firm will regularly perform an environmental analysis (of its external threats and opportunities and its internal strengths and weaknesses) and develop strategic plans, objectives, and actions for its international efforts based on that assessment. Further, all components of the business, from financial to operations to HRM, will be closely integrated into that strategic planning and will be involved with strategic planning within their own areas of responsibility. In reality this is rarely the situation.

Many of the same HRM issues arise—albeit in a more complex way—when a firm's strategic planning "goes international" as when its strategic planning is concerned only with domestic issues. When management teams begin to develop and implement global strategic plans, they also begin to concern themselves with global human resource issues.[17] Indeed, the HR issues may be the critical issues for successfully competing in the international marketplace.

Regrettably, little study has been made of the extent to which multinational firms involve their HRM functions with their global strategic planning. For example,

> An important management issue is the design of the international human resource management (IHRM) system, yet there has been little research on what determines the type of human resource management system an MNE chooses for its overseas subsidiaries. A key choice the MNE must make regarding the type of HRM system it institutes in its overseas subsidiary is whether it will allow each subsidiary to create its own HRM system, attempt to create a consistent HRM system between HQs and subsidiaries, or develop a global HRM system that is created from practices developed in both the HQs and subsidiaries. Typical ways of achieving consistency are to transfer the HQ's own HRM system to overseas subsidiaries, or to transfer HRM practices between overseas subsidiaries themselves.[18]

In the late 1970s, MNEs were only beginning to integrate HRM with their international strategic management.[19] Even this was quite limited, taking place in the context of discussions concerning acquisitions or divestitures of overseas facilities, entering or withdrawing from foreign markets, proposed corporate structures and management systems to accommodate different nations and cultures, the means for controlling relationships between overseas subsidiaries and the parent firm, and procedures for effectively managing the fundamental elements of the HRM system (e.g., staffing policies and practices in multiple countries, compensation and benefits systems, labor relations, etc.). And these discussions are most likely to occur in a context of close personal relationship between the senior HR executive and the firm's CEO.

All of these concerns are becoming increasingly important to the global firm. But anecdotal evidence and limited first-person comments in the international business and HR literature suggest that firms are not much more likely in the 1990s to incorporate their HR managers into their strategic global planning than they were in the 1970s.

HR managers can and should provide essential advice and input at every step of the traditional strategic management process (refer to Fig. 2.2). Whether formally stated or informally developed over a period of time, an organization's *strategy* is its master plan that determines the crucial courses of action that it will take in order to achieve its objectives or vision. It is the blueprint that defines how the organization will deploy its resources in order to exploit present and future opportunities and to counteract present and future threats. It is with the development of the firm's strategy that its planning for business activity should begin.

As illustrated in Figure 2.2, the HR department should provide input at each step of the strategic management process. For the international firm, this input should involve the HR department's unique knowledge and perspective about the ever-important human resource issues as they impact planning for global operations. Every step in the strategic management process, including determining the advisability of various missions and goals, assessing the threats and opportu-

34

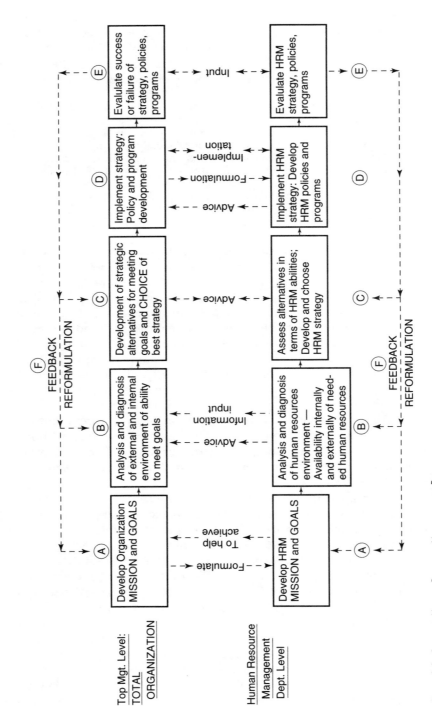

Figure 2.2. Strategic Human Resource Management Process

nities in external (global) environment and organizational strengths and weaknesses to deal with that environment, developing the alternatives and choice of overall strategies, and deciding how to implement such chosen strategies all should include analysis of firm and local labor forces, comparisons of corporate and national cultures and management systems, evaluation of local employment practices and of labor costs and tax and benefit compatibilities, among other IHRM inputs.

Therefore, a number of problems for MNEs arise that HR departments can and should help resolve. These include the HR implications in decisions about the following issues.

- Acquisition or divestiture of overseas facilities/firms;
- Entering or withdrawing from markets;
- Proposals for redesign of corporate organizational structures to accommodate different cultures or geographic areas;
- Means for controlling relationships between overseas subsidiaries and the parent company;
- Means for effectively managing the HRM system in multiple foreign locations;
- Assessment of major international events such as EC 1992, Hong Kong 1997, North American Free Trade Agreement and the like.

IHRM in Action 2.3 describes the involvement of Merck & Co.'s HR executives in the firm's international business. Merck & Co., voted America's most-admired firm by *Fortune* magazine for a number of years in a row, is a giant in the pharmaceutical industry worldwide. It is obvious from the accompanying remarks that Merck's executives expect their human resource function to play a major role in the achievement of the strategic global objectives.

IHRM IN ACTION 2.3
IHRM AT MERCK & CO.

In October 1988 over one hundred human resource managers from Merck facilities in twenty countries gathered in Montreal for the Human Resources Conference. This week-long meeting was centered on the theme "The Globalization of Management Issues: Toward the Year 2000." The program emphasized the role of human values in Merck's drive to excel in an era of intense global competition. Most of the top executives in the company journeyed to Montreal to address the conference.

Merck's CEO Roy Vagelos began his talk by quoting from Proverbs: "Where there is no vision, the people perish." He went on to emphasize that Merck focuses on the knowledge and capabilities of its people. Its goal is to be the leader of innovation in the pharmaceutical industry. To do that, Vagelos told the attendees, all Merck employees must ask themselves, "How can I add value to what I'm doing today?" The role of human resources is to provide development programs for employees so that they can grow and be capable of competing in the global marketplace.

Jerry Jackson, president of Merck, Sharp, and Dohme International, noted there is a crucial need to develop the organization's resources to meet the challenges of globalization. He stated that Merck must successfully address these key issues:

1. The growing complexity of the global market.
2. The European Community in 1992.

3. Emergence of Japan as a major global player.
4. Global product availability.
5. Launching new products while maintaining current products.

He concluded by stating, "You, human resources, will be our partners in meeting these challenges [of globalization]."

John Zabriskie, president of Merck, Sharp, and Dohme, talked about business strategies and globalization. He said, "Global opportunity is founded on several management principles. Those that strongly impact human resources are: (1) employee strength, (2) cultural harmony, (3) shared objectives, (4) training as renewal, (5) pervasive communication, (6) new value measures, (7) focus on the outside, and (8) belief in human dignity."

Noel Vichy, professor of business administration at the University of Michigan, one of a number of outside presenters, challenged the participants with the question, "How can Merck continue to get executives with a global mind-set who can cooperate cross culturally within the company, and how can Merck ensure the ongoing development of mechanisms to operate worldwide?" He told them that "to respond to your CEO's challenge, you need to mobilize."

The program focused on the idea that people are the key to success in a high-tech industry such as pharmaceuticals and emphasized that the role of human resources is absolutely critical. Again and again the theme was one of partnership between human resources and management. Vice-Chairman John Lyons put it squarely on the participants' shoulders: "You are the builders who see the vision."

Walt Trosin, vice-president of human resources, chaired a final panel discussion. In his remarks at the conclusion of the conference he said, "This week in Montreal we have heard and learned a great deal about what will be expected of us in the coming years at Merck as the company works to achieve the stretch goals that Dr. Vagelos has defined for us. The 1990s will require personal growth and development for all of us. Our roles may change; certainly we will need to become more knowledgeable of the business problems facing our clients if we are to make a full contribution. We must continue to earn the partnership we share with Merck managers worldwide."

Jack Fitz-enz, one of the outside presenters, observed about the conference: The conference speakers dwelt on strategic themes. No one talked about tactical matters such as employee testing, performance review programs, or training techniques. At Merck, they know that success is built on a common strategic focus. Tactics come after everyone understands the problems and opportunities. Merck has developed a reputation for doing things right, and this shows in its products, in its relationships with its employees, and in its profits. This type of participation of corporate human resources in the strategic management of the firm is one of the reasons for this success.

In the end, however, the critical strategic decision for the IHRM department itself is the resolution of the dilemma created by the conflict between centralization for control and international consistency of policies and decentralization to meet local requirements. As was discussed thoroughly in the first chapter, there is no easy answer to this choice: Should the MNE superimpose parent-company HRM practices on its international subsidiaries (with the local HR office run by an HR manager from the parent firm), or should it allow subsidiaries to follow local customs, laws, and practices as much as possible (with the local HR office usually run by a local national HR manager)? The experiences of long-term multinational firms suggests that the trend is to move toward more local control and management over time, which is consistent with the pattern described in the first part of this chapter. And yet, as will be discussed in greater detail later in the book, successful multinational firms have found ways (such as cross-national management training, cross-national assignments for management development, and cross-national project teams) to develop a common set of values and culture to ensure worldwide pursuit of a common corporate vision and objectives.[20]

IHRM in Action 2.4 illustrates how the human resource department of Ericsson, the Swedish global telecommunications firm, has integrated its own IHRM strategy into that of the corporation. One aspect of that integration, from which IHRM in Action 2.4 is adapted, is the brochure *Foundation for Human Resource Work in Ericsson,* published by the HR department to communicate both within and outside of Ericsson the IHRM strategy.

IHRM IN ACTION 2.4
A CORPORATE APPROACH TO
HUMAN RESOURCE
MANAGEMENT

STATEMENT FROM BRITT REIGO, CORPORATE DIRECTOR OF HUMAN RESOURCES:

The ability of Ericsson to attract, retain, and motivate competent people is fundamental to the achievement of its corporate objective—to be the leading international supplier of advanced telecommunication systems and services.

It is our obligation in the HR function to ensure that Ericsson is regarded as an Excellent Employer in all our operations throughout the world. *The employer of choice.*

This objective will be primarily achieved through the development and reinforcement of a strong corporate culture based on our values: Professionalism, Respect, Perseverance.

"The Foundation for Human Resource Work in Ericsson" derives from the statements given above. Executives, HR managers, and employees all over the world have contributed in the preparation of this document, which will serve as a guide for all of us engaged in the field of human resource management.

If all our activities are based on our values—then we will succeed in developing and making the best of Ericsson's most valuable asset—our employees.

HOW CAN THE HUMAN RESOURCE FUNCTION CONTRIBUTE?

Let us derive advantage from Ericsson's size by capitalizing on our organization's collective competence: Let us generously share our experience! This means that it is important for all of us to develop our own competence.

Build networks in the HR function! Work in projects and competence teams across borders and organizational boundaries! In this way we will be better able to ensure that Ericsson continues to develop as a modern organization.

The HR function wants to extend its activities to include tasks other than those related to traditional personnel administration. We want to widen our focus, understand business, promote change, and so contribute to the development of Ericsson. The ambition of the HR function is to be a natural, professional, and respected member of the management team, and act as the team's strategic partner.

An HR professional must be able to assert integrity. The nature of HR issues requires the ability to deal with a large number of groups, which may have contradictory interests—managers, employees, union representatives, and employers' associations, and so on.

HR professionals must be able to understand the conditions of international cooperation and respect differences. This will be emphasized through the ongoing process of change, and through increased cooperation and mobility across borders. HR professionals must function as catalysts, develop new methods and tools, influence attitudes and values, provide service to managers and their coworkers, and also act as consultants. Feedback on behavior and measures taken by managers is essential, since their behavior is always to reflect Ericsson's values: *Professionalism, Respect, and Performance.*

ERICSSON AS AN EXCELLENT EMPLOYER

To attain our objective of being regarded as an Excellent Employer, we must do much more than offer interesting tasks and fair pay. To be an excellent employer we have to satisfy other requirements too. Individual employees should feel:

- That they are respected as individuals.
- That, through their proficiency, know-how, and behavior, they join in the creation of products and services of great value to other people, and that they take part in a significant development process.
- That individual achievements contribute to progress—both within and outside the company.
- That they are recognized and rewarded for their value and enjoy an environment with rewarding interpersonal relationships.

DIRECTION FOR THE FUTURE

We will:

- Develop and practice a dynamic corporate human resource philosophy, based on our values: Professionalism, Respect, and Perseverance.
- Shape our working climate, our leadership, and our organization, to match with this philosophy.
- Emphasize everyone's freedom to take responsibility, and to communicate effectively in a flexible organizational structure.
- Broaden individuals' experience and perspectives by encouraging transfer across organizational boundaries and a limited period of service in one position.
- Overcome cultural differences by inviting employees from different countries to participate in development.

- Develop information systems into efficient channels that meet the need for a broad exchange of information within Ericsson, and enable the individual employee to acquire a sound knowledge of the Company and its operations.

Various researchers have identified three different possible approaches by MNEs to fit their IHRM activities to those of the firm.[21] These include an *adaptive* approach (fitting subsidiary HRM activities to the local environment), *exportive* (full transfer of parent-company HRM practices to foreign subsidiaries), and *integrative* (development of a worldwide HRM system, drawing on the best HRM practices from subsidiaries as well as from headquarters). The particular approach used depends on factors such as (1) whether top management believes that the firm possesses a special HRM competence; (2) the firm's administrative heritage (and thus the firm's abilities to transfer centralized policies); (3) the firm's particular global strategy as to degree of localization versus globalization; (4) whether top management believes that HRM is important to the firm's competitiveness; (5) the extent of the firm's resources to train subsidiaries in central policies or to identify and transfer policies from multiple locations; and (6) the level of centralization of the HRM system used by the MNC in its home country.

In reality, a firm's business strategy, HRM strategy, and HRM practices interact within and with an external environment of national culture, power relationships between various economic and social groups, legislation, education, employee representation, and union relations that vary from country to country.[22] The end result is that effective HRM strategies and practices also vary in response to that external environment. There is not "one best way," nor is there one best way to match HRM strategy with local and global conditions and strategies.

INTERNATIONAL MERGERS AND ACQUISITIONS

Increasingly, international businesses gain access to markets, products, and technologies around the world through a global strategy of buying or merging with existing firms in other countries.[23] Many of these international mergers and acquisitions fail, however, because of inadequate consideration of the IHRM implications. These IHRM complications often include issues such as an overestimation of the abilities—particularly the human resource abilities—of the acquired firm, an exaggerated assumption of synergies available from the merger, inadequate attention to the incompatibilities of the two firm's cultures, and unwillingness to prepare for the frequently experienced loss of productivity and staff after the acquisition is completed.

Firms can greatly increase their probabilities of success in their cross-border mergers and acquisitions if they get their HR managers involved early in the planning process. Even without recognition by top management of the strategic role that IHRM can and should play in such decisions, and the help that IHR managers can provide in the merger of different business cultures, there also are many critical IHRM concerns that need to be addressed in any proper process of "due diligence" analysis of the firm(s) to be merged or acquired. If this isn't done properly or well, it is often HRM issues that create the problems that result in failure in the end. Therefore, the following provides a short introduction to the role that IHRM can play in this process of due diligence.

Every area of IHRM responsibility needs to be examined in the firm(s) of the seller. In every area there are potential liabilities. These include attention to compensation systems and levels, benefits, labor relations and contracts, HR information systems, environmental and safety concerns, medical and health-care programs, and variances in administrative support. In addition, IHRM needs to realize and understand its multiple roles in this merger and acquisition process as fact finder, negotiator, facilitator, communicator, technical specialist, environmentalist, "good will" ambassador, and business manager. IHRM must also have access to the assistance of a number of other specialists, such as HRM legal counsel in each affected country, actuaries and benefit consultants, and environmental consultants.

An example of the type of information that must be gathered and analyzed for compatibility of the firms and the cost of the acquisition or merger would include the nature of any employment contracts, any pending employee litigation, all redundancy and termination notice and payment requirements and obligations, collective bargaining contracts and obligations, review of all employee documentation (handbooks, work rules, works councils, offer letters, etc.), pension obligations and other benefit liabilities, nature of employee insurance programs, bonus schemes, incentive programs and obligations, special perquisites (company cars, golden or tin parachutes, loans, etc.), special consultancy agreements, and so forth. This is only the surface of the types of data that need to be examined to do a thorough job of the necessary due diligence prior to completing any merger or acquisition agreement. In the end, incompatibilities in these areas can be just as significant to the failure of mergers and acquisitions, as are more purely financial concerns.

If IHRM is going to be able to provide the strategic assistance to its employer as is important to international success, it is going to have to be closely involved in every form of decision and planning for going international, including the due diligence analysis required for accurate assessment of possible mergers and/or acquisitions.

INTERNATIONAL JOINT VENTURES AND ALLIANCES

Similar issues arise for IHRM in cross-border joint ventures and other forms of alliances and partnerships. Increasingly firms are using creative forms of cooperative venture that include organizational forms involving alliances among enterprises from more than one country. There are many business reasons for doing this, usually involving the merger of technological, manufacturing, and/or marketing competences. But, as is true with mergers and acquisitions, often the degree of success of such partnerships is due more to the resolution of problems encountered in the merger of the human resources involved.

In every area of HRM responsibility, problems can arise in the implementation of successful cooperative ventures that must be resolved if the alliance is in fact to deliver benefits greater than those available for any of the parent firms, individually and separately.[24] For example, key obstacles encountered by IHRM in such strategic partnerships include the lack of involvement of the IHRM function in the planning for the joint venture, insufficient lead time to resolve critical staffing decisions for the alliance, lack of attention to cross-cultural sensitivity or training for employees assigned to the joint venture, poor understanding by the parents of the conditions for performance in the joint activity such that performance evaluation and resultant rewards and incentives are poorly constructed and administered, and inattention to problems of management assignment and career benefits from such assignments to these cooperative ventures.

According to preliminary studies of a limited number of situations, six issues appear to be among the particularly crucial ones for HRM within cooperative ventures in international settings.[25] These issues include:

- Assignment of managers to cooperative ventures: Who should be assigned where?
- The human resource transferability issue: Who "controls" a particular manager? The managers' parent firms or the new cooperative venture?
- The trade-offs in spending time between operating and strategic tasks among various managers involved in the cooperative venture. The various parents may have differing views as to how to resolve this issue. It is likely that it was not addressed in the negotiations to establish the alliance.
- Judgment calls regarding the performance of the human resource function in the established cooperative venture: How to avoid biases? The different parents are likely to have varying perceptions about how to evaluate performance, which aspects of performance to evaluate, as well as about the purposes of the cooperative venture in the first place.
- Human resource loyalty issues: To whom do the employees of the joint venture owe their loyalties—the cooperative venture or the parent?
- Individual managers' career planning issues: How can they achieve career progression through cooperative venture assignments?

The resolution of these issues is not easy. And as explained in the next section, the solutions must come out of the parent firms' global strategies and their linkages to the IHRM strategy.

LINKING IHRM TO OVERALL GLOBAL STRATEGY

In the final analysis, the critical point for IHRM and the firms it serves is to link IHRM activities to the overall global strategies of those firms.[26] International HR managers must help their firms achieve the global strategies, which can be done in a number of ways, including:

- Helping the firm to understand its multiple, national cultures;
- Providing advice to the rest of the business on how to integrate and coordinate these differing national cultures;
- Helping the firm to hire and train a truly world-quality and globally aware workforce and management team;

    • Developing career planning and management development programs that include international assignments and cultural training;

    • Understanding global business issues like exchange rates and foreign markets so that they can "talk international business" with the top management team and thus be important to the development of global business strategies and the achievement of global business objectives; and

    • Developing themselves so that they personally have the ability to communicate to the global workforce and global management team the firm's values, goals, and global strategy and how IHRM fits into them.

The international HR manager's ability to translate corporate cultural issues throughout the global firm ultimately provides the linkage between IHRM and the firm's global strategies. The quality of this translation often has a major impact on the success of the global business.

SUMMARY

Conducting business internationally presents many challenges to the multinational firm. As they expand their operations "overseas," multinational companies generally transfer their marketing first, then their production techniques, and then their management and personnel practices, from the parent company and country to their foreign affiliates and operations.[27] They presume that what works well "at home" will work well elsewhere. It is becoming increasingly clear, though, that local cultures and laws create different ways of thinking, behaving, managing, and doing business. A company's ways of managing people and providing products and services reflect that firm's (and country's) particular values, culture, management styles, and laws. Effective business operation in different countries and cultures may well require reevaluation of headquarter's way of seeing and interacting with those various locations.

    This chapter has outlined the traditional route by which businesses have traveled into the international business arena. Involvement with international commerce normally follows an evolutionary pattern, advancing from simple export to development of sales branches overseas to foreign subsidiaries to fully integrated foreign operations to becoming a global enterprise "without borders." Each successive stage of development calls for a more complex and complicated set of responsibilities by the human resource function.

    Many firms have been conducting business in more than one country for a long time (and thus have much experience with IHRM). In addition, the volume of international commerce and the number of firms thus involved are clearly increasing dramatically as we approach the turn of the century. Combine these realities with the many major changes occurring on the global scene—many unpredicted and unpredictable, such as the elimination of barriers to commerce in the European Community (EC) in 1992; the opening of Eastern Europe; the breakup of the Soviet Union; the transfer of political control in Hong Kong to the People's Republic of China in 1997; the fast-developing newly industrialized countries (NICs); the incredibly fast-developing economy of China; the opening up for commerce of countries such as Vietnam and the former republics of the Soviet Union; the formation of new trading blocks, such as Mercosur between Brazil, Argentina, Paraguay, and Uruguay, announced in March 1991; or the North American Free Trade Agreement—and it becomes obvious why HRM managers must become ever more knowledgeable about global business and how to best develop HR policies and practices to improve their firms' successes in that environment. A major component of this must be involvement by HR managers with their firms' global strategic management planning, even complete involvement in the due diligence analysis for possible mergers and acquisitions and multinational cooperative ventures.

ENDNOTES

1. See for example, Adler, N. J., and F. Ghadar, "Strategic Human Resource Management: A Global Perspective," in *Human Resource Management: An International Comparison*, ed. R. Pieper (Berlin: Walter de Gruyter, 1990); Bartlett, C. A., and S. Ghoshal, *Managing Across Borders* (Boston: Harvard Business School Press, 1989); Dulfer, E., "Human Resource Management in Multinational and Internationally Operating Companies," in Pieper, ed., *Human Resource Management*; Ghadar, F., and N. J. Adler, "Management Culture and the Accelerated Product Life Cycle," *Human Resource Planning*, 12(1), 1989, 37–42; Ohmae, K., *The Borderless World* (New York: Harper Business, 1990).

2. See, for example, Adler and Ghadar, "Strategic Human Resource Management"; Ghadar and Adler, "Management Culture and the Accelerated Product Life Cycle"; and Milliman, J., M. A. Von Glinow, and M. Nathan, "Organizational Life Cycles and Strategic International Human Resource Management in Multinational Companies: Implications for Congruence Theory," *Academy of Management Review*, 16(2), 1991, 318–339.

3. Ohmae, *The Borderless World*; Bartlett and Ghoshal, *Managing Across Borders*; Bartlett, C. A., and S. Ghoshal, "Matrix Management: Not a Structure, a Frame of Mind," *Harvard Business Review*, (July–August 1990, pp. 138–145; and Reich, R., "Who Is Us?" *Harvard Business Review*, January–February 1990, pp. 53–64; Reich, R., "Who Is Them?" *Harvard Business Review*, March–April 1991, pp. 77–88; Reich, R., *The Work of Nations: Preparing Ourselves for 21st-Century Capitalism* (New York: Alfred A. Knopf, 1991).

4. Bartlett and Ghoshal, *Managing Across Borders*; and Ohmae, *The Borderless World*.

5. Main, J., "How to go Global—And Why," *Fortune*, August 28, 1989, p. 70.

6. Solomon, C. M., "Transplanting Corporate Cultures Globally," *Personnel Journal*, October 1993, pp. 78–88.

7. Ibid., p. 78.

8. For example, Bartlett and Ghoshal, *Managing Across Borders*; Kanter, R. M., *When Giants Learn to Dance: Mastering the Challenges of Strategy, Management, and Careers in the 1990s* (New York: Simon & Schuster, 1989); Porter, M. E., *The Competitive Advantage of Nations* (New York: Free Press, 1990); Ohmae, *The Borderless World*.

9. See, for example, Schneider, S. C., "National vs. Corporate Culture: Implications for Human Resource Management," *Human Resource Management*, 27(2), 1988, 231–246; Taylor, W., "The Logic of Global Business: An Interview with ABB's Percy Barnevik," *Harvard Business Review*, March–April 1991, pp. 91–105; Townley, P., "Globesmanship" (interview with Paul Oreffice, chairman of the board of Dow Chemical, Michael Angus, chairman of Unilever, and John Young, CEO and president of Hewlett-Packard), *Across the Board*, February 1990, pp. 24–34.

10. Taylor, "The Logic of Global Business," p. 92.

11. Brandt, E, "Global HR," *Personnel Journal*, March 1991, pp. 38–44.

12. Kanter, *When Giants Learn to Dance*; Silva, M., and B. Sjogren, *Europe 1992 and the New World Power Game* (New York: John Wiley, 1990).

13. "Thriving on Chaos" seminar (course notebook), Career Track Seminars, presented in San Diego, CA, 1990, p. 21.

14. Ibid.

15. See, for example, the discussion of organizational structures of MNCs in Czinkota, M. R., P. Rivoli, and I. A. Ronkainen, *International Business*, Ch. 21, "Organization and Control in International Operations" (New York: Dryden Press, 1989).

16. Ibid.

17. Bartlett, C., "How Multinational Organizations Evolve," *Journal of Business Strategy*, Summer 1983, pp. 10–32; Dowling, P. J., and R. S. Schuler, *International Dimensions of Human Resource Management* (Boston: PWS-Kent, 1990); Lorange, P., and R. Vancil, *Strategic Planning Systems* (Englewood Cliffs, NJ: Prentice-Hall, 1977); Tung, R. L., "Strategic Management of Human Resources in Multinational Enterprise," *Human Resource Management*, 23 (1984), 129–143; and Miller, E. L., S. Beechler, B. Bhatt, and R. Nath, "The Relationship Between the Global Strategic Planning Process and the Human Resource Management Function," *Human Resource Planning*, 9 (1986), 9–23.

18. Taylor, S., S. Beechler, and N. Naiper, "Toward an Integrated Theory of International Human Resource Management," paper presented at the National Academy of International Business, Hawaii, 1993.

19. Lorange and Vancil, *Strategic Planning Systems.*

20. For references discussing these programs refer to work of Paul Evans of INSEAD in footnote 27 in Chapter 1 and Bartlett and Ghoshal, *Managing Across Borders.*

21. Taylor, Beechler, and Napier, "Toward an Integrated Theory of International Human Resource Management."

22. A good summary of approaches to HRM strategy can be found in Brewster, C., "Developing a 'European' Model for Human Resource Management," paper presented at the National Academy of International Business, Hawaii, 1993.

23. Much of this section is based on Weslock, K. A. (William M. Mercer, Inc.), and R. C. Donovan (GTE International, Inc.), *Human Resource Issues in International Mergers & Acquisitions*, a two-part report presented to the Annual Meeting of the International HR Division of the Society for Human Resource Management, San Francisco, March 12, 1991.

24. Pucik, V., "Strategic Alliances, Organizational Learning, and Competitive Advantage: The HRM Agenda," *Human Resource Management*, 27(1), 1988, 77–93.

25. Lorange, P., "Human Resource Management in Multinational Cooperative Ventures," *Human Resource Management*, 25(1), 1986, 133–148.

26. Solomon, C. M., "Transplanting Corporate Cultures Globally," *Personnel Journal*, October 1993, pp. 78–88.

27. Adler and Ghadar, "Strategic Human Resource Management"; Bartlett and Ghoshal, *Managing Across Borders*; Fayerweather, J., *International Business Strategy and Administration* (Cambridge, MA: Ballinger, 1978); Ghadar and Adler, "Management Culture and the Accelerated Product Life Cycle"; Ohmae, *The Borderless World*; Porter, *The Competitive Advantage of Nations*; and Silva and Sjogren, *Europe 1992 and the New World Power Game.*

3

Global Staffing

The staffing responsibilities for firms that operate in a multinational environment are very complex. In addition to normal domestic hiring responsibilities—which in today's global economy often involve the selection of employees from numerous nationalities and cultures—the international HR manager takes on a number of new responsibilities. The recruitment and selection of the employees by HR managers in multinational firms has traditionally been described as involving any of three different types of employee: parent-company nationals (PCNs), host-country nationals (HCNs), or third-country nationals (TCNs), the last of which can be either permanent or temporary immigrants in the countries in which they are hired.

Figure 3.1 illustrates the movement of these types of employees from one part of an MNE to another—and from a third country to either foreign subsidiaries or to the parent firm. Each of these three types of employee can be recruited and hired from any of the business locations of the MNE: either parent-company locations (headquarters or elsewhere in the parent country) or foreign subsidiaries (of all types, such as wholly owned subsidiaries either acquired by the parent or joint ventures, turn-key operations, or other types of alliances). Table 3.1 illustrates the relationships between the type of employee and the location of the organizational component of the MNE. Of course, all of these terms are from the perspective of the parent firm.

IHRM staffing, though, has become even more complex. This terminology does not adequately describe all the possible types of "hires" in the multinational firm. For example, employees who move from one foreign subsidiary to another—a situation which is increasingly common in global firms—are clearly expatriates; but they do not fall clearly within one of the three categories. This is shown in Figure 3.1 as movement from subsidiary X2 in Foreign Country B to subsidiary X1 in

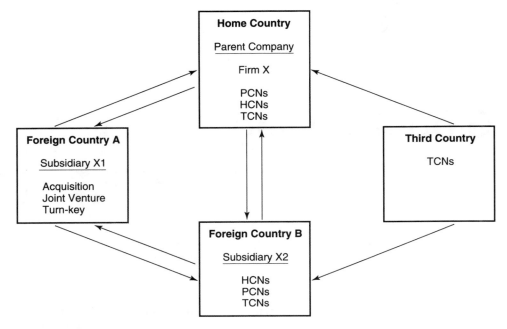

Figure 3.1. IHRM Staffing

Foreign Country A (and vice versa). These are not TCNs as that term is usually used, referring to hires from another country but who are not expatriates from another branch of the firm. And they aren't HCNs or PCNs. Individuals from the parent country who are hired in the overseas location by a foreign subsidiary are not PCNs or HCNs.[1] This group is becoming more important, particularly for American and European MNEs throughout the European Community, as labor mobility becomes easier as a result of the efforts to drop national barriers to trade. This group could be classed as TCNs, but they are not the traditional form of TCN. Employees from foreign subsidiaries who are posted to headquarters for temporary assignments are increasingly being referred to as inpatriates. But, again, they don't really fall into the categories of PCN, HCN, or TCN.

Two additional types of international employees increasingly seen in MNEs include "permanent expatriates" and "international cadre." Permanent expatriates are expatriates that stay in their overseas assignments for extended periods of time, or even permanently. Most firms reclassify their long-term expatriates as locals after five years. Primarily, this means that they are no longer compensated as parent-company expatriates but rather as local nationals. (This issue is discussed further in Chapter 5 on compensation.)

The international cadre are expatriates (most of whom originally came from the country of the parent company, but who increasingly can come from any country) who move from one foreign assignment to another, not returning for most of their careers to their home countries. European firms and firms in international

Table 3.1   Sources of Employees for MNEs

LOCATION OF FIRM	TYPE OF EMPLOYEE		
	LOCALS	IMMIGRANTS	EXPATRIATES
Parent Country	(PCNs) (native-born) (foreign-born)	TCNs	Inpatriates
"Overseas" (Foreign Subsidiary)	HCNs	TCNs	PCNs

banking are most likely to develop international cadres of managers who move from city to city in the foreign countries in which the firm operates.

Staffing for the multinational firm within its parent country as well as hiring by its foreign subsidiaries can involve seeking employees from any of the above three sources, as well as other less traditional sources, as described above. But typical employment practices for managerial and often marketing and technical positions in foreign subsidiaries place heavy emphasis on the use of expatriates.[2] There are many reasons why MNEs transfer personnel from one country to another.[3] These usually include the need to solve particular problems or to use a certain expatriate's technical expertise; to transfer technology from the parent country to foreign subsidiaries; to enhance employees' career development; to develop managers with global perspectives; to help develop a common, worldwide organizational culture; and to train and develop local managers and technicians.

> What seems clearly true is that at many big companies—Ford, Coca-Cola, and Dow, for example—putting in time abroad is increasingly a required, and critical, step in an executive's progress up the ladder. To run a global enterprise, the reasoning goes, you need the ability to psych out the foreigner as a consumer, as well as a sense of how to get things done offshore. What better training for this than a tour of duty overseas?
>
> Another, more subtle consideration may also be at work. A number of companies report finding that the personal qualities that enable an executive to negotiate his way through a job over there—an ability to think himself into the shoes of someone else, a capacity to make decisions even in the face of thorough-going ambiguity—are precisely those qualities increasingly needed at the top back here.[4]

Michigan-based Dow Chemical Co., a $16.7-billion diversified chemical manufacturer with facilities in 31 countries and 250 sales offices worldwide, illustrates how complex the movement of personnel from country to country can become. Dow has about 62,000 employees around the world, with at any point in time about 1,000 of them on assignment outside their country of origin.[5] Only 175 of these are U.S. employees based abroad. Another 175 or so are non-U.S. nationals now in the United States. The remaining 650 expatriates are non-U.S. employees based in other international locations, different from their home countries.

Pressure for the development of host-country nationals stems from the changes in attitudes in many host countries (and in many large multinationals, as well), preferring the development of local personnel and managers. The need for large numbers of highly qualified personnel has also made it increasingly necessary to use larger numbers of foreign (host country/local) nationals.

> Most multinational firms favor hiring local nationals for foreign subsidiaries, home-country nationals at headquarters, and, where a regional organization exists, a mix of foreign and home-country managers for regional positions. Within this general approach, however, the nationality mix will vary with the nature of a firm's business and its product strategy. Where area expertise plays a major role, as in the case of consumer goods and/or a limited product line, the use of home-country personnel for overseas assignments will be minimal. Where product expertise is highly important and/or industrial markets are being served, home-country personnel will be used more extensively for foreign assignments because they generally have quick access to the home-country source of supply and technical information. Service industries also tend to have more home-country personnel in foreign posts, particularly where the firm is serving home-country multinationals in foreign areas, as has been the case in banking.[6]

Thus, in the typical MNE of any size (and for international business in total), there are divergent forces operating relative to the use of expatriates. Larger MNEs use a greater number of HCNs but also need international experience among their management team. So to develop this experience, they are increasingly likely to move managers from the parent company, as well as their foreign managers, to assignments in countries other than their countries of origin. Firms which are newly developing their international business, of which there are a constantly increasing number, typically early in that development rely heavily on expatriates from the home office (or parent-country managers and technicians) for the development of their international business but also typically need the assistance of local nationals to effectively expand their foreign activities.[7]

However, in that situation where the multinational firm needs or wants to hire host-country nationals, the availability of local nationals with the necessary education and skills often becomes a major problem. Sometimes, there is simply a shortage of the needed local nationals. This can result in the heavy use of PCNs or TCNs in some countries and the ability to function almost without them in other countries.

> Among U.S. multinational enterprises, for example, about 60 percent of their employees in Saudi Arabia are expatriates, but less than 1 percent in Western Europe. Although U.S. firms have the bulk of their investments in industrial countries, more than 70 percent of the American expatriates that they employ are in the developing countries.[8]

Nevertheless, a key point that will be stressed throughout this book is that multinational firms throughout the world are increasingly concerned about hiring, developing, and retaining managers with international experience and global perspectives, with lessening regard for their countries of birth or citizenship.[9] IHRM in Action 3.1 describes one such manager, Adel Zakaria, an Egyptian-born, naturalized U.S. citizen, who is head of the world's largest manufacturing plant, the Waterloo, Iowa, plant of the John Deere Co. John Deere has a significant worldwide presence in more than eighty countries. As the feature indicates, Adel Zakaria fits the mold of the new global manager—one who can do more than one job, in more than one language, in more than one country or culture.

IHRM IN ACTION 3.1
JOHN DEERE'S COMPETITIVE
ADVANTAGE

The John Deere Co., the second oldest company in the United States, sees its foreign-born employees as an integral part of its worldwide organization. They're implanted, almost as a kind of yeast, into the workforce. They broaden the company's perspective, enabling it to see beyond the dominant cultures wherever they have operations. The company is firmly convinced that this helps it to maintain a competitive advantage as the diversity of its customer base continues to grow worldwide.

Adel Zakaria, an Egyptian-born, naturalized American, is a bona fide example of this new breed of manager for global firms like John Deere. He's extremely well qualified technically—an industrial engineer with postgraduate work and several degrees. But best of all, he fits the multicultural, multilingual, multifunctional criteria. He's a manager who can do more than one job, in more than one language, in more than one country.

Zakaria is very aware of the process that has put him where he is today—at the head of the largest plant in the world, the Waterloo Works, owned by the diversified manufacturer of farm equipment and appliances founded in 1837.

Zakaria was born into a minority status in his own country. A Coptic Christian, in the overwhelmingly Muslim country of Egypt, he has been dealing with issues of prejudice and persecution since grade school and has evolved an effective worldview. "I came to this country [the U.S.] in 1968 when I was 19 years old. I had a mechanical engineering degree from Ain Shams (Eye of the Sun) University in Cairo, and a desire to pursue my graduate studies." Zakaria is an early example of the *gold collar worker* of today, highly skilled and highly sought after employees with advanced degrees from other countries who have done research in technical fields.

Zakaria says, "Those of us from smaller countries are usually more international in outlook. We have to be to survive. Some people I meet may unconsciously label me as a foreigner. But I refuse to be alienated. I'm a fully naturalized American with great respect for the rights and privileges I enjoy here. People make assumptions when they hear my accent and ask me, 'Where are you from?' And when I say, 'Waterloo, Iowa,' they say, 'Before that?' Then I say, 'Quad Cities' and they start showing signs of frustration. 'No, I mean before that!' and I answer, 'Buffalo, NY,' before I finally tell them I was born in Egypt. . . . We [foreign-born employees] must not allow others to alienate us."

He implies that if native-born Americans paid closer attention to the overall process of acculturation (which we can learn from the foreigners who live and study in the United States—we don't necessarily have to travel abroad to acquire this sensitivity), we could learn more about the specifics of what works and what doesn't, with which groups, and why. And then, when we needed to do the adapting—for example, to the different preferences of customers in other countries—we'd already have some practice.

Zakaria went to work for John Deere at a time when they were going through major expansion into global markets, and he had opportunities to work with some of the firm's early global visionaries. The corporate engineering staff of which he was a part traveled to projects throughout the world, modernizing and expanding facilities in many manufacturing locations. And now Zakaria is one of the firm's executives who carries that vision forward. Whether speaking to business school students in Iowa universities or visiting John Deere plants in Europe and Asia or dealing with the Taiwanese, Indian, Mexican, and other foreign-born employees right here in the United States, Zakaria works with the many levels of diversity in a completely natural way. He's internalized it to the point that it is second nature to him.

It is managers and employees like Adel Zakaria that will continue to give John Deere it's competitive advantage in its global marketplace.

Source: C. F. Barnum, "John Deere's Competitive Advantage," HR MAGAZINE, February, 1992, 74–76, 107. Reprinted with permission of HR MAGAZINE published by the Society for Human Resource Management, Alexandria, VA. All rights reserved.

This chapter deals with the overall issue of staffing for multinational and global firms. Primarily, it discusses the issues of expatriation and repatriation. The transfer of personnel from one country to another appears to be necessary for a multitude of different reasons. Managing expatriates is often the principle international responsibility for IHR managers, but it is rarely an easy process. And it has always been very expensive and critically important to the success of an MNE's overseas operations. Thus most of the rest of this chapter deals with problems associated with the expatriation process. By necessity, however, some of the issues associated with the hiring of local nationals is also discussed.

MANPOWER PLANNING IN A GLOBAL ENVIRONMENT

The previous chapter discussed the importance of IHRM being integrated into the strategic management of global business. An important component of such integration involves planning for manpower needs on a global basis. Manpower planning in domestic operations typically involves assessing the demand for employees and managers (based on the strategic business plan) as well as determining the supply of people to meet that demand. The international environment adds considerable complexity to this planning.

Manpower planning for MNEs and global firms involves two levels of planning (key employees and lower-level employees) for as many locations as the business has activity, as well as the need to integrate the plans across those locations to develop a worldwide plan. To the extent that MNEs and global firms do this type of planning, most attention is placed on manpower planning for key managers and key positions.[10] This type of succession planning first identifies those positions which the business determines to be critical to its international success and then identifies high-potential and senior managers to prepare for and to fill those positions. This planning becomes important within each country of operation as well as for the global business as a whole.

As more firms expand their operations throughout the world, the problems they experience with staffing become more pronounced. This text describes IHRM theory and practice for workforces at the local level as well as for the integrated global workforce. Thus, this chapter, and the next two as well, discuss issues related to the management of expatriates, global cadres, host-country nationals, and third-country nationals. All types of international employees play important roles in the staffing of global enterprises.

EXPATRIATION

Expatriation has been historically viewed as the process of moving from the parent company or headquarters to foreign subsidiaries or overseas operations. But expatriation might better be viewed as the process of moving from one country to another while staying on the payroll of the original employer. Thus this process can take many forms (see Figure 3.1 and Table 3.1). At any particular location in the global firm, an individual manager may be a TCN and still be an expatriate from another country who is employed by and represents the parent company.

Expatriation continues to be a major concern for MNEs, even while it may be taking on new forms with large, global firms.[11] For example, some firms, such as Unilever Corporation, the large Anglo-Dutch global consumer-products firm, are now moving expatriate managers from subsidiary to subsidiary and country to country to help build global relationships and a common corporate identity and business culture among their management ranks.[12] More will be said about this in the next chapter.

Nevertheless, it is clear that there still are many firms using expatriates to develop and manage their foreign operations. Expatriates are used to beef up the skill levels in the international subsidiaries. In many firms, international experience is seen as important for executive promotion. It helps managers shake off the assumption that products or methods that work at home will automatically work in foreign lands. Tours of duty offshore are seen as necessary to understand the increasingly important international components of these businesses. The foreign duty also helps the expatriate gain insights into how foreign competitors operate. And the same skills needed to work in different cultures and markets in foreign assignments and to make decisions in the face of the type of ambiguity often faced in an unfamiliar culture are often seen as precisely those skills needed at the top of multinational corporations. The international experience is often a way to give "fast track" managers experience in running good-sized operations without close oversight from headquarters.

But all of this takes time. In many big companies, globalization is being developed division by division. These firms want to develop cultures that value the international experience. So they try to produce role models, individuals who have gone overseas and returned and subsequently done quite well in their careers.

There is also a counter concern. Good business practice and local government pressures often dictate that MNEs use and develop local nationals. But this can conflict with the desire by many MNEs to use parent-company expatriates in their

"WHEN YOU CAME TO WORK WITH US, WALSH, YOU STRESSED THAT YOU HOPED TO GO FAR WITH THE COMPANY. WELL, WE'VE DECIDED TO OPEN AN OFFICE IN TIBET, AND...."

Source: MANAGEMENT REVIEW, April 1993. Reprinted by permission of publisher, from MANAGEMENT REVIEW, © 1993. American Management Association, New York. All rights reserved.

overseas operations to help market their products, to transfer technology to their foreign subsidiaries, to provide managers with international experience, to reward long-time employees with end-of-career international assignments, and to provide better on-site control of their foreign subsidiaries. All these purposes place ongoing stress on firms to carefully select and prepare individuals for overseas assignments who will enhance the probability of the firm achieving its foreign-market objectives.

As suggested already, the roles and purpose for expatriation may well be changing. As MNEs increasingly develop local nationals to run their overseas operations, it might be suggested that the numbers of expatriates may actually be on the decrease. Countering this possibility, though, is the increased use of expatriation for individual and organizational development purposes coupled with the obvious increase in the number of firms operating internationally. And as historical experience shows, firms that are early in the evolution of their international activity tend to use more PCN expatriates to manage and develop their international sales and operations than do more internationally mature firms.

As would be expected, there are no comprehensive counts of the numbers of expatriates, either here in the United States or in other countries. But some estimates can be made. The IRS in the United States reports increasing numbers of tax returns from U.S. expatriates, from 435,000 in 1985 to 593,000 in 1989.[13] And a research group in England also concludes from their many studies that the overall numbers of expatriates is growing.[14] In contrast to these data and findings, a major American consulting firm (Organization Resources Counselors or ORC) finds from its yearly corporate surveys that the numbers of U.S. expatriates reported from their responding firms continues to decline from year to year.[15] The explanation for the different findings, though, is probably found in the pattern of evolution of multinational firms: The number of expatriates for the first couple of years after international start-up is high, grows for a short time, and then tapers off to the minimum number necessary to ensure effective continuity of the international business. The ORC survey results come from their clients, who tend to be larger, more experienced MNEs. These firms report declining use of expatriates from the home office because they are mature enough to seek increased development of local nationals and third-country nationals.

In the last chapter, the point was made that use of expatriates is high during the initial stages of foreign operations in order to accomplish technology transfer, including production and management technologies, and in order to best control the marketing of the firm's product(s).[16] The number of expatriates then usually declines as the firm's local managers, salespeople, and technical staff assimilate this knowledge and the ability to market the product effectively. The number expands again as local operations become increasingly integrated into a global operational framework. In addition, as the firm becomes more global, it develops a need for international managers with more international experience as it develops its worldwide competitive advantages. At this stage, these international managers may well come from any country, not necessarily, or even primarily, from the country of the parent company.

When an organization first begins to develop international business, it will recruit managers with international expertise from outside the firm or acquire the expertise it needs from consulting firms (of course, many firms pursue international business with their own inexperienced managers and salespeople, but this inevitably leads to months, and often years, of frustration while these managers "learn the business"). Sometimes, such expertise can be recruited from the overseas countries themselves. And, over the long-term, foreign managers can often be recruited from universities of either the country of the parent firm (i.e., foreign students) or of the countries in which the firm plans to operate.

Managers, salespeople, and technicians who are sent abroad are faced with a complex problem. Expatriates must be able to adjust to their new and often alien environments while effectively delivering their technical and managerial expertises. They must graciously accept their new cultures but not at the expense of not getting their jobs done. While technical expertise is usually important (and the primary reason most firms send a particular expatriate to a foreign assignment), the principal difficulty faced by most expatriates lies in the inability of the manager and his or her family to adapt to the foreign culture.

The firm must select managers who, with their families, will be most able to adapt overseas and who also possess the necessary expertise to get the job done in that foreign environment. In trying to increase their foreign sales, many firms that lack experience in international operations overlook the importance of the cultural variations in other countries. This attitude, combined with firms' inclinations

Table 3.2   Reasons for Expatriate Failure

1. Inability of spouse to adjust
2. Inability of expatriate to adjust
3. Other family-related problems
4. Expatriate's personality or lack of emotional maturity
5. Expatriate's inability to cope with overseas work
6. Expatriate's lack of technical competence
7. Expatriate's lack of motivation to work overseas

to choose employees for the expatriate experience because of their technical abilities, generally leads to international assignments being made without the benefit of training or help in acculturation, or even concern about this as an issue.[17] For example, even the most recent survey of MNE practices shows that in nearly all cases (92 percent of the time), line managers select employees for international assignment primarily on the grounds of technical and professional competence.[18] This may—and all too often does—lead to failure in the foreign assignment with premature return to the parent company and country, or even dismissal in the foreign locale. Table 3.2 lists the most common reasons for expatriate failure, when defined as early return or termination from foreign assignment.

A number of surveys and studies have found the most important factors in the early return of expatriates to lie in the inability of their families (and/or themselves) to adjust to the foreign environment.[19] To the extent that preparation is provided, often the parent company will typically provide that preparation for the new assignment only to the relocating expatriate, not to his or her family. In addition, after arrival in the foreign location, the individual expatriates have the advantage of personal contacts with their colleagues at work, while their spouses and families are often left on their own to "figure out" their new surroundings and to develop local relationships, often with little understanding of the culture and an inability to speak the language. Thus the individual expatriate often finds adjustment easier and less lonely than does his or her spouse and family.

The expatriate's own ability to adjust and/or difficulty in merging with the new culture can also be a major handicap. Too often, expatriates bring stereotypes and prejudices—as well as strongly felt biases in favor of their own culture's way of doing things—that keep them from feeling comfortable in their new foreign assignments. IHRM in Action 3.2 describes some of the experiences of one expatriate, Fred Bailey, as he tried to cope with a move from Boston to Tokyo for his firm, Kline & Associates, a large multinational consulting firm.

IHRM IN ACTION 3.2
FRED BAILEY: AN INNOCENT
ABROAD

It had been only six months since Fred Bailey had arrived with his wife and two children for this three-year assignment as the director of Kline & Associates'

Tokyo office. Kline & Associates was a large multinational consulting firm with offices in nineteen countries worldwide. Fred was now trying to decide if he should simply pack up and tell the home office that he was coming home or if he should try to somehow convince his wife and himself that they should stay and finish the assignment.

Seven months ago, Dave Steiner, the managing partner of the main office in Boston, offered Fred the position of managing director of the firm's relatively new Tokyo office, which had a staff of forty, including seven Americans. Steiner implied to Fred that if this assignment went as well as his past projects, it would be the last step before becoming a partner in the firm.

When Fred told his wife about the unbelievable opportunity, he was shocked at her less than enthusiastic response. His wife, Jennifer, thought that it would be rather difficult to have the children live and go to school in a foreign country for three years, especially when Christine, the oldest, would be starting middle school the next year. Besides, now that the kids were in school, Jenny was thinking about going back to work, at least part time.

Fred explained that the career opportunity was just too good to pass up and that the company's overseas package would make living overseas terrific. After two days of consideration and discussion, Fred told Mr. Steiner he would accept the assignment.

Fred and his family had about three weeks to prepare for the move. Between transferring things at the office to his replacement and getting furniture and the like ready to be moved, neither Fred nor his family had much time to really find out much about Japan, other than what was in the encyclopedia. After a few days of just settling in after arriving in Japan, Fred spent his first full day at the office.

Fred's first order of business was to have a general meeting with all the employees of associate consultant rank and higher. All the Japanese staff sat together and all the Americans sat together. After Fred introduced himself and his general idea about the potential and future directions of the Tokyo office, he called on a few individuals to get their ideas about how things for which they were responsible would likely fit into his overall plan. From the Americans, Fred got a mixture of opinions with specific reasons about why certain things might or might not fit well. From the Japanese, he got very vague answers. When Fred pushed to get more specific information, he was surprised to find that a couple of the Japanese simply made a sucking sound as they breathed and said that it was "difficult to say."

After they had been in Japan about a month, Jennifer complained about the difficulty she had getting certain everyday products (at a reasonable price) such as maple syrup, peanut butter, and good-quality beef. And unless she went to the American Club in downtown Tokyo, she never had anyone to talk to.

One of the most frustrating experiences for Fred had been the efforts to sign a major contract with a significant prospective client, a top 100 Japanese multinational company. The original meeting, in which Fred and colleagues presented the team from the Japanese firm with a specific proposal, resulted in only the vaguest of responses. And the subsequent five months had produced little progress. When Fred asked one of the promising Japanese research associates in his office to prepare a report on the potential client, impressing on him the importance of the project and the great potential they saw in him, he was again presented with frustration. The young associate was unable to finish the report in the requested week, but had not let Fred know that he was unable to complete it in the requested time period.

There were other incidents, big and small, that had made especially the last two months frustrating. To Fred it seemed that working with the Japanese both inside and outside the firm was like working with people from another planet. Fred felt he just couldn't communicate with them, and he could never figure out what they were thinking. It drove him crazy.

Then on top of all this, Jennifer told him she wanted to go home, and yesterday was not soon enough. Even though the kids seemed to be doing all right, Jennifer was tired of Japan—tired of being stared at, of not understanding anybody or being understood, of not being able to find what she wanted at the store, of not being able to drive and read the road signs, of not having anything to watch on television, of not being involved in anything. The company had led them to believe this was just another assignment, like the last two years they spent in San Francisco, and it was anything but that!

And, lastly, when the employer makes a mistake by assigning an employee who lacks the necessary technical abilities or motivation to perform the foreign requirements, the expatriate may be sent home early.

The rate of early return for American expatriates varies in different companies from 10 percent to as high as 80 percent (with a common failure rate in the 20 to 30 percent range) with the average cost per failure to the parent company ranging from $50,000 to $150,000 or more, depending on the expenses involved with moving the expatriate and his or her family to a foreign location.[20] Many expatriates cost their firms as much as $350,000 the first year, if they and their families are moved to expensive locales such as Paris, London, Stockholm, Buenos Aires, or Tokyo. These costs will be addressed in more detail in Chapter 5, International Compensation and Benefits. Nevertheless, under any circumstances, these are conservative estimates, since these figures don't include the costs to the overseas operations of the loss of such key personnel nor the resulting career costs for the firm or the individual who experiences an early return from such an assignment.

In contrast, European and Japanese multinationals rarely experience failure rates over 10 percent.[21] Better selection, preparation, language skills, and longer foreign assignments all lead to better experience with expatriates among European and Japanese MNEs. Even so, expatriates from European and Japanese firms also can experience culture shock and adaptation problems that result in bad experiences for themselves or their families. For example, even though it has not received much attention, the typical Japanese executive being expatriated to the United States, even though he (it essentially always is a "he") may have received substantial and substantive training and preparation for the assignment, has a very jarring experience.[22] Japanese executives and their families routinely face severely disorienting experiences in their dealings with Americans. Japanese and American approaches to personal and business interactions and relationships vary greatly. These encounters impede the Japanese executives' effectiveness and hamper their abilities to manage the businesses they came to the United States to manage.

Success or failure for expatriates is usually defined in terms of early return to the home country. But success or failure is a more complex issue than this.[23] Expatriate failure can also be defined in terms of characteristics such as poor overall performance in the foreign assignment, personal dissatisfaction with the experience, lack of adjustment to local conditions, lack of acceptance by local nationals, or the inability to identify and train a local successor (see Table 3.3). All of these can be important to IHRM in planning the selection, preparation, and placement of expatriates. Even if an expatriate does not return early from his or her foreign assignment, any one of the above problems could create major problems for the firm. If expatriates or their families return from overseas totally negative about their experiences, it will make it much more difficult to recruit new expatriates. And if returning expatriates have left a very negative impression among local nationals in the foreign subsidiary, it will be a long time before new expatriates are accepted easily into that subsidiary.

In addition, a number of factors seem to influence the severity of expatriate failure rates (and help to explain why Japanese and European firms don't tend to experience the high rates of expatriate failure experienced by many American firms). These include length of assignment (longer assignments appear to be based on the employer's willingness to provide the expatriate with more time to adjust and to "get up to speed" in terms of performance, which is more common among Japanese and European multinationals), receipt of training and orientation (with training and orientation about the new country and culture being associated with more successful adaptation and, again, being more common among Japanese and European MNEs),[24] and too much emphasis placed in selection on the expatriates' technical expertise to the exclusion of attention to his or her other attributes that

Table 3.3 Expatriate Failure

- Usually defined in terms of early return home or termination
- But could also be defined in terms of:

- Poor quality of performance in foreign assignment
- Personal dissatisfaction with experience (by expatriate or family)
- Lack of adjustment to local conditions
- No acceptance by local nationals
- Inability to identify and/or train a local successor

COMPOUNDING FACTORS

1. Length of assignment
2. Concern about repatriation
3. Overemphasis in selection on technical competence with disregard of other necessary attributes
4. Lack of training for overseas assignment

might aid in adaptation to the new foreign assignment (which is most common among American MNEs).

The process of adjustment itself has been classified into the three related but separate facets of adjustment to (1) work, (2) interacting with host nationals, and (3) the general environment.[25] The selection and preparation of employees for overseas assignments needs to consider all three facets of expatriate adjustment.

Further, the process of adjustment is a complex phenomenon.[26] Three modes of the adjustment process have been identified: integration, reaction, and withdrawal, any of which can be used to adjust to work, host nationals, and the general environment. In the case of integration, the individual takes steps to bring his or her behavior into harmony with the environment. That is, the individual learns to behave appropriately in the new culture. In the reaction mode, the individual takes steps to change the environment to be in greater congruence with the behavior and attitudes of the expatriate. In the case of withdrawal, the individual takes steps to reduce the pressures felt from the new environment, for example, by spending as much time as possible with home-country nationals. This might also be a form of psychological withdrawal, with the expatriate focusing on the temporariness of the assignment or in other ways trying to insulate him or herself from the "foreignness" of the experience.

Three tasks appear to facilitate the adjustment process for expatriates as described above.[27] The first task which confronts expatriates is to learn about the new environment. Firms can facilitate both the awareness of the need for this as well as the actual learning itself. The second task relates to the processes described above, that is, shaping or adapting to the new environment. And, lastly, the individual must manage the stress experienced during the transition to the foreign assignment. Obviously, these tasks are interrelated, as the first two tasks facilitate managing the experienced stress.

Selection and Preparation of Expatriates

This section primarily describes the process of selecting expatriates. A key aspect of creating successful expatriate experiences is the extent and nature of training and preparation that expatriates and their families receive prior to and during their stays overseas. The next chapter is devoted to an examination of training and development issues (for expatriates and for local workforces). So most of the discussion here is focused on the expatriate selection process.

In terms of the parent company, it is most important for the performance of expatriates in their foreign assignments that they be seen as able to perform the specific tasks to which they will be assigned as well as to perform well in a different cultural environment. That is, it is not just a case of one issue or the other: Both are important. Thus, the first consideration in the process of identifying individuals for overseas assignments should be for their firms to fully understand the requirements of those overseas assignments in both technical and cultural terms (refer to Figure 3.2 on successful expatriate experience). As with all HRM activities, a thorough job analysis (including an examination of the work environment) is necessary in order to make correct expatriate selection decisions.

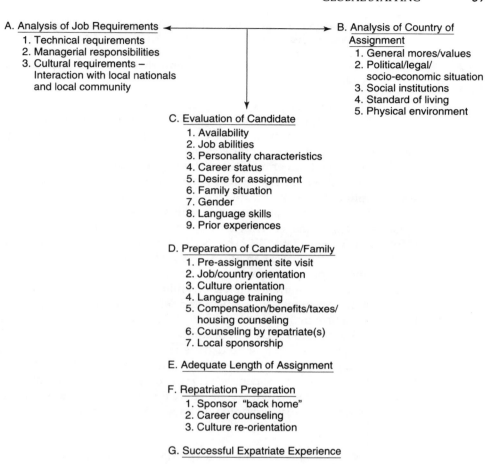

A. Analysis of Job Requirements
    1. Technical requirements
    2. Managerial responsibilities
    3. Cultural requirements –
       Interaction with local nationals
       and local community

B. Analysis of Country of
   Assignment
    1. General mores/values
    2. Political/legal/
       socio-economic situation
    3. Social institutions
    4. Standard of living
    5. Physical environment

C. Evaluation of Candidate
    1. Availability
    2. Job abilities
    3. Personality characteristics
    4. Career status
    5. Desire for assignment
    6. Family situation
    7. Gender
    8. Language skills
    9. Prior experiences

D. Preparation of Candidate/Family
    1. Pre-assignment site visit
    2. Job/country orientation
    3. Culture orientation
    4. Language training
    5. Compensation/benefits/taxes/
       housing counseling
    6. Counseling by repatriate(s)
    7. Local sponsorship

E. Adequate Length of Assignment

F. Repatriation Preparation
    1. Sponsor "back home"
    2. Career counseling
    3. Culture re-orientation

G. Successful Expatriate Experience

Figure 3.2. Successful Expatriate Experience
Source: D. R. Briscoe and G. M. Gazda, "The Successful Expatriate," PROCEEDINGS, Managing in a Global Economy, Third Biennual International Conference, Eastern Academy of Management, Hong Kong, November 1989.

In addition to basing their choices for overseas assignments on a clear understanding of the technical and cultural requirements of the foreign job, MNEs should also base their expatriate choices for foreign positions on a number of personal and family considerations. Because of the nature of most overseas assignments, selections for international transfer are most successful when based on factors such as the following:[28]

- The maturity of the candidate (i.e., the candidate should be a self-starter, be able to make independent decisions, have emotional stability, be sensitive to others who are different, and have a well-rounded knowledge of on- and off-the-job subjects to facilitate discussion with foreign colleagues and contacts who are often quite knowledgeable and interested in such topics);
- Ability to handle foreign language(s) (see discussion below);

- Possession of a favorable outlook on the international assignment by the expatriate and his or her family (i.e., he or she wants to go overseas); and
- Appropriate personal characteristics (excellent health, desire for the assignment, this is an appropriate time in the individual's career, individual resourcefulness, adaptability).

From the viewpoint of the persons being considered for transfer, studies suggest that two specific factors—in addition to strong personal interests in foreign experiences, which are usually based on their having previously enjoyed living overseas—are primary in their decisions to take on such an assignment: increased pay and improved career mobility.[29] This suggests that multinational firms need to pay close attention to these factors when making their selections for overseas positions. Both of these factors are discussed in later chapters.

From the company side, the problem of selection of expatriates increasingly involves finding managers with the necessary skills to function successfully in the new global environment. Table 3.4 exhibits the skills that are being cited as important for the twenty-first-century expatriate manager. The core abilities of being able to develop a multinational perspective while maintaining skills in line management, decision-making skills, and international resourcefulness, adaptability, and sensitivity will be the foci of management development and selection for the effective multinational or transnational firm in the latter half of the 1990s and on into the next century.

According to Ed Dunn, corporate vice president of Whirlpool Corp,[30] "The top 21st-century manager should have multi-environment, multicountry, multi-functional, multicompany, multi-industry experience." Michael Angus, chairman of Unilever PLC, adds, "Most people who rise toward the top of our business will have worked in at least two countries, probably three. They will probably speak another language and they most certainly will have worked in different product areas."

Language

As important as it is for the expatriate to have a working knowledge of the language of the country to which he or she is assigned, English is rapidly becoming the international language of business. This has happened because English is not only the major language spoken in the home country of many MNEs (e.g., those that come from England, Canada, Australia, and the United States) but also English is the first or second language in many other important countries, such as South Africa, Nigeria, India, Malaysia, the Netherlands, New Zealand, and the like. In addition, many companies from countries whose languages are not widely known internationally, such as Japan, Korea, Hong Kong, Sweden, Norway, and the newly opened Eastern and Central European countries of Hungary, the Czech Republic, Slovakia, Poland, the Baltics, and the Commonwealth of Independent States, have found it necessary for their managers to speak English in order to be able to interact in international markets.

Not all interactions are likely to take place in English, particularly within the host country. But transnational exchanges are more and more expected to take place in English. When the top worldwide staff of ABB Asea Brown Boveri (a Swiss-Swedish firm) meets, the common language for their joint sessions is English. And

Table 3.4   The 21st-Century Expatriate Manager Profile

CORE SKILLS	MANAGERIAL IMPLICATIONS
Multidimensional Perspective	Extensive multiproduct, multi-industry, multifunctional, multicompany, multicountry, and multi-environment experience.
Proficiency in Line Management	Track record in successfully operating a strategic business unit(s) and/or a series of major overseas projects.
Prudent Decision-Making Skills	Competence and proven track record in making the right strategic decisions.
Resourcefulness	Skillful in getting him or herself known and accepted in the host country's political hierarchy.
Cultural Adaptability	Quick and easy adaptability into the foreign culture—individual with as much cultural mix, diversity, and experience as possible.
Cultural Sensitivity	Effective people skills in dealing with a variety of cultures, races, nationalities, genders, religions. Also sensitive to cultural difference.
Ability as a Team Builder	Adept in bringing a culturally diverse working group together to accomplish the major mission and objective of the organization.
Physical Fitness and Mental Maturity	Endurance for the rigorous demands of an overseas assignment.

AUGMENTED SKILLS	MANAGERIAL IMPLICATIONS
Computer Literacy	Comfortable exchanging strategic information electronically.
Prudent Negotiating Skills	Proven track record in conducting successful strategic business negotiations in multicultural environment.
Ability as a Change Agent	Proven track record in successfully initiating and implementing strategic organizational changes.
Visionary Skills	Quick to recognize and respond to strategic business opportunities and potential political and economic upheavals in the host country.
Effective Delegatory Skills	Proven track record in participative management style and ability to delegate.

Source: C. G. Howard, "Profile of the 21st-century Expatriate Manager," HR MAGAZINE, June, 1992, 96. Reprinted with permission of HR MAGAZINE, published by the Society for Human Resource Management, Alexandria, VA. All rights reserved.

when the Italian middle manager for the Milan, Italy, branch of Commerz Bank of Germany phones headquarters in Frankfurt—which she must do many times a day—the conversation takes place in English. Of course, all the worldwide managers above a particular level for firms like Unilever, ABB Asea Brown Boveri, IBM, or Ford Motor Company, all of which operate in seventy or more countries, must speak English. And, even though it was controversial, when Euro-Disney opened outside of Paris, France, in April 1992, all 12,000 employees were required to be able to speak English, French, and, of course, the language of their home countries, if it wasn't French or English.

It is in fact now estimated that English is spoken worldwide by more people than any other language, by at least one billion persons.[31] The end result of this may be that employing local nationals that are fluent in English may be as important as requiring expatriates to be fluent in the local language(s). Even so, it is clear that an ability to speak the local language is still quite important—for expatriates to deal with local nationals and local customers and suppliers, as well as to adapt to the host culture (and be accepted into that culture), both of which are major keys to successful expatriate experiences.

Gender

In the past (and still true), most expatriates have been men. In surveys of large MNEs, the number of women expatriates has been found to be between 3 and 10 percent of the total number of expatriates.[32] The evidence suggests that the fact that there are so few women working overseas for MNEs may be due more to bias and stereotyping in the parent country and company about foreign acceptance of women in professional or managerial roles than to actual prejudice in the host country or foreign subsidiary (refer to Figure 3.3).[33] As Figure 3.3 illustrates, the perception of American managers is that there is strong prejudice

Figure 3.3 Managers Perceive Greater Barriers to Women in International Versus Domestic Management

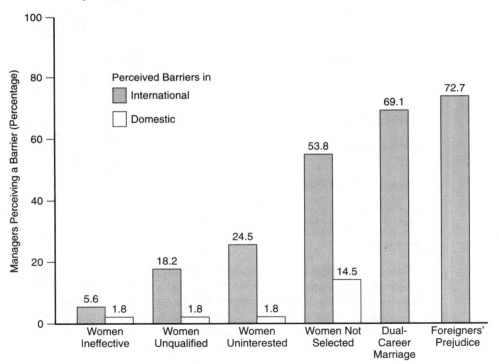

against women as managers in foreign countries and that women are uninterested in such assignments and/or are handicapped by being in dual-career marriages. Experience and limited research, however, suggests that women not only welcome such opportunities (for the same reasons their male counterparts seek them) but also often perform better than their male colleagues, even in traditionally male-dominated cultures, such as in the Far East.[34] Typically, female expatriates are treated first as representatives of their parent firms and rarely experience the prejudice that the stereotypes from their home firms presume. Nevertheless, women expatriates frequently also do have trailing spouses and families to consider, and thus need to be given the same considerations received by their male counterparts.

In recent years the number of women who have successfully taken on foreign assignments, even to countries such as Japan, Brazil, and China (which are usually presumed to be hostile to women managers and professionals), has risen considerably. Of course the use of women expatriates, except in very specialized professional positions, is likely to remain very limited in some countries such as Saudi Arabia.[35]

The limited number of female expatriates seems mostly to be due to the incorrect assumptions by most firms that women don't want foreign assignments and that they will not be accepted in the foreign countries of assignment. That is, the main problem appears to be that the MNEs themselves maintain prejudices against the use of women in foreign assignments.

New Types of Expatriates

Increasingly, multinational firms, particularly American MNEs, are confronted with new types of potential expatriates based on the new types of workforces they must draw from at home. As MNEs make foreign assignments a critical step in employees' career development, and as laws require MNEs to give equitable treatment to all employees, even in their assignment of employees to foreign positions, firms find themselves having to consider all their employees for such assignments.

Thus, the diverse workforces from which firms, particularly in the United States, must draw their expatriates include: managers in dual-career couples (which create special family needs and which involve problems with "trailing spouses" who have career concerns of their own and who follow their husbands/wives to the foreign assignments; a recent survey[36] showed that 46 percent of expatriate spouses work before the foreign assignment while only 10 percent work during the assignment);[37] potential expatriates with unresolved problems with their adolescent children, health, dependent parents, or psychological difficulties (such as a flying phobia); male expatriates with wives who are trying to reenter the labor force (which will be difficult to do in the foreign location); potential expatriates with special education requirements for their children (such as gifted children or children looking for colleges to attend); individuals with unmarried partners (homosexual or otherwise); women; individuals with physical or mental disabilities; and minority (African-American, Hispanic, Asian, Native American) managers and technicians. Ultimately, the consideration of potential expatriates (or members of their families) with medical problems like AIDS, substance abuse, or even alcohol abuse, or problems like multiple sclerosis, can cause what may seem like insurmountable problems for IHRM. These types of individual or family problems are both a problem in expatriate selection and a problem for acceptance into and adaptation to foreign cultures. And yet, firms, in order to find the numbers of expatriates they need and to stay away from possible charges of illegal discrimination, must accept and find ways to accommodate these types of problems.

Many of these concerns make a health screening of the expatriate and his or her spouses and family members advisable, to determine if a health problem exists that might either preclude relocation or be aggravated by a relocation. Often even minor health problems are not treatable in the foreign country because qualified health professionals or facilities are not available.

Recent research by ORC (Organization Resources Counselors, Inc., a major IHRM consulting firm) found that international HR managers believe that overseas assignments of dual-career couples will be one of the top five challenges they must face during the 1990s.[38] According to a survey by Bennett Associates of accompanying career spouses, active involvement in the career of the accompanying spouse is the type of assistance preferred worldwide by dual-career couples above all other possible interventions.[39]

According to recent surveys by Runzheimer International and ORC, nearly 50 percent of firms offer some form of spouse assistance for dual-career international assignees.[40] Of those firms, 87 percent provide *ad hoc* interventions (helping as and in ways that seem necessary) and 13 percent have formal policies. Programs fall into three broad categories: personal adjustment (helping trailing spouses adjust to the foreign assignment); career maintenance (helping trailing spouses find jobs or other ways to maintain their career status); and offset of loss of income (due to trailing spouses having to quit their jobs while following their expatriate spouses overseas). The types of interventions found in these surveys—that firms use when they find it necessary—included the following:

- Pre-acceptance assessment sessions and site visits.
- Career and life planning counseling.
- Pre-departure and reentry job hunting trips.
- Couple/family counseling.
- Specially adapted cross-cultural/language training.
- Relocation assistance to help spouse settle in and network quickly.
- Search firm retained.
- Company employment or consulting opportunities.
- Intra and inter-company networking and job search assistance.
- Access to E-mail and Internet capabilities.
- Visa and work permit assistance.
- Shorter-term assignments for expatriate employee.
- Commuter marriage support.
- Tuition and/or training reimbursement.
- Professional development trips.
- Child care provisions.

- Partial compensation replacement for spouse.
- Increased employee compensation, bonus, and noncash benefits.
- Reentry outplacement.
- Tax equalization for second income.
- Spouse "inconvenience" or incentive payment.
- Set allowance to be applied to a cafeteria selection of assistance programs.

REPATRIATION

Repatriation is the opposite of expatriation: It involves the move of the expatriate back to the parent company and country from the foreign assignment. For many expatriates, the move "back home" is even more difficult than the original move overseas—and is a concern that is generally overlooked in the total expatriation process.[41] Because repatriation is often so difficult, it is just as important to manage the repatriation process as it is to manage the expatriation process.[42]

The overseas experience is generally challenging, exciting, highly developmental, and full of visibility and exposure for the expatriate. The expatriate is the representative of the parent company (i.e., headquarters) and is therefore looked to for perspective, help, and favors. In addition, because the compensation practices of most MNEs reward their expatriates quite well, the expatriate and family typically have a high standard of living in the overseas location, often better than they have "at home." Thus expatriates usually return from such experiences quite "charged." They expect their employers to use their new experiences and excitement.

But the reality is more likely to be "out-of-sight, out-of-mind." Firms often fail to use the experience or knowledge gained in the foreign assignment and most likely have not thought about the career implications of this experience. Repatriates often feel out of touch with the corporate culture they experience when they return, which may have changed considerably while they were overseas. Their "sponsor" may have relocated, retired, or left the firm. Their spouses are still bitter toward the firm for having to uproot their own careers. Typically, repatriates are reassigned to positions similar to the ones they left two or three years before. In addition, repatriates and their families often also have trouble readjusting to the home life style. Most people are changed by the foreign experience and not only must relearn their original cultural and life style, but probably view it very differently than when they left. And, finally, repatriates are often offered great positions with competitors who wish to take advantage of their overseas skills. This might even include an opportunity to go back overseas, which might seem very desirable at that point.

Just as MNEs need to provide their expatriates with preparation for the move abroad, so must they prepare their expatriates for the move back home and prepare themselves to use these individuals' overseas experiences in their home assignments. This preparation can make the difference between an overall favorable attitude by the repatriates about the whole experience and a failed expatriate experience. Ultimately, an unfavorable attitude will likely lead to the individual resigning and seeking a position with another employer that will utilize that individual's foreign experiences and skills.

The kinds of practices that MNEs have used to ensure a successful expatriation and repatriation experience include giving the expatriate a written job guarantee, or contract, upon successful return from the foreign assignment, assigning a "sponsor" back home to look after the expatriate while he or she is away (including keeping the expatriate informed about significant events and changes back home and looking after the expatriate's career interests, such as putting the expatriate's name into consideration for key openings when the expatriate is ready to return home), providing career counseling to ensure job assignments upon return that meet the needs of the repatriate, orientation for the expatriate and his or her family for adjustment back into the home culture, use of the skills acquired overseas in special task forces and projects, and special support networks for the repatriate and his or her family both during the overseas assignment and upon return home.[43] These steps go a long way toward ensuring a successful readjustment. IHRM in Action 3.3 describes how Monsanto Corporation has redesigned its repatriation efforts—adapting many of these ideas—in order to more effectively use its expatriates and their international experiences, integrating them with their domestic operations.

IHRM IN ACTION 3.3
REPATRIATION AT MONSANTO

In 1992, Monsanto Corporation undertook a detailed change of its repatriation policy, concentrating on the logistical planning, the kinds of skills and cultural development the company wanted its expatriates to learn, and the placing of its repatriates in projects where overseas experience was needed. "They're out there to do the job, but they're also there to develop personally and culturally," says John Amato, manager of human resources, international assignments.

Amato says that repatriation begins six to eighteen months prior to return in both the host and the home countries, so that expatriates return to planned jobs for which the operating unit is responsible. An extensive debriefing program is also run for the employees and their families.

The employee debriefing is exceptionally thorough: He or she is debriefed with peers and managers in the new job and is expected to provide recommendations about global development and to provide a view other than that of domestic Monsanto. Peers are expected to discuss the differences and changes in the organization that occurred while the expatriate was abroad. Managers are encouraged to free up repatriates for committees, work groups, and demonstrations where their knowledge is needed, over and above the employee's regular job. Repatriates need to see how much they've changed when they come back.

Source: Barbara Ettorre, "A Brave New World: Managing International Careers." Reprinted with permission of publisher from MANAGEMENT REVIEW, April, 1993, © 1993. American Management Association, New York. All rights reserved.

SUCCESSFUL EXPATRIATION

Everything discussed thus far in this chapter in terms of the management of the expatriation process involves the close and active participation of the IHRM depart-

ment. In order for the expatriation process to result in successful expatriation—
that is, the expatriate effectively fulfills his or her job responsibilities in the foreign
assignment, the expatriate and his or her family successfully adapt to the foreign
environment and enjoy the experience, and the expatriate and his or her family successfully return to the home country and the firm effectively assigns the expatri-
ate/repatriate to a parent-company position that uses his or her new skills—IHRM
must be involved.[44] Every one of these steps requires the active participation of an
IHRM department that oversees the total process and ensures that the necessary
actions are taken at appropriate times. Firms that assign basic IHRM responsibilities to line managers and/or don't integrate their IHRM responsibilities well with
their overall global strategies are not likely to ensure the close involvement of IHRM
with the management of their expatriates and are thus more likely to experience
significant problems with their expatriates.

HIRING HCNS AND TCNS

In general, MNEs staff their subsidiaries—below the top management level—with
local nationals (host-country nationals, HCNs). At times, these workers may be sup-
planted by TCNs, particularly in areas where there is either a shortage of the necessary type of workers (e.g., the use of Koreans in Saudi Arabia for construction
projects by Western oil companies or Turks in Germany for unskilled jobs) or where
there is relatively free movement of people from one country to another (e.g., within
the European Community). Of course, the presence of potential employees with
adequate training, education, and skills is always of utmost importance to an HR
strategy of staffing with HCNs. In the case where the strategic decision has been
made to locate a subsidiary in a country where the local population lacks the necessary education or training, then HR must find other ways to staff with the necessary work force, for example, by training locals or hiring TCNs.

The Global Labor Force

Hopefully, the HR manager has been involved in making the decisions as to where
to locate foreign operations. One of the questions that ought to be addressed in the
making of such decisions has to do with the qualifications of the local labor force.
Just as cultures vary considerably from country to country, so also do basic educational systems and levels of training and industrial experience. And as workers
throughout the world become increasingly mobile, HR managers and their firms
will need to increasingly reach across borders to find the skills they need.

These movements of workers will be driven by the growing gap between
the world's supplies of labor and the demands for it. While much of the world's
skilled and unskilled human resources are being produced in the developing world,
most of the well-paid jobs are being generated in the cities of the industrialized
world. This mismatch has several important implications for the 1990s:

- It will trigger massive relocations of people, including immigrants, temporary
  workers, retirees, and visitors. The greatest relocations will involve young well-
  educated workers flocking to the cities of the developed world.

- It will lead some industrialized nations to reconsider their protectionist immigration policies, as they come to rely on and compete for foreign-born workers.
- It may boost the fortunes of nations with "surplus" human capital. Specifically, it could help well-educated but economically underdeveloped countries such as the Philippines, Egypt, Cuba, Poland, and Hungary.
- It will compel labor-short, immigrant-poor nations like Japan to improve labor productivity dramatically to avoid slower economic growth.
- It will lead to a gradual standardization of labor practices among industrialized countries. By the end of the century, European standards of vacation time (five weeks) will be common in the United States. The 40-hour work week will have been accepted in Japan. And world standards governing workplace safety and employee rights will emerge.[45]

Much attention has been focused on the current or looming labor shortages in the industrialized world, particularly in the United States, Europe, and Japan, due to the aging of the populations in these locales.[46] Yet the overall world labor supply continues to grow (primarily in the developing world). In addition, the growth in the labor force in the developing world is magnified by the entrance of women into the labor force, a phenomenon which has pretty well worked itself out in much of the developed world. When these demographic differences are combined with the different rates of economic growth between the developed and developing world, it becomes likely that firms in the developed world will increasingly seek workers among the excess in the developing world.

Just as product and service markets have become or are becoming global, such will also happen to the labor market. In one sense, this may alleviate the labor surpluses among the developing countries of the world; but in another sense it may well exacerbate the economic differences between the countries of the developed world and those of the developing world as MNEs hire the educated and trained citizens of the developing countries, lessening those countries' available human resources for their own needs.

Relying on Local Managerial Talent

The expensive expatriate failure problem and a general trend toward geocentrism (a truly global approach to resources, customers, and employees) in recent years have resulted in a greater reliance on local managers in foreign operations. Foreign nationals already know the language and culture and do not require huge relocation expenditures. In addition, host-country governments tend to look favorably on a greater degree of local control and the development and use of local personnel. On the negative side, however, local managers may have an inadequate knowledge of home-office goals and procedures and have difficulty with the parent-company language. Thus the staffing of foreign positions—particularly key managerial and technical ones—is necessarily decided on a case-by-case basis.

In some ways this strategy may not be as easy as is sometimes suggested, either by the firms that want to follow it or the governments that encourage it. For example, in some countries with their own successful multinational firms, such as Japan, the best candidates take positions with their own country's companies. This leaves the foreign MNEs with having to rely on the "rejects" or the more risk-oriented local nationals, often those who have gone to school overseas. Other categories of possible candidates for hiring by foreign MNEs in countries like Japan include young women graduates who prefer Western firms because they find more career opportunities than may be possible in local firms and individuals who are fluent in the language of the multinational. However, one problem that sometimes arises with such bilingual candidates is that they may get hired for their language skills rather than because of a thorough screening of their technical skills. Nevertheless, MNEs are increasingly likely to have to compete locally for managerial and technical talent at the same time that local firms are increasing their own demands for these employees.

Multinational firms also find the recruiting of host-country managers difficult for these reasons:[47]

- Lack of knowledge about the local labor markets;
- Ignorance about the local education system and the status of various qualifications;
- Language and cultural problems at interviews; and
- Trying to transfer recruitment methods which work well in the home country but might not work so well in the foreign locale.

The end result is that unless there is an extremely strong interest, that is, even a strategic interest, in hiring and developing local managers, the international firm is still likely to rely most heavily on the use of expatriates from the home office, at least to staff top positions in its foreign offices.

An extension of this focus on local managers involves an increasing willingness to look for managers from all countries for assignment to any country. These TCNs are often the solution to overseas staffing problems. It was described earlier how Bechtel Corporation needed to recruit and hire employees from around the world in order to fulfill its contract to put out the oil well fires in Kuwait after the Gulf War. IHRM in Action 3.4 shows how a number of other American MNEs have recently increased their use of TCNs.

IHRM IN ACTION 3.4
FIRMS WOO EXECUTIVES
FROM "THIRD COUNTRIES"

Multinational firms are tapping more "third-country nationals" for overseas posts.

Nationality matters less as businesses race to enlarge their ranks of global managers. So-called TCNs—neither Americans nor local nationals—often win jobs because they speak several languages and know an industry or a foreign country well. The average number of third-country nationals per U.S. company rose to 46 last year from 33 in 1988, say consultants Organization Resources Counselors.

Pioneer Hi-Bred International employs 29 TCNs in key jobs abroad, triple the number of five years ago, partly because they accept difficult living conditions in Africa and the Middle East. Raychem has a dozen such foreigners in top European posts, up from eight in 1986. "The numbers are going to increase" as Europe's falling trade barriers ease relocation, suggests Edward Keible, a senior vice president. A Frenchman runs the company's Italian subsidiary, a Belgian is a sales manager in France, while a Cuban heads the unit in Spain.

Scott Paper, whose ranks of TCN managers have leaped to 13 from 2 in 1987, will step up recruitment of young foreigners "willing to move around Europe or around the Pacific," says Barbara Rice, personnel chief.

Source: "Firms Woo Executives from 'Third Countries'," by J. S. Lublin, THE WALL STREET JOURNAL, Sept. 16, 1991, B1. Reprinted by permission of THE WALL STREET JOURNAL, copyright © 1991, Dow Jones & Company, Inc. All rights reserved worldwide.

Inpatriates

Inpatriates are HCNs or TCNs hired by global enterprises in their foreign subsidiaries that are subsequently assigned to the parent company (usually to headquarters or parent-country research facilities) for typically two- or three-year periods. The common reason for these assignments is to immerse these local nationals in the culture, attitudes, and often products and marketing approaches of the parent firm. These inpatriates are chosen because they are seen as key future managers for the MNE back in their home countries, and this parent-company experience is seen as important to their learning the firm's strategic perspective. Indeed, these individuals may then be assigned as part of the international cadre of managers that the firm can draw on for assignments anywhere in the world.

CROSS-BORDER COMMUNICATIONS

Firms that operate in more than one country are constantly faced with problems of communication between the parent company and its foreign offices. Almost all of the writing about cross-cultural communication problems in this type of setting is from the perspective of expatriates (and, very recently, inpatriates) having to adjust to a foreign assignment and culture. An issue that has received essentially no attention concerns the problems that employees in the parent country have in normal, day-to-day communications with their counterparts in foreign subsidiaries (or, for that matter, between subsidiaries). So far, no one has given attention to the training of all employees who must interact with employees from other countries, even if it is only by telephone, E-mail, FAX, or memo. To some extent this is a language problem, and to a large extent it involves sensitivity to the cultural values and norms and ways of doing business in the foreign locales. As many possibilities for misunderstanding exist in these circumstances as is true for situations that involve those employees who are in personal contact (whether short- or longer-term) with their colleagues in other countries.

APPLYING PARENT-COUNTRY LAWS OVERSEAS AND COMPLYING WITH LOCAL LAWS AND CUSTOMS

In most countries of the world, human resource activities are highly regulated. This is particularly true in industrialized countries. As would be expected, the regulations in one country are often very different from those in other countries. Thus, multinational firms are often confronted with concerns about the conflict between employment practices and laws in their parent countries and those experienced in the foreign locations in which they operate.

There appear to be at least two components to these concerns. For example, from the perspective of U.S. MNEs, one concern is whether U.S. law applies to the management of its American employees in its foreign subsidiaries and, on a more ethical or philosophical level, whether to follow U.S. law or practice in foreign locations for host-country nationals when it is perceived that the U.S. approach is "better." Of course, these issues are also confronted by MNEs from other countries, from their parent-country perspectives. These questions are particularly difficult when dealing with laws against discrimination in employment practices, an area of law where one might argue that U.S. law is more "developed." And it works in both directions: application by American firms in their overseas operations and by foreign firms in the United States.

The American Firm Overseas

In the U.S. Civil Rights Act (CRA) of 1991, the American Congress affirmed its policy that American civil rights laws (specifically Title VII of the 1964 Civil Rights Act and the 1990 Americans with Disabilities Act) do apply to the employment practices of American multinationals relative to their U.S. citizens employed in their foreign operations. That is, American MNEs cannot discriminate on the grounds of an individual's sex, race, religion, color, or national origin against American citizens who they employ in their overseas subsidiaries. (The Age Discrimination in Employment Act of 1967 was amended in 1984 to protect American workers over the age of forty against discrimination by U.S. companies abroad.)

The action in the CRA of 1991 reversed the decision of the U.S. Supreme Court in *EEOC v. Arabian American Oil Co.*,[48] which had concluded that Congress had not intended to apply Title VII of the Civil Rights Act of 1964 (which outlawed discrimination in employment practices on the basis of race, color, religion, sex, and national origin) to the foreign operations of American multinational firms. The original case involved an American, Ali Boureslan, claiming unlawful discrimination in his dismissal by ARAMCO while in its employment in Saudi Arabia.[49]

Related to this issue is the ongoing problem for all multinationals of whether or not to apply their parent-country laws, values, and management practices to their foreign subsidiaries. The very success of most multinational firms in their domestic economies reinforces the ethnocentric attitude that "what works well at home should work well abroad." And yet it is clear that from the perspective of the foreign country, its laws, values, and practices should take precedence in its locales, just as the United States insists that American laws, values, and practices take precedence in the United States. Indeed, international law recognizes the rights of nations to regulate conduct within their national borders. At some point, for example, this could end up causing conflict with the Civil Rights Act of 1991, in which Congress applied American nondiscrimination law to the employment practices of American MNEs in other countries, albeit only in their employment of American expatriates. From the perspective of that American MNE, conflict could arise between the application of American law in the foreign country (in their treatment of their American expatriates) and the local law which might require different employee decisions.

Because of the potential conflict between foreign and local practices in such MNE situations, the general practice that has evolved is for foreigners (such as expatriates and their families) to comply with the laws and mores of the countries to which they are assigned, whether or not they conflict with the individual's home-country laws or mores. Thus, for example, women expatriates (or female family members) while in Saudi Arabia, are expected to cover their arms and legs at all times, avoid wearing shorts, driving vehicles, walking unescorted, or chatting casually in public with men who are not their husbands. Women in Saudi Arabia can be expected to ride in the back of public transportation and may be excluded from some stores. In addition, they may well be restricted in terms of professional or work roles they can occupy. The local workforce should also be recruited and managed in accordance with local laws and practices, although not all MNEs have historically followed this approach.

The Foreign Firm in the United States

A parallel to the above discussion is the applicability of American law to the personnel practices of foreign-owned subsidiaries in the United States. Just as American MNEs must abide by local laws in their foreign operations, particularly as they make employment decisions about local nationals, so must foreign subsidiaries in the United States abide by U.S. laws as they make employment decisions about their U.S. employees. This has become of particular concern with Japanese and Korean firms in the United States, but it has also raised questions in other situations. This is not a trivial concern for either the American subsidiaries of foreign MNEs nor for their U.S. HR managers. There are about 5 million Americans employed in the United States by foreign MNEs in hundreds of offices, stores, and plants (and this doesn't take into account the millions of Americans that work in American firms that have been acquired by foreign firms).

For many reasons having largely to do with significant cultural and managerial differences, Japanese firms have perhaps received the most attention to the conflicts between their management and HRM practices and those traditionally and legally followed in the United States. As many as one third of Japanese firms with operations in the United States have been confronted with lawsuits for discrimination in their employment practices relative to their American employees in the United States.[50] Part of the problem may be a lack of knowledge about U.S. employment laws. But more to the point (and one which must concern all multinational firms) is the conflict between the national culture and employment practices of the parent firm and the employment laws in the overseas locations. As is true with the MNEs from some other countries as well,

Japanese firms tend to use only parent-country (i.e., Japanese) executives to run their American subsidiaries, providing few of the perquisites and no opportunities for promotion to the top management slots for their American managers. In addition, all major decision making tends to be made by the Japanese managers, often in consultation with their colleagues back in Japan, rather than in conjunction with their American counterparts. At least three Japanese firms have settled discrimination suits for multimillion-dollar figures (Honda of America, Sumitomo Corporation, and Quasar, a division of Matsushita Electric Corporation of America). And a number of other suits are still pending (against, for example, Fujitsu, DCA Advertising, C. Itoh & Company, Nikko Securities Co., and Mitsubishi Bank).[51]

The preceding discussion notwithstanding, Japanese firms in the United States may well be protected in their staffing practices, at least at their top tiers of management. The seventh circuit court of appeals has ruled that Japanese subsidiaries operating in the United States may legally prefer Japanese citizens over U.S. citizens and Civil Rights Act prohibitions against discrimination on the basis of national origin do not apply.[52] According to the ruling in *Fortino v. Quasar Co.*,[53] Title VII of the 1964 Civil Rights Act is preempted by a treaty between Japan and the United States which permits companies of either country to prefer their own citizens for executive positions in subsidiaries based in the other country. This ruling clarifies a 1982 Supreme Court decision in *Sumitomo Shoji America Inc. v. Avagliano*[54] and, by extension, applies to both Japanese firms in the United States as well as to American firms in Japan, although U.S. multinationals are less interested in pursuing such "parent-company-executive-only" strategies.

In a slightly different example, but illustrating the same type of problem with non-U.S. multinational firms not adhering to U.S. laws, in the 1980s, the International Association of Machinists and Aerospace Workers (IAM) had a labor dispute with El Al Israel Airlines, Ltd., in New York. Refusal to bargain, the importation of strike breakers from Israel, and other unfair labor practices have been charged by the American union, but this has received little sympathy from the U.S. administration.[55] The Israeli management of El Al has followed traditional Israeli labor relations practices in dealing with their American union at their New York operations, rather than pursuing union relations in New York that are consistent with American practices. In the United States as elsewhere, political considerations can override purely economic or domestic legal considerations.

U.S. IMMIGRATION LAW

A last topic of concern to IHRM staffing is the nature and application of immigration law. This issue becomes important to HR managers as they hire new immigrants, acquire visas for inpatriates, and work with HR managers and government officials in other countries as they get work visas for the managers and technicians they send abroad as expatriates. It is beyond the scope of this book to examine immigration regulations in other countries, but IHR managers of U.S. MNEs have to gain some knowledge of the laws of each of the countries to which they plan to send expatriates. Because this area of responsibility is so complex, the typical IHR manager will likely retain external expertise, for example, local (foreign) law firms, to help with this.

The next few paragraphs provide a short introduction to U.S. immigration laws, which have undergone considerable change in recent years. Knowledge of these regulations are important to all U.S. HR managers as they work to staff their firms with the best available employees, many of whom may come from other countries.

American immigration law primarily involves two recent laws: the Immigration Reform and Control Act of 1986 (IRCA) and the Immigration Act of 1990 (IMMACT 90). IRCA, for the first time in U.S. history, essentially makes it necessary for American employers to ensure that all of their employees are either U.S. citizens or have some form of work visa providing permission to work in the United States.[56] Thus HR managers must acquire at time of hiring and keep on file evidence of U.S. citizenship (or work visa) for every employee. Failure to do so can lead to sizable fines. A "pattern or practice" of violations can lead to criminal penalties. In addition, the firm must complete a government I-9 form for every hire, providing a summary of the evidence retained for proof of citizenship.

IMMACT 90 rewrote the rules for visas for entry as permanent or temporary immigrants into the United States.[57] Under the new regulations, the number of employer-sponsored permanent-resident visa allotments (traditionally referred to as "green cards") have been increased to 140,000 per year. It is hoped that these new, higher allotments will alleviate the backlogs that exist for immigration applications for particularly educated and skilled employees (for example, there are an estimated 200,000 vacancies for registered nurses, alone, many of which are filled by immigrants). There are now five categories under which employers can apply for such status for an immigrant:

1. Priority workers (40,000 visas per year), which include persons of extraordinary ability in the arts, sciences, business, education, or athletics; outstanding professors and researchers; and executives and managers of multinational firms.
2. Professionals with advanced degrees and persons with exceptional ability (40,000 visas per year). In this category, employers must first get Department of Labor certification before applying for the green card. The employer must verify to the satisfaction of the Department of Labor that there is no American available for the position in which the alien is sought.
3. Professionals, skilled workers, and other workers (40,000 visas per year). This category also requires Labor Department certification. There is a limit of 10,000 green cards under this category for unskilled workers, which is expected to increase the existing four- to five-year backlog for such workers.
4. Special immigrants (10,000 visas per year). This is a category for special immigrants that do not fall into the other categories, such as religious workers, that is, missionaries.
5. Investors (10,000 visas per year). This is a new category for individuals who invest at least $1 million in a new business and employ at least ten workers.

The new law also makes many changes in the existing system of nonimmigrant or temporary visas. Most employees who are sponsored by their employers for green cards are already present in the United States working on temporary professional visas (referred to as "H-1B" visas). Under the new law the temporary work visa categories include (presented in alphabetical order, but which does not reflect their most common usage):

1. B-1 for business visitors, working for and paid by business abroad, for short periods;
2. E for people from countries with "treaty of commerce and navigation" with the United States (E-1 for conducting trade and E-2 for overseeing investment in the United States);
3. F-1 for foreign students, including students in practical training (twelve months pregraduation and twelve months postgraduation);
4. H-1A for registered nurses;
5. H-1B for persons in other specialty occupations, including individuals of extraordinary ability in the arts, sciences, business, education, and athletics, and performers (a limit of 65,000 per year);
6. H-3 for training programs (classroom or on-the-job or both when training is unavailable in the alien's home country);
7. J-1 for visitor-exchange programs, including industrial and business trainees;
8. L-1 for intracompany transfers with parent, subsidiary, affiliate, or branch abroad, available to managers, executives, and those with specialized knowledge;
9. M-1 for foreign students in nonacademic training programs; and
10. Q for international exchange programs, eligible for practical training and employment, primarily for entertainment theme park industry.

Other than the numerical limits placed on the various categories for work-related visas, the additional major new impact of IMMACT 90 is the application process for "certification" to the Department of Labor. This application now requires that employers attest to the following for each H-1B worker:

1. It will pay the H-1B worker the actual wage level for the occupation at the facility or the prevailing wage for the occupation in the area of employment, whichever is higher;
2. It will provide working conditions that will not adversely affect the working conditions of other similarly situated workers;
3. There is no strike or lockout in the course of a labor dispute involving the occupational classification at the place of employment; and
4. It has provided notice of the filing of the application with the local union bargaining representative, or if the facility is not unionized, it has posted notice in conspicuous locations at the place of employment.

The application must specify the number of workers sought, their occupational classifications, and the wage rate and conditions of work. Thus this process is open to complaints by unions or other interested parties, leading to Department of Labor investigations. Nevertheless, these new immigration regulations should provide U.S. employers better opportunities for employing quality employees from around the world.

SUMMARY

This chapter focused on the IHRM responsibility for staffing, primarily on the issue of expatriation and repatriation, the movement of employees of multinational firms from either the parent company to a foreign subsidiary or from a foreign subsidiary to another subsidiary or to the parent firm. In the development of their early international activities, typical MNEs rely heavily on the use of PCNs. As they mature, they rely more heavily on the use of HCNs and eventually evolve toward staffing with employees and managers hired worldwide for worldwide needs.

This chapter examined the difficulties experienced in the selection and management of expatriates and repatriates and suggested some of the approaches successful MNEs use to ensure positive experiences with those expatriates and repatriates. In addition, the chapter discussed problems that MNEs are experiencing with women and other types of nontraditional expatriates and the hiring of host-country and third-country nationals.

The chapter also provided an overview of legal problems associated with the use of expatriates in overseas subsidiaries as well as the problems that foreign MNEs face in dealing with American laws in their HRM practices in their U.S. subsidiaries. Even though recent American law (the Civil Rights Act of 1991) applies American civil rights law to American multinational treatment of their American employees in their overseas operations, in general international law respects the rights of nations to enforce their laws within their own borders, even against foreign firms operating there, which is exactly what the United States is doing to the foreign firms that operate in the United States.

Finally, the chapter examined the question of immigration, particularly from the perspective of the American firm hiring foreign citizens or those who immigrate either permanently or temporarily to the United States. The international HR manager must become familiar with the U.S. laws toward immigration as well as those of other countries, particularly as his or her firm moves employees from country to country.

ENDNOTES

1. See, for example, Parker, B., "Employment Globalization: Can 'Voluntary' Expatriates Meet U.S. Hiring Needs Abroad?" *Journal of Global Business,* Fall 1991 pp. 39–46.

2. For more complete discussion of the management of expatriates, refer to Black, J. S., H. B. Gregersen, and M. E. Mendenhall, *Global Assignments* (San Francisco: Jossey-Bass, 1992); Brewster, C., *The Management of Expatriates* (London: Kogan Page, 1991); and Tung, R. L., *The New Expatriates: Managing Human Resources Abroad* (Cambridge, MA: Ballinger, 1988).

3. See footnote 2 plus Deutsch, C. H., "Losing Innocence Abroad," *The New York Times: Business,* July 10, 1988, Sec. 3, pp. 1, 26; Barham, K., and C. Rassam, *Shaping the Corporate Future* (Ashridge, U.K., Ashridge Research Management Group, July 1989); and Shahzad, N., "The American Expatriate Manager," *Personnel Administrator,* July 1984, pp. 23–30.

4. Kiechell, M., III, "Our Person in Pomparippu: The Successful Expatriate Executive Learns to Cool Heels, Live with Servants—and Come Home Again," *Fortune,* October 17, 1983, p. 213.

5. Brandt, E., "Global HR," *Personnel Journal,* March 1991, pp. 38–44.

6. Robock, S. H., and K. Simmonds, *International Business and Multinational Enterprises,* 3rd ed. (Homewood, IL: Richard D. Irwin, 1983), p. 559.

7. For a discussion of the decision by midsized U.S. firms to send expatriates abroad, refer to Toll, E. E., "Someone to Talk To," *World Trade,* February 1994, pp. 46–50.

8. Quoted from Daniels, J. D., E. W. Ogram, Jr., and L. H. Radebaugh, *International Business: Environments and Operations* (Reading, MA: Addison-Wesley, 1982); original data from Reynolds, C., "Expatriates in a Changing World Economy," paper presented to the Academy of International Business, November 15, 1978.

9. Howard, C. G., "Profile of the 21st-Century Expatriate Manager," *HR Magazine,* June 1992, pp. 93–100; Laabs, J. J., "The Global Talent Search," *Personnel Journal,* August 1991, pp. 38–43; Marsick, V. J., and L. Cederholm, "Developing Leadership in International Managers—An Urgent Challenge!" *Columbia Journal of World Business,* Winter 1988, pp. 3–11.

10. Swaak, R. A., "Key Manpower Planning for the Global Enterprise," *Journal of International Compensation & Benefits,* January–February 1994, pp. 38–42.

11. Refer to the introduction in Brewster, *The Management of Expatriates.*

12. Bartlett, C. A., and S. Ghoshal, *Managing Across Borders* (Boston: Harvard Business School Press, 1989); Maljers, F. A., "Inside Unilever: The Evolving Transnational Company," *Harvard Business Review,* September–October 1992, pp. 46–52; Townley, P., "Globesmanship" (interview with Paul Oreffice, chairman of the board of Dow Chemical, Michael Angus, chairman of Unilever, and John Young, CEO and president of Hewlett-Packard), *Across the Board,* February 1990, pp. 24–34; and the work of Paul Evans as referenced in footnote 27 in Chapter 1.

13. Rehak, J., "IRS Takes Close Look at U.S. Expatriates," *International Herald Tribune,* August 24–25, 1991, p. 15.

14. Brewster, *The Management of Expatriates.*

15. Yearly survey reports from Organization Resources Counselors, Inc., for example, as reported in Reynolds, C., "HR Must Influence Global Staff Strategy," *HR News: International HR,* March 1991, Sec. C, pp. 1–2.

16. See, for example, Franko, L. G., "Who Manages Multinational Enterprise?" *Columbia Journal of World Business,* Summer 1973, pp. 30–37. This discussion is adapted from R. Grosse and D. Kujawa, *International Business,* 2nd ed., Homewood, IL: Irwin, 1992.

17. See, for example, Baker, J. C., and J. M. Ivancevich, "The Assignment of American Executives Abroad: Systematic, Haphazard, or Chaotic?" *California Management Review* 1971, pp. 39–41; Hixon, A. L., "Why Corporations Make Haphazard Overseas Staffing Decisions," *Personnel Administrator,* March 1986, pp. 91–94; Mendenhall, M., E. Dunbar, and G. R. Oddou, "Expatriate Selection, Training, and Career-Pathing: A Review and Critique," *Human Resource Management,* Fall 1987, pp. 331–345; Mendenhall, M., and G. Oddou, "The Dimensions of Expatriate Acculturation: A Review," *Academy of Management Review,* 10(1), 1985, 39–47; Miller, E. L., "The Overseas Assignment: How Managers Determine Who Is to Be Selected," *Michigan Business Review,* 24(3), 1972, 12–19; Miller, E. L., "The International Selection Decision: A Study of Some Dimensions of Managerial Behavior in the Selection Decision Process," *Academy of Management Journal,* 16 (1973), 239–252; Tung, R. L., "Selection and Training of Personnel for Overseas Assignments," *Columbia Journal of World Business,* 16(1), 1981, 68–78; Tung, R. L., *The New Expatriates: Managing Human Resources Abroad* (Cambridge, MA: Ballinger, 1988); Zeira, Y., "Overlooked Personnel Problems of Multinational Corporations," *Columbia Journal of World Business,* 10(2), 1975, 96–103.

18. Windham International and the National Foreign Trade Council, *International Relocation Trends Survey,* authors, 1994.

19. Refer to notes 17 and 18; plus Black, J. S., and H. B. Gregersen, "The Other Half of the Picture: Antecedents of Spouse Cross-Cultural Adjustment," *Journal of International Business Studies,* Third Quarter, 1991, pp. 461–477; Black, J. S., and M. Mendenhall, "The U-Curve Adjustment Hypothesis Revisited: A Review and Theoretical Framework," *Journal of International Business Studies,* Second Quarter, 1991, pp. 225–247; Conway, M. A., "Reducing Expatriate Failure Rates," *Personnel Administrator,* July 1984, pp. 31–32, 37–38; De Cieri, H., P. J. Dowling, and K. F. Taylor, "The Psychological Impact of Expatriate Relocation on Spouses," paper presented to the Annual Meeting of the Academy of International Business, Singapore, November 19–22, 1989; Foxman, L. D., and W. L. Polsky, "HR Approaches for the Age of Globalization," *Personnel Journal,* April 1991, pp. 38–41; Fuchsberg, G., "As Costs of Overseas Assignments Climb, Firms Select Expatriates More Carefully," *The Wall Street Journal,* January 9, 1992, B1, B5; "Gauging a Family's Suitability for a Stint Overseas," *Business Week,* April 16, 1979, pp. 127, 130; Gómez-Mejía, L., and D. B. Balkin, "The Determinants of Managerial Satisfaction with the Expatriation and Repatriation Process," *Journal of Management Development,* 6(1), 1987, 7–17; Greene, W. E., and G. D. Walls, "Human Resources: Hiring Internationally," *Personnel Administrator,* July 1984, pp. 61–66; Harris, J. E., "Moving Managers Internationally: The Care and Feeding of Expatriates," *Human Resource Planning,* 12(1), March 1989, 49–53; Lanier, A. R., "Selecting and Preparing Personnel for Overseas Transfers," *Personnel Journal,* March 1979, pp. 160–163; Lee, Y., and L. Larwood, "The Socialization of Expatriate Managers in Multinational Firms," *Academy of Management Journal,* 26(4), 1983, 657–665; Murray, F. T., and L. H. Murray, "SMR Forum: Global Managers for Global Businesses," *Sloan Management Review,* Winter 1986, pp. 75–80; Oddou, G. R., M. E. Mendenhall, and P. Bedford, "The Role of an International Assignment on an Executive's Career: A Career Stages Perspective," paper presented at the Academy of International Business Conference, San Diego, CA, October 20–22, 1988; Savich, R. S., and W. Rodgers, "Assignment Overseas: Easing the Transition Before and After," *Personnel,* August 1988, pp. 44–48; Tung, R. L., "Career Issues in International Assignments," *Academy of Management Executive,* 2(3), 1988, 241–244; and Tung, R. L., "Expatriate Assignments: Enhancing Success and Minimizing Failure," *Academy of Management Executive,* 1(2), 1987, 117–126.

20. Conway, "Reducing Expatriate Failure Rates"; Harvey, M. G., "The Multinational Corporation's Expatriate Problem: An Application of Murphy's Law," *Business Horizons,* January–February, 1983, p. 72; Henry, E. R., "What Business Can Learn from Peace Corps Selection and Training," *Personnel,* 42(4), 1965, 17–25; Misa, K. F., and J. M. Fabricaatore, "Return on Investment of Overseas Personnel," *Financial Executive,* 47(4), 1979, 42–46; Murray, F. T., and A. H. Murray, "SMR Forum: Global Managers for Global Businesses," *Sloan Management Review,* Winter 1986, pp. 75–80; Rahim, A., "A Model for Developing Key Expatriate Executives," *Personnel Journal,* April 1983, p. 312; Tung, "Selection and Training of Personnel for Overseas Assignments"; Tung, "Expatriate Assignments."

21. Tung, R. L., "Selection and Training Procedures of U.S., European, and Japanese Multinationals," *California Management Review,* Fall 1982, pp. 57–71; Tung, R. L., *Key to Japan's Economic Strength: Human Power* (Lexington, MA: D. C. Heath, 1984).

22. Linowes, R. G., "The Japanese Manager's Traumatic Entry into the United States: Understanding the American-Japanese Cultural Divide," *Academy of Management Executive,* 7(4), 1993, 21–40.

23. Nasif, E. G., M. S. Thibodeaux, and B. Ebrahimi, "Variables Associated with Success as an Expatriate Manager," *Proceedings,* Academy of International Business, Southeast Region, Annual Meeting, New Orleans, November 4–7, 1987, pp. 169–179.

24. See, for example, Feldman, D. C., and H. B. Thompson, "Expatriation, Repatriation, and Domestic Geographical Relocation: An Empirical Investigation of Adjustment to New Job Assignments," *Journal of International Business Studies*, Third Quarter, 1993, pp. 507–529.

25. See, for example, Black, J. S., "Work Role Transitions: A Study of American Expatriate Managers in Japan," *Journal of International Business Studies*, 19(2), Summer 1988, 277–294; Black, J. S., and H. B. Gregersen, "Antecedents to Cross-Cultural Adjustment for Expatriates in Pacific Rim Countries," *Human Relations*, 44 (1991a), 497–515; Black, J. S., and H. B. Gregersen, "The Other Half of the Picture: Antecedents of Spouse Cross-Cultural Adjustment," *Journal of International Business Studies*, 22(3), 1991b, 461–478; Black, J. S., M. Mendenhall, and G. Oddou, "Toward a Comprehensive Model of International Adjustment: An Integration of Multiple Theoretical Perspectives," *Academy of Management Review*, 16(2), 1991, 291–317; Black, J. S., and G. K. Stephens, "The Influence of the Spouse on American Expatriate Adjustment in Overseas Assignments," *Journal of Management*, 15(4), 1989, 529–544; Janssens, M., *International Job Transfers: A Comprehensive Model of Expatriate Managers' Cross-Cultural Adjustment*, PhD. dissertation at Catholic University of Leuven, Leuven, Belgium, Psychology Department; Kauppinen, M., and H. Gregersen, "Towards a More Comprehensive Approach to Expatriate Adjustment Research: Mode Can Make a Difference," paper presented at the National Academy of International Business, Hawaii, November 1993.

26. Berry, J. W., U. Kim and P. Boski, "Psychological Acculturation of Immigrants," in *Cross-Cultural Adaptation: Current Approaches*, eds. Y. Y. Kim and W. B. Guddykunst (San Francisco: Sage, 1988); Black, Mendenhall, and Oddou, "Toward a Comprehensive Model of International Adjustment"; and Kauppinen and Gregersen, "Towards a More Comprehensive Approach to Expatriate Adjustment Research."

27. Newman, L. V., "A Process Perspective on Expatriate Adjustment," *Proceedings*, Third Conference on International Personnel and Human Resource Management, July 2–4, 1992.

28. See, for example, Black, J. S., and M. Mendenhall, "Cross-Cultural Effectiveness: A Review and a Theoretical Framework for Future Research," *Academy of Management Review*, 15 (1990), 113–136; Blocklyn, P., "Developing the International Executive," *Personnel*, March 1989, pp. 44–48; Callahan, M., "Preparing the New Global Manager," *Training and Development Journal*, March 1989, pp. 29–31; Cateora, P. R., *International Marketing* (Homewood, IL: Richard D. Irwin, 1983); Conway, "Reducing Expatriate Failure Rates"; Foxman and Polsky, "HR Approaches for the Age of Globalization"; Fuchsberg, "As Costs of Overseas Assignments Climb"; Gilroy, E. B., D. M. Noer, and J. E. Spoor, "Personnel Administration in the Multinational/Transnational Corporation," in *PAIR Policy and Program Management*, ASPA Handbook of Personnel and Industrial Relations, Vol. VII, eds. D. Yoder and H. G. Heneman, Jr. (Washington, DC: Bureau of National Affairs, 1978); Hixon, "Why Corporations Make Haphazard Overseas Staffing Decisions"; Hogan, G. W., and J. R. Goodson, "The Key to Expatriate Success," *Training and Development Journal*, January 1990, pp. 50–52; Lanier, A. R., "Selecting and Preparing Personnel for Overseas Transfers," *Personnel Journal*, March 1979, pp. 160–163; Stuart, K. D., "Teens Play a Role in Moves Overseas," *Personnel Journal*, March 1992, pp. 71–78; Tung, "Expatriate Assignments"; Tung, *The New Expatriates*.

29. Miller, E. L., and J. Cheng, "A Closer Look at the Decision to Accept an Overseas Position," *Management International Review*, 1978, pp. 25–33.

30. Quoted in Howard, C. G., "Profile of the 21st-Century Expatriate Manager," *HR Magazine*, June 1992, pp. 93–100.

31. Naisbitt, J., and P. Aburdene, *Megatrends 2000* (New York: William Morrow, 1990).

32. Adler, N. J., "Women Managers in a Global Economy," presentation at the 1994 Global Congress on Personnel Management, San Francisco, February 28, 1994; Adler, N. J., "Competitive Frontiers: Women Managing Across Borders," in *Competitive Frontiers: Women Managers in a Global Economy,* eds. N. J. Adler and D. N. Izraeli (Colchester, VT: Blackwell Publishers, 1993); Windham International and the National Foreign Trade Council, *International Relocation Trends Survey,* authors, 1994.

33. Adler, N. J., "Competitive Frontiers"; Adler, N. J., "Expecting International Success: Female Managers Overseas," *Columbia Journal of World Business,* 19(3), Fall 1984a, 79–85; Adler, N. J., "Pacific Basin Managers: A Gaijin, Not a Woman," *Human Resource Management,* 26(2), 1987, 169–191; Adler, N. J., "Women Do Not Want International Careers: And Other Myths About International Management," *Organizational Dynamics,* 13(2), Autumn 1984b, 66–79; Adler, N. J., "Women in International Management: Where Are They?" *California Management Review,* 26(4), Summer 1984c, 78–89; Adler, N. J., "Women Managers in a Global Economy," *HR Magazine,* September 1993, pp. 52–55; Adler, N., and D. Izraeli, eds., *Women in Management Worldwide* (Armonk, NY: M. E. Sharp, 1988); "Corporate Women: A Rush of Recruits for Overseas Duty," *Business Week,* April 20, 1981, pp. 120+; Golesorkhi, B., "Why Not a Women in Overseas Assignments?" *HR News: International HR,* March 1991, p. C4; Jelinek, M., and N. J. Adler, "Women: World-Class Managers for Global Competition," *The Academy of Management Executive,* 2(1), 1988, 11–19; Kirk, W. Q., and R. C. Maddox, "International Management: The New Frontier for Women," *Personnel,* March 1988, pp. 46–49; Rossman, M. L., *The International Businesswoman of the 1990s* (New York: Praeger, 1990).

34. See above, plus Maital, S., "A Long Way to the Top," *Across the Board,* December 1989, pp. 6–7.

35. Abraham, Y., "Personnel Policies and Practices in Saudi Arabia," *Personnel Administrator,* April 1985, p. 102; Thal, N., and P. Caleora, "Opportunities for Women in International Business," *Business Horizons,* December 1979, pp. 21–27.

36. Windham International and the National Foreign Trade Council, 1994.

37. See, for example, Ball, L. L., "Overseas Dual-Career Family an HR Challenge," *HR News: International HR,* March 1991, p. C8; "Problems for Dual-Career Expatriates," *Personnel Journal,* September 1990, p. 17; Reynolds, C., and R. Bennett, "The Career Couple Challenge," *Personnel Journal,* March 1991, pp. 46–49.

38. Reported in Bennett, R., "Solving the Dual International Career Dilemma," *HR News,* January 1993, p. C5.

39. Ibid.

40. Ibid.

41. Black, J. S., "Repatriation: A Comparison of Japanese and American Practices and Results," *Proceedings,* Eastern Academy of Management Bi-Annual International Conference, Hong Kong, 1989, pp. 45–49; Clague, L., and N. Krupp, "International Personnel: The Repatriation Problem," *Personnel Administrator,* 23 (1978), 29–33; Harvey, M., "The Other Side of Foreign Assignments: Dealing with the Repatriation Problem," *Columbia Journal of World Business,* 17 (1983), 53–59; Harvey, M., "Repatriation: An Ending and a Beginning," *Business Horizons,* 24 (1981), 21–25; "Weigh the Risks First on That Job Abroad," *U.S. News and World Report,* December 2, 1985, p. 82.

42. Black, J. S., "Returning Expatriates Feel Foreign in Their Native Land," *HR Focus,* August 1991, p. 17; Black, J. S., and H. B. Gregersen, "O Kairinasai: The Role of Job Expectations During Repatriation for Japanese Managers," *Proceedings,* Third Conference on International Personnel and Human Resource Management, Ashridge, England, July 2–4, 1992; Brewster, *The Management of Expatriates*; Dowling, P. J., and R. S. Schuler, *International Dimensions of Human Resource Management* (Boston: PWS-Kent, 1990); Harvey, M. G., "Repatriation of Corporate Executives: An Empirical Study," *Journal of International Business Studies,* Spring 1989, pp. 131–144; Howard, C. G., "Out of Sight—Not Out

of Mind," *Personnel Administrator,* June 1987, pp. 82–90; Mandell, M., "Robust Repatriation," *World Trade,* February 1994, pp. 40–44; Moynihan, M., "Bringing Expatriates Home: A Fresh Look at Returnees' Problems," *Business International,* February 11, 1991, pp. 13–17; Moynihan, M., "How MNCs Ease Expatriates' Return to Home Countries," *Business International,* February 25, 1991, pp. 21–24; Shilling, M., "How to Win at Repatriation," *Personnel Journal,* September 1993, pp. 40–46; Welds, K., "The Return Trip," *HR Magazine,* June 1991, pp. 113–114.

43. Brewster, *The Management of Expatriates.*

44. Tiemann, C., "Involvement of Human Resources Is Key To Successful Expatriation," *Journal of International Compensation & Benefits,* January–February 1994, pp. 53–58.

45. Johnston, W. B., "Global Work Force 2000: The New World Labor Market," *Harvard Business Review,* March–April 1991, pp. 115–127.

46. For example, refer to ibid.; Richman, L. S., "The Coming World Labor Shortage," *Fortune,* April 9, 1990, pp. 70–77; and Templeman, J. D. C. Wise, E. Lask, and R. Evans, "Grappling with the Graying of Europe," *Business Week,* March 13, 1989, pp. 54–56.

47. Scullion, H., "Strategic Recruitment and Development of the Global Manager," *Proceedings,* Third Conference on International Personnel and Human Resource Management, Ashridge, England, July 2–4, 1992.

48. *EEOC* v. *Arabian American Oil Co.,* 111 S.Ct. 1227 (1991).

49. For a good overview of the issues and historical development related to application of national laws against employment discrimination in overseas operations, refer to Cherian, J., "Current Developments in Transnational Employment Rights," *Labor Law Journal,* May 1989.

50. Garland, S. B., "Were Civil Rights Laws Meant to Travel?" *Business Week,* January 21, 1991, p. 36; Hoerr, J., L. N. Spiro, L. Armstrong, and J. B. Treece, "Culture Shock at Home: Working for a Foreign Boss," *Business Week,* December 17, 1990, pp. 80–84; Jacobs, D. L., "Suing Japanese Employers," *Across the Board,* October 1991, pp. 30–37; Lambert, W., "Sumitomo Sets Accord on Job Bias Lawsuit," *The Wall Street Journal,* November 8, 1990, p. B1; and Payson, M. F., and P. B. Rosen, "Playing by Fair Rules," *HR Magazine,* April 1991, pp. 42–43.

51. Ibid.

52. Society for Human Resource Management, "Court Rules Japanese-Owned Company Not Bound by Title VII," HR: *Issues in HR,* March–April 1992, pp. 1–2.

53. *Fortino* v. *Quasar Co.,* 950 F.2d 389 (7th Cir. 1991).

54. *Sumitomo Shoji America Inc.* v. *Avagliano,* 102 S.Ct. 2374 (1982).

55. Reichel, A., and J. F. Preble, "The El Al Strike in New York," *Journal of Management Case Studies,* 1987, pp 270–276.

56. For information on IRCA, refer to any human resource legal manual or to any of a number of articles that have appeared in the HR press, such as Berry, D. P., and J. T. Appleman, "Policing the Hiring of Foreign Workers: Employers Get the Job," *Personnel,* March 1987, pp. 48–51; Bradshaw, D. S., "Immigration Reform: This One's for You," *Personnel Administrator,* April 1987, pp. 37–40; "The Immigration Reform and Control Act of 1986," *IMPACT,* June 11, 1987, pp. 1–8; May, B. D., "Law Puts Immigration Control in Employers' Hands," *Personnel Journal,* March 1987, pp. 106–113; Ortman, J., "Employer Sanctions: 25 Questions," *Personnel Journal,* October 1987, pp. 60–63; Shusterman, C., "Understanding Immigration Law," *Personnel Journal,* August 1991, p. 43; Skrentny, R., "Immigration Reform—What Cost to Business?" *Personnel Journal,* October 1987, pp. 53–60; and Sullivan, F. L., "Immigration Legislation: An Update," *Personnel,* December 1987, pp. 26–32.

57. Bower, B. L., "New Immigration Law Places New Burdens on Employers," *HR Focus,* December 1991, p. 15; Klasko, H. R., "Immigration Act Demands New Strategies," *HR*

News: International HR, March 1991, pp. C6–C7; Miller, H. N., "Guide to Revised U.S. Immigration Law," *Journal of International Compensation & Benefits,* 1(4), January–February 1993, 31–36; Moore, S., "Mixed Blessings," *Across the Board,* March 1991, pp. 45–49; Nice, A. M., "Skilled Workers Find Easy Access," *HR Focus,* March 1991, pp. 3–4; and Shusterman, C., "A Welcome Change to Immigration Law," *Personnel Journal,* September 1991, pp. 44–48.

4

Training, Management Development, and Performance Appraisal in the International Arena

Firms that operate in the international arena confront a number of special problems related to the training and development of workforces and managers. Responsibility for training and development is traditionally one of the human resources department's core functions. So when a firm's international activity reaches a significant level, where it is involved with multiple subsidiaries in other countries, with the transfer of technology to other countries, and with the movement of a large number of expatriates from country to country, the training and development function takes a new and more complex nature.[1]

In this chapter, the international nature of training and development is examined from the perspective of the multinational firm. This includes discussion of the problems associated with developing a management group with a global perspective, the special training needs of expatriates and their families, and the training and development of host-country workforces and managers, and the special problems involved with evaluating the performance of this international workforce, particularly managers and senior technicians. Issues of language interact with all of these topics and are, therefore, discussed first.

LANGUAGE

In today's shrinking world, the ability to communicate accurately and effectively takes on increasing importance. Even though English has become the language in which much of the world's business transactions take place (as discussed in Chapter 3), it is also clear that being able to sell, negotiate, discuss, and manage in the languages of one's neighbors, customers, and employees can improve the probabilities of successful communication and successful business transactions. Those firms which are the most global—such as Coca-Cola, described in IHRM in Action 4.1—are learning how important foreign-language skills are. As the feature shows, at least for Coca-Cola, the ability to speak another language is seen as so important it has become a major plus when recruiting new employees. Other features in this text have also illustrated how important foreign-language skills are. Indeed, a recent survey of the readers of an international business magazine found that 85 percent of polled readers felt that ability to speak a foreign language was very or somewhat important to success as an international manager.[2] This is a reversal of the attitudes found in the past in other surveys of (mostly American) executives who often felt that the ability to speak English was enough.[3]

IHRM IN ACTION 4.1
LANGUAGE SKILLS
AND THE COCA-COLA COMPANY

[In 1990] the Coca-Cola Company transferred more than 300 professional and managerial staff from one country to another under its leadership development program. And the number of international transferees is increasing, says Mike Semrau, assistant vice president and director of international human resources for Atlanta-based Coca-Cola. For most of its 100-year history, the company has been global. It now has operations in 160 countries and employs nearly 400,000 people. "As you look to the future, the people who are running companies are going to be people who have operated in more than one company and in more than one culture," says Semrau. "We recently concluded that our talent base needs to be multilingual and multicultural. Years ago we never thought about that. Today, we do. To use a sports analogy, you want to be sure that you have a lot of capable and competent *bench strength*, ready to assume broader responsibilities as they present themselves."

Everything the company does, he says, is built around that concept: the ability to develop and supply globally, people who have the experience, skills, and values to help the company achieve its objectives. Coca-Cola even includes an HR recruitment forecast in its annual and long-term business strategies. Although vital, "It's not rocket scientist stuff. It's looking out and anticipating whom you're going to need in the future, the same way you do with finances or materials," explains Semrau.

In addressing that goal, Coca-Cola's HR department has set selection standards on which managers can focus when recruiting and hiring. For instance, the company prefers applicants who are fluent in more than one language. Although the language of business is English, says Semrau, candidates who have additional language skills often are more valuable to the company in its transnational dealings than those who speak only English.

"If I'm out recruiting somebody and they speak Spanish, that facilitates our ability to move them into certain areas where Spanish is critical," he says. "We increasingly are hiring people who are broader-based." Testament to that fact is the company's own Cuban-born CEO Roberto Goizueta, who started with Coca-Cola in Cuba and became chairman in 1979. His philosophy? Successful companies need people with the mind of a strategist: "We must recruit and nurture the growth of associates to match the needs of the business. In the 1990s, internationalists having multilingual and multicultural capabilities will be the norm." Applying this philosophy, of the directors of the company's twenty-one divisions, only four are Americans.

This new importance placed on being multilingual is well stated in the words of George Gourlay, the assistant vice president of corporate manufacturing operations for the Coca-Cola Company: "Understanding how to function in different cultures and different languages is fundamental to our success. Knowing how to give our customers what they expect—consistently, wherever we operate, regardless of local conditions—is our challenge."[4] His point, which would be echoed by all global firms, is that the quality of the product is in the perception of your customer. And this is only going to be influenced effectively when you understand the culture of your consumer. Gourlay goes on to say, "Language study . . . opens the door to deeper cultural understanding. Speech patterns, thought patterns, and behavior [i.e., consumer] patterns are all interlinked."[5]

This ability to speak two or more languages is seen as so important, in fact, that chief executives of a number of multinational American firms are learning a second language.[6] For example, Du Pont Chief Executive Edgar S. Woolard, Jr., took a crash course in Japanese and a number of his executive colleagues (at Du Pont and other firms such as Eastman Kodak, Citicorp, and General Electric's Medical Systems division) are also taking cram courses in second languages. French, German, and Japanese appear to be the favorites among Americans attending major language schools,[7] but overall Spanish probably maintains a lead in numbers of Americans who speak it as a second language. And, of course, an increasing number of U.S. citizens speak Spanish as a first language, in effect making Spanish the "local language" in many locations across the United States.

One aspect of language that has not received much attention, but which often falls under the IHR manager's responsibilities, involves translation, the use of interpreters, and adaptation of business and training materials into foreign languages and cultures.[8] Selection of interpreters and translators needs to be given special attention, for being good at interpretation and translating requires more than training in the original and the foreign language. It also requires deep familiarity with the nature of the business and any technical and special managerial terminology which may not translate easily into the foreign language or back into the original language.

THE TRAINING OF EXPATRIATES

The first major international training responsibility for HR managers usually concerns the preparation of expatriates (and their families) for overseas assignments. Indeed, even for large multinationals, this may be the only attention paid to international training issues for quite some time (and in many firms, even this receives very little attention). Management development will remain the purview solely of managers from the parent firm (and may not seriously involve international experience), and the training of local workforces will stay the concern of local-national HR managers. Nevertheless, at some point, the firm will come to recognize how important is the preparation of its expatriates (and their families).

As discussed in the previous chapter, the preparation of expatriates prior to going overseas is at least as important as selecting the right candidate and family in the first place (refer to Figure 3.2). A lot of evidence suggests that MNEs do not do a very thorough job of this, and yet the inability to adjust, in one form or another—which can often be improved through training and orientation—is generally the reason for "failure" in an overseas assignment.[9] "There is too much emphasis on executives' technical abilities and too little on their cultural skills and family situation," says Roger Herod, vice-president of international human resources at Campbell Soup Company.[10] "When international executive relocations fail, they generally fail either because expatriates can't fathom the customs of the new country or because their families can't deal with the emotional stress that accompanies relocation." In both cases, orientation to the "culture shock" they will experience in their new environments seems particularly important.

Experienced international HR managers think it is absolutely necessary for expatriate success in foreign assignments to give the candidate and his or her family enough adequate, accurate information about the assignment and location for them to be able to make informed decisions about the desirability of such an assignment.[11] This needs to be more than a week-long familiarization trip to the proposed location, even though this is important. Both the employee and spouse should be well briefed on the new assignment's responsibilities as well as on the firm's policies regarding expatriate compensation, benefits, taxes, security procedures, and repatriation.

In addition, the employee and family need to be provided with all the information, skills, and attitudes which they will need to be comfortable, effective, and productive in the overseas assignment. Much of this orientation and training must be focused on the cultural values and norms of the new country and their contrast with those of the home country. Figure 4.1 provides a model for understanding this overall development of expatriates. Given a number of different types of problems that expatriates and their families might face plus a number of possible development objectives, the particular methods chosen for the training or development should vary as well.

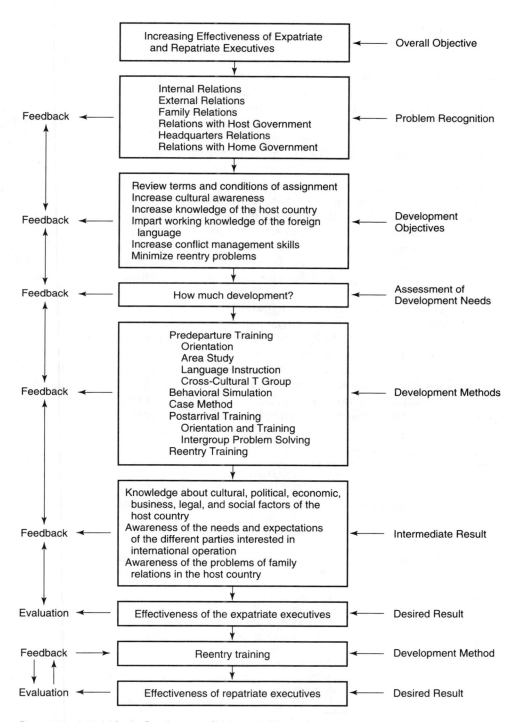

Figure 4.1. A Model for the Development of Multinational Management

Source: A Model for Developing Key Expatriate Executives," by A. Rahim, © April 1983. Reprinted with permission of PERSONNEL JOURNAL, ACC Communications, Inc., Costa Mesa, CA. All rights reserved.

The model, for example, suggests that first management (or IHRM) must recognize the various types of problems that exist for expatriate executives. These range from difficulties with business relationships (either within or external to the subsidiary or with headquarters), difficulties within the expatriate's family, or difficulties with either host or home governments. Each of these potential sources of difficulty has its own particular solutions with its own specific objectives that will help overcome the problems. For example, developing a working knowledge of the foreign language that will be needed can lead to improvements in a number of the possible relationship concerns. The particular development methods chosen need to be matched to the specific development needs. And, of course, at every step in the development model, evaluation of progress and feedback into the process (for possible changes in focus and methods, when necessary) are important. Ultimately, the objective is for the expatriate to be successful in his or her assignment, to remain in the foreign location for the duration of that assignment, and to return to the parent firm to an assignment that effectively uses the repatriate's new skills and motivation.

A number of authors have suggested that cross-cultural training ought to be matched to the nature of the particular need.[12] Table 4.1 shows one author's matching of method and technique to purpose in the training of expatriates. In particular, these authors are concerned that as the differences between the culture of the expatriate (and his or her family) become greater when compared to that of the new overseas assignment, the length and rigor of the training should become greater.

At a minimum, training and orientation on the following topics should be provided to facilitate the ever-crucial cultural adjustment process:[13]

Table 4.1 Training the International Assignee

METHOD	TECHNIQUE	PURPOSE
Didactic-Informational Training	Lectures Reading material Videotapes Movies	Area studies, company operation, parent-country institutions
Intercultural Experiential Workshops	Cultural assimilators Simulations Role playing	Culture-general, culture-specific negotiation skills; reduce ethnocentrism
Sensitivity Training	Communication workshops T groups Outward-bound trips	Self-awareness, communication style, empathy, listening skills, nonjudgmentalism
Field Experiences	Meeting with ex-IAs Minicultures Host-family surrogate	Customs, values, beliefs, nonverbal behavior, religion
Language Skills	Classes Cassettes	Interpersonal communication, job requirements, survival necessities

Source: "Training the International Assignee," by Simcha Ronen, in TRAINING AND DEVELOPMENT IN ORGANIZATIONS, by I. L. Goldstein and Associates, eds. Reprinted with the permission of Jossey-Bass, Inc., Publishers. Copyright 1989 by Jossey-Bass, Inc., Publishers. All rights reserved.

- Intercultural business skills (e.g., negotiation styles in different countries and cultures);
- Culture shock management (e.g., what to expect and how to deal with the stress of adaptation);
- Life-style adjustment (e.g., how to deal with different shopping and transportation systems and the differing availability of familiar foods and entertainment);
- Host-country daily living issues (e.g., any unfamiliar problems with water or electricity);
- Local customs and etiquette (e.g., what to wear and different behavior patterns for men and women);
- Area studies (e.g., the political and religious environment);
- Repatriation planning (e.g., how to stay in touch with the home office and how to identify an appropriate assignment prior to repatriating back home); and
- Language learning strategies, both before leaving for the new assignment as well as after arrival.

In the broader picture, many firms divide their preparation of expatriates into two categories: counseling and training. The counseling component deals primarily with the mechanics of a move abroad while the training tries to develop skills and sensitivities to national and cultural issues that will better enable the expatriate and family to adapt to and enjoy their new situation. Increasingly, firms are realizing how important such preparation is to the international business success of their expatriates.[14] CIBA-GEIGY (a Switzerland-based international pharmaceutical company) does a particularly fine job of this type of preparation.[15] The types of topics covered by their typical counseling and training sessions include the following:

COUNSELING

- Compensation, benefits, and taxes;
- Travel;
- Shipping and storage of household goods;
- Housing and property management;
- Local transportation;
- Allowances;
- Vacations and home leaves;
- Language training and orientation; and
- Children's educational expenses and options.

TRAINING

- Local customs, politics, religions, attitudes;
- Local laws;
- Safety;
- Cultural sensitivity, food, water, and so on; and
- Background briefing on company: history, policies, individuals.

IHRM in Action 4.2 illustrates how the thorough preparation of expatriates and their families impacts the IHR manager at a firm like Ferro Corporation of Cleveland.

IHRM IN ACTION 4.2
HR ASSISTANCE
FOR EXPATRIATES AT FERRO
CORPORATION

One frequent responsibility of global human resource managers is facilitating international placements. At Cleveland-based Ferro Corporation (described in IHRM in Action 2.1), the HR department assists in numerous ways its U.S. managers who are about to become expatriates. "We have a positively daunting checklist," says David Woodbury, Ferro's vice-president of human resources. A *few* of the department's tasks include:

- Developing an overseas compensation and benefits plan, taking into account cost-of-living differences and any special needs;
- Giving tax advice and financial counseling;
- Supervising the sometimes-extensive paperwork involved;
- Assisting with housing and the selection of good schools;
- Helping the employee set up banking accounts and make cash transfers;
- Transferring medical, dental, and school records, and assisting with inoculations;
- Helping with absentee ballots and international driving licenses;
- Providing language training, often through "immersion" courses;
- Assisting with moves of household furniture and goods abroad; and
- Helping the trailing spouse get work permits and jobs abroad, if possible.

Source: "Global HR," by E. Brandt, © March 1991. Reprinted with permission of PERSONNEL JOURNAL, ACC Communications, Inc., Costa Mesa, CA. All rights reserved.

Another firm recommends that a thorough preparation program include all of the following:[16]

1. A pre-visit to the new site;
2. Language training;
3. Intensive area study;
4. Country-specific handbooks that include both country and company facts and where to get additional information;
5. In-company counseling on issues such as taxes, legal matters, compensation, the move, and the like;
6. Meetings with repatriates who have recently returned from the location to which the transferee is moving; and
7. Local sponsorship and assistance for arrival and orientation to the new locale and assignment.

Such an extensive program of preparation can minimize the high level of premature returns and bad experiences due to maladjustment to foreign assignments by expatriates and/or their families.

Even though there is much controversy as to the ability of people to learn about other cultures through training programs (some authors suggest one must experience a culture first-hand in order to gain a real understanding and/or adaptation to it), at least some evidence suggests that they do help.[17] Indeed, the experience of the American University–based Business Council for International

Understanding in its work with Shell Oil Company shows that predeparture training can reduce dramatically the expatriate failure rate (as described in the previous chapter).[18] Prior to providing any training for the employees it sent to Saudi Arabia, Shell was experiencing a 60 percent early return rate. With three days of training, that rate dropped to 5 percent. With a six-day predeparture program, the figure dropped to 1.5 percent! Actually, without predeparture cross-cultural training, it is estimated that only about 20 percent of Americans sent overseas do well.[19]

Expatriates and their families must learn to cope with—depending on the country—a varying number, importance, and criticality of disruptions to their normal routines and ways of living. Thus effective training must vary its content and intensity with the distance between what is normal and expected and what will be experienced in the new assignment. The greater the distance between the parent culture and that of the new country, the more extensive and lengthy the training should be.

The University of Michigan has begun running a program for executives from around the world, and the executives themselves report that the program is quite successful in helping them to become more sensitive to multiple cultures as well as to learn more about global management.[20] In the Michigan program, the executives learn about other cultures through interaction with fellow participants from multiple countries and through problem-solving projects in other countries. The value of this training in other cultures is illustrated by the success of firms like Canada's Northern Telecom in countries such as Japan, as described in IHRM in Action 4.3.

IHRM IN ACTION 4.3
THE SECRET TO NORTHERN'S
JAPANESE SUCCESS: WHEN
IN TOKYO . . .

When Northern Telecom Ltd. installed its first central-office switches in Japan in 1989, the Canadian company's U.S. technicians were fast but not fastidious. Tools were scattered around. Packaging materials got left at installation sites. And while Japanese co-workers switched into slippers before entering the office, the Americans kept on their boots. That style flopped with Japanese customers. Says John D. MacDonald, chairman of Northern Telecom Asia/Pacific: "We managers weren't paying attention to the right details."

Today, Northern has mastered Japanese etiquette and a lot more. Its U.S. technicians are better trained [in Japanese etiquette and work practices, in particular], and the company bows to Japan's grueling technical specifications. It's also matching the competition point for point on quality. As a result, Northern has penetrated deeper into Japan's tough telecommunications market than any other foreign suppler. . . . After navigating the ins and outs of Japanese culture for five years, Northern looks set to begin enjoying more of the rewards.

INTERNATIONAL MANAGEMENT DEVELOPMENT

There comes a point in the development of multinational firms when they begin to examine their management development programs from an international perspective—beyond what they might already have been doing to prepare their expatriates. At this point, they realize that not only is international experience important for their parent-country managers, but these firms also begin to recognize the importance of developing their managerial talent from all over the world. Michael Angus, chairman of Unilever PLC (a joint Anglo-Dutch MNC and the world's largest consumer-products firm with over 300,000 employees worldwide), states that "most people who rise to the top of our business will have worked in at least two countries, probably three [and] will probably speak another language."[21] Preston Townley, CEO of the U.S. Conference Board (a membership organization of most of America's largest firms), reflects the views of many senior U.S. executives when he makes the point like this: "The successful managers of the future will probably be those who speak both Japanese and English [no matter which other languages they speak], who have a strong base in Brussels and contacts in the Pacific Rim, and who know the cafes and bars of Singapore."[22]

In the words of Alain Gomez, chairman and CEO of France's global electronics giant, Thomson (in response to a question about managing the multiculturalism which Gomez sees as crucial to the firm's global success):

> Product development will be one measure. . . . Management is the other metric I watch. We must develop a natural system of promotion that will produce leaders in proportion to the nationalities that are part of Thomson. Right now we have two Americans and one German national among our top eight management positions. That is not bad, but it is not good enough. When you drop down in the management ranks, the proportion is even lower.[23]

Indeed, probably the most formidable task in the human resource area facing many global firms today is the development of a cadre of managers and executives who have a deep understanding of the global market environment, have the capability to transfer this knowledge into resolute action, and who expect to see their rewards and personal growth linked to opportunities for global careers in which to exercise this understanding.[24] Many global firms have invested well in the development of local staff and can thus find competent managers who are well qualified to handle local operations in most of their principle markets (this is also true, of course, for the home market). At the same time, though, they are short of seasoned executives with broader international skills who are closely attuned to the firm's global strategy.

Too much localization has often resulted in insufficient globalization. But reversing this trend is not easy, in terms of both the cost and complexity of developing a new breed of global executives and the challenge this creates for the established process of management development.

As important as management development with an international focus has become for MNCs, there has not been much research into patterns or methods employed by the major firms. Nevertheless, one author (Paul Evans of INSEAD, Europe's largest corporate-based MBA and executive training program) has, in conjunction with colleagues, identified a number of key elements.[25]

The most important of these common elements for the major MNCs is the priority placed on identifying and developing management talent.[26] At firms such as IBM, Shell, Philips, and Unilever, responsibility for international executive development is so important that it is specifically a board concern and the individual in charge of this activity reports directly to the CEO. These firms have found that the lack of management talent has been a major inhibitor in setting up businesses or developing new projects, even in some cases preventing them from staffing projects which have been technically feasible. Even smaller firms have come to understand its importance. In the words of Graham Corbett, senior partner for Peat Marwick's Continental European practice: "We are on a fast growth track, and our major task is to attract and develop enough professional talent to enable us to support the growth rates we are experiencing."[27]

Firms from different countries appear to have evolved varying approaches to management development. Yet there appear to be some common elements among them. These include practices such as (1) the early identification of individuals with executive potential, either through early-in-career assessment procedures and close monitoring of job performance or recruiting at only elite universities and "grand écoles" or the use of in-house apprenticeships that lead to increasing levels of management responsibility; and (2) the use of close monitoring of those individuals identified through whichever procedure to be candidates for positions of executive leadership. The primary purpose of the close monitoring is to manage the careers and job assignments of these high-potential employees. The movement (or mobility) of these individuals is controlled so as to ensure that they experience job assignments of adequate variety and challenge (to include multiple functional, product, and country experiences, many of which will be away from the individual's area of proven expertise) and length (so as to ensure the individuals learn how to achieve results through other associates, colleagues who are possibly more technically expert in the particular assignment and who may be from other countries and cultures). A number of observers have also noticed that many of the large multinational firms have realized that this mobility among their international workforces creates informal networks that enable information and problem solving to be shared worldwide in a more effective way than formal, hierarchical structures appear to provide.[28]

For example, Unilever Corporation has long been committed to the development of its human resources as a means of attaining durable competitive advantage. As early as the 1930s, the company was recruiting and developing local employees to replace the parent-company managers who had been running most of its overseas subsidiaries.[29] Although Unilever was delighted with the talent that began working its way up through the organization, it soon realized that by reducing the transfer of parent-company managers abroad, it had diluted the powerful "glue" that had bound its diverse organizational groups together and had linked its dispersed operations.

In order to address this problem, Unilever began to increase, again, its cross-border assignments for high-achieving managers, this time without as much attention to their countries of origin. And it developed a major management development and training center near London (referred to as "Four Acres"). The ultimate aim of these actions was to facilitate the development of contacts and relationships among its managers worldwide. In the words of a senior personnel manager at Unilever:

> By bringing managers from different countries and businesses together at Four Acres, we build contacts and create bonds that we could never achieve by other means. The company spends as much on training as it does on R&D not only because of the direct effect it has on upgrading skills and knowledge but also because it plays a central role in indoctrinating managers into a Unilever club where personal relationships and informal contacts are much more powerful than the formal systems and structures.[30]

Developing a Global Perspective

Increasingly, as more firms become global in their business activities, a major strategic concern is to create a managerial group that has a global perspective. An international management development program alone may not achieve this objective. This global perspective includes sensitivity to multiple cultures and their differences, work experience in more than one country, and willingness to seek customers, financial resources and supplies, technology, innovations, and employees throughout the world. The efforts being made by different MNCs and global firms to develop this global perspective vary considerably from each other. For example, France's Thomson, a firm which has in the last few years established itself as a major player in the world's electronics business, including consumer electronics and semiconductors, presents one such approach. Alain Gomez, again in response to a question about how Thomson is managing its necessary multiculturalism, states:

> To address that, we insist on the internationalization of in-house training. We have instituted seminars for senior managers in which half of the seminar takes place in Europe and half takes place in the United States. Next year [1991], those seminars will include our Asian managers, and half the time will be spent in the Far East, with the other half in either Europe or the United States. Each year we also hold several sessions that bring together groups of 150 or so young engineers and executives who have been with the company for three years. They come to France from all over Thomson and all over the world.[31]

IHRM in Action 4.4 shows how General Electric's Medical Systems Group (GEMS) uses a worldwide training effort to integrate its global workforce in a way that focuses on achieving the firm's global strategy.

IHRM IN ACTION 4.4
GEMS' GLOBAL LEADERSHIP
PROGRAM

Among the most sophisticated global human resources programs is that of Milwaukee-based GE Medical Systems Group (GEMS). A $3-billion division of the

$49.7-billion General Electric Co., GEMS has 15,000 employees, 7,000 of whom are located outside the United States. Integrating its HR efforts was a matter of necessity, says Toby S. D'Ambola, the company's manager of human resources and a 35-year GE veteran. In 1985, only 13 percent of GEMS' revenues came from outside the United States. By 1990, that proportion had soared to more than 40 percent and continues to grow.

The centerpiece of the company's international HR effort is its Global Leadership Program, also called G.L.P. It's a multiyear process by which several international managers from each of GEMS' three regions—the Americas, Europe, and Asia—get together with a highly organized framework to work on important business projects, such as improving worldwide engineering productivity, sharing technical expertise among international units, and developing a strategy for a global network of suppliers.

Human resources professionals are not only administering the G.L.P. Along with managers from other disciplines, they're actively participating in work groups. One G.L.P. team, for example, worked on worldwide employee integration to increase employee commitment and sense of belonging at all levels throughout the international organization.

Whirlpool Corporation, when it significantly increased its international presence by purchasing the $2-billion appliance division of N.V. Philips Gloeilampenfabrieken of the Netherlands in 1989, realized it needed a way to develop a global perspective for both its U.S. managers and its new European associates.[32] The solution for Whirlpool was to organize a conference in Montreux, Switzerland, for its top 140 executives from 16 different countries of North America and Europe. The conference was designed to achieve four objectives:

- Advance a unified vision of the company's future;
- Instill the idea of embracing the future as one global company;
- Establish a keen sense of responsibility within the leadership group for creating the company's future; and
- Identify and initiate explicit steps toward integrating various activities and ideas throughout Whirlpool's worldwide operations into a unified whole.

The conference architects determined that the first goal of the conference was to encourage managers to think of each other not as *foreigners*, but rather as business partners.[33] The second goal was to give them the amount of time and tools they needed to identify the company's challenges and create solutions to move Whirlpool's worldwide businesses forward. The conference was so successful, the next year another conference was convened in Washington, DC, and the decision has been made to make these annual events.

In the words of Ed Dunn, Whirlpool's corporate vice president of HR, "The first day these were 140 strangers, but by the last day, they were 140 very close col-

Table 4.2 Tips on How to "Globalize" Management

- Select a small number of rising "superstars" and send them on meaningful over-seas assignments. Repatriate them after two or three years.
- Bring the best overseas talent into headquarters for meaningful interim assign-ments followed by repatriation.
- Recruit staff out of universities worldwide and place them in entry-level posi-tions overseas early in their careers. Pay these recruits as close to local hiring rates as possible—do not give them standard expatriate pay packages.
- Reserve one or more positions in your international HR activity for returning ex-patriates. Too many international HR departments lack credibility.
- Move some of the best talent of all nationalities, including HR professionals, in-ternationally.
- Develop a longer-range view of management development, including overseas assignments.
- Consider moving certain businesses, units, or functions to another country for more effective global interaction.

Source: C. Reynolds, "HR Must Influence Global Staff Strategy," HR NEWS: INTERNATIONAL HR, March, 1991, C2. Reprinted with permission of HR NEWS published by the Society for Human Resource Management, Alexandria, VA. All rights reserved.

leagues."[34] Dunn continues, "You can't globalize your company unless you first globalize your people. To be effective, employees need to know and understand each other before they can work together."

An innovative, multifirm approach to helping executives develop a global perspective has been developed at the University of Michigan, as was mentioned earlier.[35] This program brings fast-track executives from twenty-one different firms from around the world together for five weeks of intensive multicultural team building and focuses on opportunity assessment and problem solving in a number of situations and countries. For the firms and individuals involved, this too appears to be a successful approach to helping individuals develop global perspectives about their jobs and their companies.

A major consulting and corporate survey firm has summarized the actions it has found among American firms that appear to be successfully globalizing their managements. These tips are reproduced in Table 4.2 and show the importance of international mobility and experience for individual managers, rather than focus-ing on the type of central conference experiences outlined above.

IHRM in Action 4.5 provides an example of the development of an inter-national perspective by a manager in a much smaller business. Even for smaller and medium-sized businesses, having an international perspective can be critical to success.

IHRM IN ACTION 4.5
THE GLOBAL CEO

Talk about a hands-on chief executive. When Dick Rubin decided to take Boston Metal Products global, in 1990, he and his wife picked up and moved—to the Hague. "I could have delegated the job to someone else," says Rubin, "but what would I be delegating? I didn't know *anything* about doing business in Europe. All I knew was that we belonged there, that there was a market for our products." Three years later international sales account for about 20 percent of the company's profits and revenues, the latter of which totaled more than $20 million in 1993.

Along the way, Rubin made a surprising discovery about what he calls "the power of the presidency." "Everywhere I go, I run into middle managers of U.S. companies," he says. "I've yet to meet an American CEO. Evidently, people just don't realize the respect accorded presidents in Europe. It opens doors; it instills confidence that promises will be kept."

Rubin thinks he has benefited as much as his company has from going global. "I took over my father's business in 1967. Today I feel as if my personal clock has gone back 25 years; I'm building something from scratch again, and I'm thriving on it. I feel revitalized." So when will he come home? "We're not coming home. I'm having too much fun. This move is permanent."

Source: "The Global CEO," December, 1993. Reprinted with permission of INC. magazine. Copyright 1993 by Goldhirsh Group Inc., 38 Commercial Wharf, Boston, MA 02110.

And for a final example of how a major global firm has implemented a strategy to broaden the international experience of its managers, which is itself a major component of the firm's strategy to become a truly transnational or global firm and be a leader in its industry, ICI Pharmaceuticals, a division of ICI PLC of the United Kingdom, the fourth largest chemical company in the world, shows an approach that incorporates many of the points already discussed.[36] ICI Pharmaceuticals realizes that it must do more than provide senior managers a two- to three-year assignment abroad. As its business becomes more transnational, many more employees require experience of cultural differences and international teamworking. The strategies being adopted to broaden the level of international experience at ICI Pharmaceuticals include:

- Internationalize the headquarters staff to a greater extent through increased transfers from abroad to the headquarters;
- Extend the use of international assignments (two to three years) and of short-term international assignments (six to twelve months);
- Make greater use of extended business visits (one to two months) and international project teams (indeed involving managers in multinational teams from as early a date in their careers as possible plus providing training in successful teamwork in such international teams);
- Identify and use international coordination roles across the business for purposes of broadening the participants' global view of the business;
- Make greater use of cultural awareness and language training and business briefings to increase knowledge of the international aspects of the business.

ICI Pharmaceuticals is even providing cross-cultural training for secretarial and support staff in the U.K. and other major countries, such as Italy, who have frequent interactions with staff from other countries.

TRAINING OF LOCAL WORKFORCES AND MANAGEMENT

As multinational firms establish increasing numbers of foreign subsidiaries and joint ventures and hire increasing numbers of HCNs and TCNs, the training of those local workforces takes on increasing importance. Training always seems to be a controversial program among top executives. Even though their rhetoric usually expresses the importance of maintaining a highly trained workforce, only some firms provide the resources to give training the priority the executive statements and annual reports suggest is necessary. This is just as true on the international level as it is on the purely domestic level.

In addition, not much has been written about the problems confronted or the programs developed to meet those problems in the delivery of training in multiple countries and cultures.[37] Nevertheless, this section provides an overview of issues related to training in the MNE as well as a sample of some of the approaches taken by major American MNEs.

Basic Issues

The types of problems confronted by the multinational firm when it begins to confront the demand for training its local workforces around the world include the following:[38]

- Who should deliver the training in the foreign subsidiaries? Trainers from headquarters? Local trainers? Independent trainers?
- How should the training be delivered? Are there local cultural differences that need to be considered?
- What are the effects of language differences? Translation problems (for both written and orally presented materials)? Are there differences in the meanings of words? Are there terms that don't exist in the "foreign" languages?
- Should training programs be exported from headquarters? Or should overseas personnel be brought to centralized training facilities? What are the effects of the various options?
- Should courses for management development be handled differently than training for HCNs and TCNs?
- To ensure respect for each host country's culture, should each subsidiary develop its own training?
- How do you adapt a training program (in terms of both the content and the process of the training) to different countries and cultures?

The difficulty for MNEs, of course, is that there are no absolute answers to these questions. Most firms appear to be developing international training practices that fit their particular needs, resources, and assumptions about what should work best. IHRM in Action 4.6 presents the practices of a number of major American MNEs (Johnson Wax, IBM, 3-M, McGraw-Hill, and Merck) and illustrates both the variety in approaches and also some of the types of problems confronted and some of the complexities in managing this international training.

IHRM IN ACTION 4.6
INTERNATIONAL TRAINING
AT JOHNSON WAX, IBM, 3-M,
MCGRAW-HILL, AND MERCK

The following short descriptions of the international training programs at five major MNEs shows clearly both the complexities in managing and delivering workforce training on a global basis as well as some of the very different approaches which are taken to this activity.

Thomas Newman, corporate director of training for Johnson Wax in Racine, Wisconsin, designs and, in some cases, delivers training for forty-five subsidiaries around the world. Newman does not ordinarily adapt courses to fit the cultures of the various countries in which the subsidiaries are located. Johnson Wax wants to maintain a strong corporate culture and believes this is one way to cultivate it.

Still there are differences among countries that necessitate some changes. For instance, a team-building course that has been delivered at Johnson Wax locations around the world hasn't been delivered in Brazil. The reason, Newman says, is that Brazilian advisers have told him that the country's culture is imbued with the idea of teamwork. Asking Brazilian employees to take a team-building course would be redundant and might be insulting.

In other cases, corporate imperatives sometimes require that Johnson Wax buck the country's culture—albeit however slowly—in order to achieve its goals, says Newman. For instance, the Chinese culture is so infused with the concept of destiny that the idea of self-development seems pointless. After all, if you are destined to be a supervisor, it's fruitless to try to develop yourself into a middle manager or top executive. Setting objectives and doing performance appraisals are other concepts common in the United States but uncommon—and sometimes considered inappropriate—in other countries.

Johnson Wax stations human resource directors in regions around the world who advise Newman on whether, when, and how a program should be delivered. "They're pretty culturally sensitive," he says. In addition, he'll check with the general manager of the subsidiary to determine whether his training agenda is appropriate for the trainees there. Ideally, Newman would like to have a full-time trainer in each subsidiary who could deliver all the training in the native language. But some of the subsidiaries are quite small, and a full-time trainer would be an extravagance.

It's a budgetary tug-of-war that is familiar to a lot of international companies that simply can't support a training department in every location. Most companies would probably like to emulate IBM, which has an education department in each of its worldwide locations. But that's expensive.

IBM organizes its education functions from 132 countries into 5 geographic units. In each unit, there is an education organization that acts as the coordinating hub. Then, within each country, there is an education operation. Some countries have as few as 5 trainers, while the United States' education division contains about 2,000 people, says Ursula Fairbairn, director of education for IBM worldwide.

Fairbairn directs meetings of the education directors from each region, who collectively agree on an overall education strategy. Each director is responsible for implementing that strategy and delivering whatever courses are needed.

3-M is even more decentralized in its approach than IBM. The company, based in St. Paul, Minnesota, has subsidiaries in fifty-two countries, each of which is responsible for its own training, says Benton Randolph, manager of human resources development, international operations.

Often the subsidiaries develop and deliver their own courses. However, sometimes they will ask for consulting help from the corporate training staff. Or they might need training connected with a new product developed in the United States. Or they might ask for a particular type of generic course, with the understanding that it will be adapted for the country. "We expect them to say, 'These are good ideas but we will draw on them and create our own approach,' " says Randolph. Curious to see how much the courses on a particular topic varied, Randolph examined some of them and found they had a great deal in common. It is not true, he says, that training courses need to be developed here because the United States is more advanced in understanding management principles and training methods. There is no reason that training cannot be developed in subsidiaries and imported into the United States. In fact, that fall, top executives would be traveling from St. Paul to Europe to participate in a management development course prepared in Europe for delivery in Europe. In the future, says Randolph, he envisions the same sort of initiatives coming from Asia and Latin America. That is as it should be, he adds. "Not all goodness and knowledge rests here."

Some companies take a more centralized approach, sending headquarters trainers around the world to deliver training. But they typically try to adapt the instruction as much as possible. Kermit Boston, a vice president of New York City–based McGraw-Hill, is in charge of the publishing company's international training. He often delivers training in the company's seventeen locations, largely in Europe and Asia.

About five years ago, McGraw-Hill merged its domestic and international operations. Shortly thereafter, corporate executives decided that all employees needed training that, if done properly, could bind the two divisions together and help to nourish a corporate culture.

Before 1984, very little training was done in McGraw-Hill's foreign locations. Now the units request whatever training they think they need, and it's usually delivered by a trainer from corporate headquarters. Boston says he hopes to be able to develop someone in each unit as an instructor eventually.

In the meantime, he says he tries hard not to be an "ugly American" while delivering training at foreign units. Before he began training abroad, he talked to about twenty people who had done international training. Then he talked with international McGraw-Hill managers about training needs for their divisions and how they preferred to have training delivered. For each location, he spent weeks working with each managing director, then arrived several days in advance to get a feel for the place and spend time with the participants.

Some global firms that don't maintain training departments in each subsidiary but still believe in the importance of training delivered locally, sometimes cultivate independent trainers in the various countries. That is one of the approaches taken by MSD Agvet, a division of Merck and Co. Inc., which produces and markets livestock and agricultural products. It does business in more than 100 countries and has subsidiaries in 21 of them.

Richard S. Miller, manager of training and conference services, says that most of Agvet's training programs are developed centrally and pilot tested in the United States. But they're delivered in different ways. Marketing and sales managers come together for their training in each of the regions in which Agvet operates. But to train salespeople in each subsidiary, Agvet takes one of three approaches.

In subsidiaries with at least twenty-five people, it will often train a line manager to deliver the training. Local managers have the advantage of knowing the trainees and being able to adapt the courses to mesh with the local culture. In smaller subsidiaries, in which there is no one available to deliver training but the subsidiary's general manager wants the training delivered by a local person, Miller will turn to a local, independent trainer, someone he has cultivated in advance who can deliver the course in the native language and is able to make any necessary adaptations.

The third approach is to send someone from central headquarters in Rahway, New Jersey, to conduct the training. Miller often selects this option for new-product releases because local trainers lack the knowledge to conduct the training and Miller lacks the time to instruct them. Sometimes, this requires simultaneous translation during a training course, but Miller doesn't think that's an insurmountable problem. Nearly all trainees know English as a second language, he says. If their language skills are weak, Miller frequently breaks them into small groups and encourages them to use their own native tongue.

Varying Country Needs

One of the reasons that the provision of training to multiple subsidiaries around the world is so complex is because the basic educational infrastructure varies so much from country to country. The basic level of literacy varies dramatically; the nature of the educational system and the type of education it provides varies significantly; the level and nature and availability of higher education varies; the availability of vocational education varies considerably; and teaching and learning styles vary from culture to culture as well. In addition, familiarity with various teaching techniques and media as well as relationships between students and instructors also vary so much that it is often impossible to transfer directly either the content or the method of instruction from one place to another.

These issues are not trivial. Not only do they need to be understood by the multinational firm providing training to its existing subsidiaries, but the opening up of Eastern/Central Europe and the republics of the former Soviet Union, as well as renewed attention to helping developing countries, has placed new emphasis on the training of these sometimes well-educated workforces in new technologies. All of the above problems, plus additional cultural problems (such as the merging of various company and national cultures, coping with increased cross-national diversity due to increased numbers of cross-border mergers, acquisitions, joint ventures, and alliances, and the many problems of cross-cultural work teams and training practices) make the management of international training programs a very complex responsibility, indeed.

PERFORMANCE EVALUATION

A critical component in the development of international management is the system of performance evaluation (PE) used by the MNE. The PE system, of course, also relates to other IHRM responsibilities, such as selection of and pay increases for expatriates. But the PE system plays a particularly important role in individual job assignments, development plans, and training decisions. Expatriates and other managers in global firms are critical to the success of the multinational enterprise.

However, one of the most serious stumbling blocks to the career paths and development of these managers is the frequent lack of recognition of the value of expatriation and the informality with which firms evaluate these managers' overseas experiences.

Appraising performance in an international environment is particularly difficult.[39] There are many reasons for this, including: (1) choice of evaluator (e.g., local or home company) and that person's amount of contact with the expatriate; (2) host-country management's perceptions of performance (there are often considerable differences between headquarters and foreign locales in what is valued in terms of performance and in terms of perceptions of the actual behavior);[40] (3) difficulties with long-distance communication with headquarters (for example, in the time and the timeliness of the communications and the understanding of the communications); (4) inadequate establishment of performance objectives for the foreign operations and means for recording levels of individual and organizational performance; (5) parent-country enthnocentrism and lack of understanding of the foreign environment and culture; and (6) frequent indifference to the foreign experience of the expatriate and to the importance of the international business, in general.

The end result all too often is that parent-company bosses either ignore performance evaluation all together for their individual expatriate and foreign managers or they pay attention only to overall financial results of the subsidiary with little or no understanding of the individual behaviors that were (or had to be) exhibited in order to achieve those results.[41] The individual may have performed under extremely difficult circumstances and achieved highly favorable and unexpected results, given the situation, but the bottom line doesn't show it. Without headquarters appreciating that results would have been much worse except for these efforts of the expatriate manager, what gets evaluated are the resulting mediocre financial figures.

From the standpoint of the expatriate, his or her performance is based on his or her overseas judgment, technical know-how, and various relevant environmental factors.[42] His or her actual performance, though, tends to be evaluated in terms of perceived performance (either locally or from the parent company, or both), which is based on a set of fairly complex variables usually below the evaluator's level of awareness. Depending on whether the manager (local or headquarters) who is assessing the expatriate's performance has had personal overseas experience or is otherwise sensitive to problems associated with overseas work, the performance appraisal will be more or less valid.

Because the appraisal will have a major impact on the expatriate's promotion and career potential, type of assignment upon repatriation back home, training and development opportunities, and probably on compensation bonuses, it is of major concern to him or her. Expatriates generally return from their overseas experiences having learned and exercised valuable managerial skills. Therefore, it behooves multinational firms to carefully review their procedures for appraising their expatriates and foreign managers and their evaluation criteria themselves or they risk losing these valuable managerial resources.

In establishing performance criteria, issues should be considered such as the operating language of the foreign assignment, the cultural "distance" to be experienced, and the stability and controllability of major performance factors such as the nature of the workforce, rates of inflation and currency exchange rates.[43] The local manager ought to have major input into the evaluation, but if the evaluation is actually developed by the home-site manager, the assistance of a former expatriate from the location under consideration can be quite valuable in developing an understanding of the local factors that are significant in the expatriate's performance. Evidently, those multinational firms which use appraisal systems, rely on a wide variety of actual appraisal techniques, ranging from a mix of formal and informal procedures, visits to and from headquarters, and examination of operating and financial statistics. In most firms, considerable weight is given to the "gut feel" of specialist HRM or senior line executives from headquarters.[44]

SUMMARY

This chapter has focused on training and development issues as they relate to the MNE. As in domestic firms, in MNEs this HRM responsibility does not always receive the priority and resources that seem necessary.

This chapter first covered the importance of language ability and the increasing awareness in international firms of being able to speak the native language of their customers and employees. Language issues cut across all training and development activities. Secondly, the chapter discussed the training and preparation of expatriates and their families. This particular responsibility tends to get most of the training and development attention of HR managers in global firms. Sophisticated global firms have come to realize the importance of this type of preparation and to provide their employees going to overseas assignments both counseling for problems associated with the move and training in language and cultural issues to facilitate adaptation.

Next the chapter presented the types of programs that MNEs are using to develop their managers on an international basis. Related to this is the concern expressed in many firms for developing managers with global perspectives so as to better function in today's worldwide economy. The chapter described both the centralized and decentralized training, conference, and management mobility programs used by a number of global firms.

The chapter then discussed corporate practices in providing training on an international basis. The whole topic of international training and development has not received much research. This particular component of that topic—the training of local workforces, has received even less. Nevertheless, the procedures followed by a number of major American firms were described.

Lastly, the chapter discussed the particularly different problem of performance evaluation in the international context. From both the MNE's and the expatriate's perspectives, effective evaluation of expatriates and foreign managers is important and typically not handled very well, if at all. An understanding of the difficulties contributed by working in foreign cultures is necessary for all concerned in order to improve the validity of performance appraisal in a multinational environment.

ENDNOTES

1. Recent texts that describe international human resource training and development include Marquardt, M. J., and D. E. Engel, *Global Human Resource Development* (Englewood Cliffs, NJ: Prentice Hall, 1993); Odenwald, S. V., *Global Training: How to Design a Program for the Multinational Corporation* (Alexandria, VA: The American Society for Training and Development, and Homewood, IL: Business One Irwin, 1993); and Reynolds, A., and L. Nadler, eds., *Globalization: The International HRD Consultant and Practitioner* (Amherst, MA: Human Resource Development Press, 1993).

2. "Faxback: What Makes a Great International Manager?" *North American International Business,* May 1991, p. 79.

3. For example, Baker, J. C., "Foreign Language and Predeparture Training in U.S. Multinational Firms," *Personnel Administrator,* July 1984, pp. 68–70.

4. Gourlay, G., "Of Coke and Cargo Cults," *Across the Board,* November 1989, pp. 59–60.

5. Ibid.

6. "Language: One Way to Think Globally," *Fortune,* December 4, 1989, p. 11.

7. Ibid.

8. See, for example, Nadler, Z., "Coping with the Language Barrier: Using Interpreters Effectively"; Pellet, M. R., "Adapting U.S. International Media for Foreign Users"; and Reynolds, A., "Adapting Technology-Based Instruction"; all in Reynolds and Nadler, eds., *Globalization.*

9. See references on expatriates in Chapter 3, plus Baker, J. C., "Foreign Language and Predeparture Training in U.S. Multinational Firms," *Personnel Administrator,* July 1984, pp. 68–72; Houghton, D., "The New ABCs: Foreign Education for Executives," *San Diego Executive,* April 1990, pp. 14–17.

10. Quoted in Blocklyn, P. L., "Developing the International Executive," *Personnel,* March 1989, pp. 44–45.

11. See, for example, Foxman, L. D., and W. L. Polsky, "HR Approaches for the Age of Globalization," *Personnel Journal,* April 1991, pp. 38–41; and Houghton, "The New ABCs."

12. Black, J. S., and M. Mendenhall, "Selecting Cross-Cultural Training Methods: A Practical yet Theory-Based Approach," *Human Resource Management,* 1989, 28(4), 511–540; Kitsuse, A., "At Home Abroad," *Across the Board,* September 1992, pp. 35–38; Landis, D., and R. Brislin, *Handbook on Intercultural Training,* Vol. 1 (New York: Pergamon Press, 1983); Ronen, S., "Training the International Assignee," in *Training and Career Development,* ed. I. Goldstein (San Francisco: Jossey-Bass, 1989); Tung, R. L., *The New Expatriates: Managing Human Resources Abroad* (Cambridge, MA: Ballinger, 1988).

13. See Blocklyn, "Developing the International Executive." In addition, good coverage of the training necessary for cross-cultural adaptation in the expatriate environment can be found in Black, J. S., H. B. Gergersen, and M. E. Mendenhall, *Global Assignments* (San Francisco: Jossey-Bass, 1992); and Harris, P. R., and R. Moran, *Managing Cultural Differences,* 2nd ed. (Houston: Gulf Publishing, 1992).

14. See, for example, Schell, M. S., and M. Stoltz-Loike, "Importance of Cultural Preparation to International Business Success," *Journal of International Compensation & Benefits,* January–February 1994, pp. 47–52.

15. See, for example, Blocklyn, "Developing the International Executive."

16. Lanier, A. R., "Selecting and Preparing Personnel for Overseas Transfers," *Personnel Journal,* March 1979, pp. 160–163.

17. Black, Gregersen, and Mendenhall, *Global Assignments;* Black, J. S., and M. Mendenhall, "Cross-Cultural Training Effectiveness: A Review and a Theoretical Framework for Future Research," *Academy of Management Review,* 15(1), 1990, 113–136; Caudron, S., "Training Ensures Success Overseas," *Personnel Journal,* December 1991, pp. 27–30;

Copeland, L., "Cross-Cultural Training: The Competitive Edge," *Training*, July 1985, pp. 49–53; Earley, P. C., "Intercultural Training for Managers: A Comparison of Documentary and Interpersonal Methods," *Academy of Management Journal*, 30(4), 1987, 685–698.

18. Kohls, L. R., "Preparing Yourself for Work Overseas," in Reynolds and Nadler, eds., *Globalization*.

19. Ibid.

20. Main, J., "How 21 Men Got Global in 35 Days," *Fortune*, November 6, 1989, pp. 71–77; Tichy, N. M., "Global Development," in *Globalizing Management: Creating and Leading the Competitive Organization*, eds. V. Pucik, N. M. Tichy, and C. K. Barnett (New York: John Wiley, 1992); Tichy, N. M., M. I. Brimm, R. Charan, and H. Takeuchi, "Leadership Development as a Lever for Global Transformation," in Pucik, Tichy, and Barnett, eds., *Globalizing Management*.

21. Quoted in Reynolds, C., "HR Must Influence Global Staff Strategy," *HR News: International HR*, March 1991, p. C1.

22. Ibid.

23. McCormick, J., and N. Stone, "From National Champion to Global Competitor: An Interview with Thomson's Alain Gomez," *Harvard Business Review*, May–June 1990, p. 135.

24. Pucik, V., "Globalization and Human Resource Management," in Pucik, Tichy, and Barnett, eds., *Globalizing Management*.

25. Evans, P. A. L., "Human Resource Management and Globalization," keynote address presented to the Third Conference on International Personnel and Human Resources Management, Ashridge Management College, Berkhamsted, Hertfordshire, U.K., July 2–4, 1992; Evans, P., E. Lank, and A. Farquhar, "Managing Human Resources in the International Firm: Lessons from Practice," in *Human Resource Management in International Firms*, eds. P. Evans, Y. Doz, and A. Laurent (London: Macmillan Press Ltd., 1989).

26. This section is based primarily on Evans, Lank, and Farquhar, "Managing Human Resources in the International Firm."

27. Quoted in Ibid.

28. For example, Evans, Lank, and Farquhar, "Managing Human Resources in the International Firm"; Bartlett, C. A., and S. Ghoshal, *Managing Across Borders* (Boston: Harvard Business School Press, 1989); and Maljers, F. A., "Inside Unilever: The Evolving Transnational Company," *Harvard Business Review*, September–October 1992, pp. 46–52.

29. This is described in Bartlett, C. A., and S. Ghoshal, "Matrix Management: Not a Structure, a Frame of Mind," *Harvard Business Review*, July–August 1990, pp. 138–145.

30. Quoted in Bartlett and Ghoshal, "Matrix Management," p. 143.

31. McCormick and Stone, "From National Champion to Global Competitor," p. 135.

32. Laabs, J. J., "Whirlpool Managers Become Global Architects," *Personnel Journal*, December 1991, pp. 39–45.

33. Ibid.

34. Quoted in Ibid.

35. Galagan, P. A., "Execs Go Global Literally," *Training and Development Journal*, June 1990, pp. 58–63; Main, "How 21 Men Got Global in 35 Days."

36. Carr, R. E., and D. R. Plowright, "From International to Transnational: A Strategy for People Development," *Proceedings*, Third Conference on International Personnel and Human Resource Management, Ashridge, England, July 2–4, 1992.

37. See, for example, Geber, B., "A Global Approach to Training," *Training*, September 1989, pp. 42–47; Harris, P. R., and R. T. Moran, *Managing Cultural Differences*, 3rd ed. (Houston: Gulf Publishing, 1991); Probably the best reference yet published for this purpose is Reynolds, A., and L. Nadler, eds., *The Global HRD Consultant's and Practitioner's Hand-*

book (Amherst, MA: Human Resource Development Press, 1993). This book provides many readings about training and development issues, programs, and practices in numerous countries.

38. Adapted from Geber, "A Global Approach to Training."

39. See, for example, Brewster, C., *The Management of Expatriates*, Ch. 4, "Monitoring Performance—And Coming Home" (London: Kogan Page Limited [in association with the Cranfield School of Management, Cranfield, England], 1991); Dowling, P. J., and R. S. Schuler, *International Dimensions of Human Resource Management*, Ch. 4, "Performance Appraisal" (Boston: PWS-Kent, 1990); and Oddou, G., and M. Mendenhall, "Expatriate Performance Appraisal: Problems and Solutions," in *International Human Resource Management*, eds. M. Mendenhall and G. Oddou (Boston: PWS-Kent, 1991).

40. See, for example, Trompenaars, F., *Riding the Waves of Culture: Understanding Diversity in Global Business* (New York: Richard D. Irwin, 1993 and 1994). Dr. Trompenaars found that managers from various countries ranked qualities for evaluation in significantly different orders.

41. For example, see survey results reported in Brewster, *The Management of Expatriates*.

42. Oddou and Mendenhall, *"Expatriate Performance Appraisal."*

43. Ibid.

44. Brewster, *The Management of Expatriates*.

5

International Compensation and Benefits

The design and maintenance of a firm's compensation system is always a critical responsibility for human resource managers. When businesses take on international activity, this responsibility becomes much more complex and difficult. The determination of individual and organizational pay and benefits on an international basis becomes extremely complicated because of considerations such as developing pay and benefits for expatriates who are serving in many different countries, having to cope with subsidiary workforces in more than one country, having to manage employees from numerous countries (HCNs and TCNs), having to understand varying country approaches to and levels of pay and benefits, and having to deal with problems with multiple currencies, exchange rates, inflation rates, tax systems and rates, and differing standards and costs of living.

Even though much space in this text has already been devoted to many other IHRM responsibilities, the majority of the time of headquarters-based international HR managers is spent creating and managing the compensation packages for expatriates.[1] When development of compensation systems for subsidiaries is added to IHRM responsibilities, it is easy to see why this area of concern is so important.

One of the reasons that this area of IHRM responsibility is so complex is that salary levels and benefit provisions invariably differ significantly among the various countries in which an MNE operates.[2] Employees performing essentially similar jobs in different countries will receive varying amounts and forms of compensation. This is due to differing costs of living and general pay levels throughout these economies and varying traditions and values for particular jobs. Thus, it is increasingly difficult to develop and maintain a compensation package that attracts and retains qualified expatriates and local managers, copes successfully with changing exchange rates and varying inflation rates, and is consistent yet fair to both expatriates and local employees. In addition, the cost of attracting and maintaining expatriates and an international cadre of managers and technicians in the traditional ways has become so expensive that MNEs are now looking for new ways to handle international compensation.[3] But the effective design of just such a compensation philosophy and package is absolutely necessary for successful human resource management in the multinational firm.

How an MNE copes with these issues tends at least partially to be a function of its level of international development. In the early stages of development, the firm's primary international involvement will be with a limited number of expatriates sent abroad to market its products, transfer its technology, and manage relatively small operations. At this stage of development, compensation concerns are largely limited to providing adequate remuneration and incentives for expatriates. But as the firm's international involvement develops even further, concerns about compensation programs for employees from multiple countries moving around the world for the firm as well as equity among work forces in many different global locations present many new problems.

Therefore, the main objectives for the typical MNE international compensation program include:

1. Attraction and retention of employees who are qualified for foreign assignments (from the perspective of the parent company, but includes PCNs, HCNs, and TCNs);
2. Facilitation of transfers between foreign affiliates, between foreign affiliates and the parent company (usually headquarters), and between parent-company and foreign locations;
3. Establishment and maintenance of a consistent and reasonable relationship between the compensation of employees of all affiliates, both at home and abroad; and
4. Maintenance of compensation that is reasonable in relation to the practices of competitors yet minimizes costs to the extent possible.

One of the most important considerations for multinational firms in the design of their compensation programs is the problem of comparability (although cost is probably a very close additional and primary consideration). Indeed, in at least one recent survey, 77 percent of the expatriates surveyed were dissatisfied with expatriate salaries and benefits and their international compensation packages in general.[4] (As will be discussed later, not all surveys find this level of dissatisfaction, but these results suggest that among some samples of expatriates it is possible to find a large number of expatriates who are unhappy with their compensation.) And a significant portion of this dissatisfaction was due to feelings of inequity in their salaries and benefits.

This problem of comparability has at least two significant components: (1) maintaining comparability in salaries and benefits (to similar employees in other firms and to peers within the firm) for employees who transfer from one country to another (either from the parent company to foreign subsidiaries or from one subsidiary to another or to headquarters) and (2) maintaining competitive and equitable salaries and benefits among the various foreign operations of the organization.

Until recently, most MNEs felt it was necessary for expatriates to receive a salary and benefit package at least comparable to what they were receiving in their countries of origin. (Because of the high cost of expatriates and because of changing attitudes about the use and purpose of expatriates, this view about expatriate compensation is being questioned. This will be discussed in more detail later in the chapter.) But comparisons between local nationals and expatriates (and between local nationals in different locales of the multinational firm) are inevitably made. In a globally competitive economy (or even a regionally competitive one, such as within Europe), recruiting and holding on to the best employees will require developing a compensation strategy and policy that will minimize problems associated with such comparisons. This chapter discusses both of these issues: wage determination and comparability for expatriates and compensation program design and comparability for subsidiaries in multiple countries.

For firms that are newly developing their international presence, the answers to these three questions may help establish their overall compensation policies:

1. Who (which other companies) provides their competition for people (local firms or international firms)?
2. How much should the compensation and benefits conform to headquarter's goals and practice versus practice at the overseas location?
3. To what extent does the firm want to set precedent for its future presence in the international arena (does the firm want any particular practice or policy to be its program for all future situations or does it want to customize compensation packages for each expatriate/inpatriate and subsidiary)?

IHRM in Action 5.1 illustrates how difficult these issues are for one multinational high-tech firm headquartered in San Jose, California. Even though there seem to be many reasons to maintain company-wide pay scales and comparable benefit packages so that, for example, all marketing managers for consumer products worldwide are paid within the same pay scale, not adapting wage scales to local markets presents numerous problems.[5] In the first case, such marketing managers are less likely to feel inequities among themselves around the world and the problems associated with keeping track of disparate country-by-country wage rates is simplified.

In the second case, problems are created because it is much more expensive to live in some countries (such as Japan) than others (like Greece). If these cost-of-living differences aren't considered, it may be almost impossible to get expatriates to accept postings to the high-cost locales particularly. But paying marketing managers in different countries different salaries based on the local cost of living won't solve all problems either. New problems are thus created by, for example, moving a highly remunerated marketing manager from, say, Tokyo to Athens. (In all cases, an assumption underlying the approach is that the firm can determine fairly accurately

what the community pay levels are within each of the countries of its subsidiaries—
an assumption that is clearly not always correct.)

IHRM IN ACTION 5.1
PAY FOR A GLOBAL WORKFORCE

Expanding the international workforce to include non-U.S. employees has
brought increased capabilities and decreased costs—along with a new set of compensation problems. For example, John Brown, director of international personnel
for a large multinational company, faced just such a dilemma.

"It seems as though our international over-base compensation program has
gotten out of hand. I have US expatriates, third-country nationals, and inpatriates
(as international HR experts now call foreign nationals working in the US) yelling
at me about their allowances. [In addition] headquarters management is yelling at
me because the costs are too high," says Brown. "Quite frankly, I can't seem to get
any answers from our consultant, and no one else in the industry seems to know
how to approach the problem."

Brown told the firm's international division director that he had forty U.S.
expatriates working as field engineers and marketing managers in fourteen countries. He also said he had foreign national employees from the Philippines, Japan,
and Bolivia working alongside the U.S. employees in eight locations worldwide.
Finally, he added, that he had foreign nationals from Thailand and the Philippines
working with U.S. nationals at the organization's San Jose, California, headquarters. In all cases, it was the firm's policy to send such employees out on foreign assignments for less than five years and then return them to their home countries.

An example of the type of complaints that were being received from the
expatriates involves the following inpatriate employees working at the San Jose
headquarters.

"We have a field engineer from the Philippines who's earning the equivalent of $15,000 US in Manila. I have another field engineer from Thailand who's
earning the equivalent of $20,000 US in Bangkok. They've been relocated to our
San Jose facility and are working side by side with American field engineers who
earn $30,000 for the same job. Not only do they work side by side, but they live
near each other, shop at the same stores and eat at the same restaurants. The problem is that I'm spending a lot of money for cost-of-living data for two different
home countries going to San Jose, and yet their current standard of living is the
same. They're angry because their allowances don't reflect how they live in San
Jose. Their allowances also don't reflect how they lived in their home countries,
either.

"So what we have are two employees, one earning $15,000 and the other
earning $20,000, working and living side by side with US counterparts who are
earning $30,000. The solution that most companies have tried is to simply raise the
foreign nationals' salaries to the $30,000 US level, thereby creating a host-country
pay system for a home-country employee.

"Unfortunately, there's nothing more pathetic than the tears of your foreign nationals when it's time to return home, and you have to tell them you're cut-
ting their salary to the pre-US assignment level. What you . . . are looking for is a
pay system that will compensate your foreign nationals either by pay or by provided benefits [including, e.g., housing and local transportation], in a consistent,

fair and equitable manner, and will allow you to repatriate them with minimal trauma."

Source: "Pay for a Global Work Force," by L. P. Crandall and M. I. Phelps, © February 1991. Reprinted with permission of PERSONNEL JOURNAL, ACC Communications, Inc., Costa Mesa, CA. All rights reserved.

The rest of this chapter explains how MNEs try to cope with this complexity as they design country systems for their international operations. First the chapter looks at the problem associated with compensation for expatriates. Second, the chapter looks at the design of global compensation programs. And last, the chapter examines the problems associated with the design of worldwide benefit and taxation programs and policies.

COMPENSATION AND BENEFITS FOR EXPATRIATES

Just as there are objectives for an overall international compensation program, the component that involves expatriates must also meet certain objectives in order to be effective. These include (1) providing an incentive to leave the home country for a foreign assignment; (2) maintaining a given standard of living (although this is being questioned by many MNEs as the cost of sustaining expatriates overseas gets too high); (3) taking into consideration expatriates' career and family needs; and (4) facilitating reentry into the home country at the end of the foreign assignment.[6] To achieve these objectives, MNEs typically pay a high premium over and beyond base salaries to induce managers to accept overseas assignments. The costs to firms are often 2 to 2.5 times the cost of maintaining the manager in a comparable position at home.[7]

Types of Expatriates for the Purpose of Compensation

Most multinational firms have compensated all their expatriates with policies that assumed they were alike. With increasing numbers of expatriates being posted abroad, firms are recognizing that not all expatriates are the same (and should not be compensated as if they were).

In essence, larger firms, with a number of years' experience sending employees overseas, are realizing that they have at least five distinct types of overseas employees. These include (1) temporaries (employees who are given short-term assignments, e.g., less than six months); (2) young, inexperienced expatriates (with assignments for six months to five years) who can be compensated and managed similar to local hires; (3) older, experienced expatriates (moved for their technical or managerial skills) who are compensated with incentives, add-ons, and adjustments; (4) international cadre (expatriate employees from throughout the firm that move from one foreign assignment to another and need to be compensated with a global salary and benefits); and (5) permanent expatriates (posted to a foreign country but who stay there for extended periods—beyond the normal five-year limit for expatriates) who need to be reclassified as locals.

Each of these types of foreign-assignment employees has different needs and can be compensated on different schedules. Many MNEs are just beginning to realize this and thus looking to design more flexible expatriate compensation systems. The next section describes some of these varying approaches.

Approaches to Compensation for Expatriates

There appear to be six basic approaches followed by MNEs and global firms to compensate their expatriates.[8] These include:

Negotiation

When firms first start sending expatriates abroad and while they still have only a few expatriates, the common approach to determining compensation and benefits for those expatriates is to negotiate a separate (and usually unique) compensation package for each individual expatriate. This *ad hoc* approach is quite simple initially, and, given the limited amount of information available about how to design a compensation system for expatriates and the many complexities in such a compensation package compared to domestic compensation and benefits, it is easy to see why HR managers follow this approach.

Balance sheet

The approach followed by most multinationals when their international business expands to the point where the firm has a larger number of expatriates (maybe in the vicinity of twenty or so) is what is referred to as the balance sheet approach. At this point, the negotiation approach has led to too many inconsistencies between the many expatriates and the firm realizes it needs to develop policy and practice that will apply to all expatriates. (In addition, the *ad hoc* approach is probably at this point seen as taking too much time to negotiate, develop, and manage the unique package for each individual.)

In essence, the balance sheet approach involves an effort by the multinational to ensure that its expatriates are "made whole." That is, at a minimum, expatriates should be no worse off for accepting an overseas assignment. Ideally, the compensation package not only should make the expatriate whole but also should provide incentive to take the foreign assignment, to remove any worry about compensation issues while on that assignment, and to ensure that the individual and his or her family feel good about having been on the assignment. Making all of this complicated, of course, is that it takes place in an environment that increasingly asks IHRM to control all employment costs, including the costs of expatriation.

Figure 5.1 provides a model that helps to understand the balance sheet approach to expatriate compensation. This has particularly been the approach of MNEs with significant international activity but prior to becoming what was referred to earlier as a global or transnational firm. This approach is primarily used when the MNE is sending expatriates from the parent firm to its foreign subsidiaries. The approach becomes much more complex as the firm evolves to moving individuals between foreign subsidiaries and from its foreign subsidiaries back

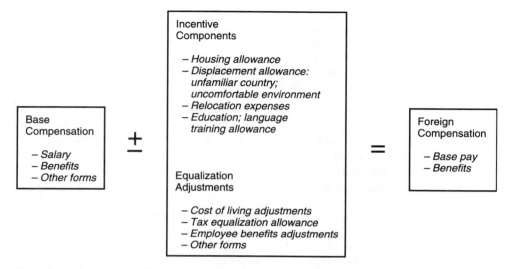

Figure 5.1. International Compensation Balance Sheet Approach

Source: Adapted with permission of Macmillan College Publishing Company from PERSONNEL/HUMAN RE-SOURCE MANAGEMENT by Terry L. Leap and Michael D. Crino. Copyright © 1989 by Macmillan College Publishing Co., Inc. All rights reserved.

to its headquarters or other home-country locations (as illustrated in IHRM in Action 5.1). Firms that are also developing an international cadre of managers who move from foreign assignment to foreign assignment add even another level of complexity to expatriate compensation.

The balance sheet approach is particularly used for experienced senior- and mid-level expatriates and keeps them whole compared to their home-country peers while encouraging and facilitating their movement abroad and return home at the end of their assignments. But with large numbers of expatriates, this can become complex to administer too. Some firms have found that this approach begins to lead managers to view the incentives and adjustments as entitlements that are sometimes difficult to change. And some expatriate managers have complained that this approach to determining their overseas compensation is much more intrusive into their personal lives (basically determining their appropriate standards of living, etc.) than is true for the traditional domestic compensation package.

The balance sheet approach to determination of an expatriate's compensation (and, even in large firms, this is still pretty much customized for each expatriate) begins with the employee's existing parent-company compensation (salary, benefits, and any other forms of monetary or nonmonetary remuneration). To this is added two other components: a series of incentives to accept and enjoy the foreign posting and a series of equalization components that ensure the expatriate does not suffer from foreign-country differences in salary or benefits.

One of the key complications in this balance sheet approach is the determination of the base upon which to add incentives and adjustments. A number of possibilities exist, including basing the expatriate's salary on:

- Parent-country salaries;
- International standard;
- Regional standard (e.g., the European Community, United States, Latin America, Southeast Asia);
- Host-country salaries; or the salaries of other expatriates—peers and/or colleagues—in the host location.

The choice of base to use may be best related to the nature of the firm. That is, if the international assignment is long (three to five years) and assignees often go from one foreign-country assignment to another, then an international standard is probably most appropriate (but it will still probably be based on the parent-country/company base, particularly if the MNE is from a high-wage, developed country). If assignees go to foreign assignments for relatively short assignments and then return to the parent country, then a home-country base makes more sense. For truly global firms, such as Coca-Cola, it may make sense to use regional bases (although these may in reality be some percentage of the home-country base, with the intent of eventually merging the regional bases with the parent-country base).

To date, most companies compensate their expatriates based on either a home- or a host-country philosophy.[9] Interestingly, however, even with all the attention given to designing these compensation packages for expatriates, surveys (in contrast to that reported earlier) show that expatriate managers tend to be pretty satisfied with their financial packages but dissatisfied with the limited career planning, life-style support, and cultural training that is provided.[10] This suggests, as discussed in previous chapters, that more attention ought to be paid to these non-compensation factors.

DETERMINING THE TYPE AND AMOUNT OF INCENTIVES.   Once the base salary has been determined, then the firm must decide which incentives it feels are necessary to convince its employees that it will be to their financial advantage (or, at least as is being increasingly maintained, not to their disadvantage),[11] to take the foreign assignment. One of the key issues that has arisen, here, at least for more experienced MNEs, is the high cost of expatriation. In the past (and still normally for less developed multinational firms), many incentives were offered, often with sizable monetary benefit to the expatriate.

For example, one of the most common incentives has been a large "overseas premium," used to (1) compensate the expatriate for all the adjustments that he or she will need to make; (2) compensate the expatriate and his or her family for the "dislocation" of having to move to an unfamiliar country and to live in what might be seen as an uncomfortable environment; (3) provide an incentive to take the foreign assignment; and (4) keep up with the practices of other MNEs. These premiums used to average about 25 percent of the expatriate's base pay. Today, it is more common for this premium to be about 15 percent of base pay. Also, these premiums were higher for high cost-of-living postings, such as Tokyo, Geneva, or Brussels (see the State Department indexes in Table 5.1). As an example of the disparities from one city to another, the comparable annual cost of living for a family of four having a U.S. salary of $75,000 in 1991 was $63,898 in Mexico City, $74,176 in Moscow, $83,766 in Stockholm, $107,621 in London, and $207,246 in Tokyo![12]

Table 5.1   U.S. State Department Indexes for Cost of Living and Housing Allowances for Selected Cities (Indexes for living costs—excluding housing and education, October 1990)

LOCATION (%)	COL INDEX (D.C. = 100)	MAXIMUM ANNUAL HOUSING ALLOWANCE	HARDSHIP (%)	DANGER
Buenos Aires, Argentina	113			
Canberra, Australia	123			
Vienna, Austria	152			
Brussels, Belgium	146	$25,700		
Rio de Janeiro, Brazil	127			
Montreal, Canada	105	18,900		
Beijing, China	105		25	
Copenhagen, Denmark	150		25	
Cairo, Egypt	77		15	
Paris, France	139	30,700		
Frankfurt, Germany	136	20,200		
Athens, Greece	98	13,400	10	
Hong Kong	118			
New Delhi, India	98		15	
Tel Aviv, Israel	137			
Rome, Italy	128	22,500		
Tokyo, Japan	184	54,500		
Seoul, Korea	136	18,000		
Beirut, Lebanon	80		25	25
Mexico City, Mexico	78	24,100	10	
Riyadh, Saudi Arabia	125		20	
Singapore	115			
Madrid, Spain	128	30,600		
Stockholm, Sweden	171			
Geneva, Switzerland	158	39,800		
Taipei, Taiwan	142			
London, United Kingdom	142	30,000		

Source: Department of State Publications, Bureau of Administration, Allowances Staff, "U.S. Department of State Indexes of Living Costs Abroad, Quarters Allowances, and Hardship Differentials—October 1990" (Washington, DC: Government Printing Office, 1990).

Increasingly, firms are questioning whether it is necessary to pay this premium for an overseas assignment.[13] Critics argue that in a truly global economy with improved communication and transportation and accepted international business norms, there is no longer as much trauma and dislocation associated with an overseas transfer. Still, the great majority of MNEs continue to pay such a premium.[14]

Additional forms of incentives include premiums for "hardship" postings or dangerous postings, which could include many assignments to developing countries, to locations where the threat of kidnapping or terrorist activity is high, or to remote locations (such as the outback of Indonesia or on an ocean oil-drilling platform) or locations with primitive conditions. The three broad areas typically considered in evaluating the extent of hardship include physical threat, level of discomfort, and inconvenience.[15] The physical threat category includes potential or actual violence, hostility to foreigners from the local population, prevalence of disease, and the adequacy of local medical facilities and services. The discomfort category evaluates the physical environment and climate, as well as geographical, cultural, and psychological isolation. And the inconvenience category rates the local education system, the availability and quality of local housing, the access to recreational and community facilities, and the availability, quality, and variety of consumer goods and services.

Hardship allowances typically range from 5 to 25 percent of base pay with danger pay perhaps adding another 25 percent to base pay. Most U.S. MNEs use U.S. State Department tables for determining these amounts. Table 5.1 shows for a few locations what the State Department determines for hardship and danger pay. Depending on the location (such as Beirut, Lebanon), these two incentives could add as much as 50 percent to an expatriate's income.

An example of what corporations provide for hardship pay is provided by these results of a recent survey of MNEs in the Middle East for the percentages of base pay added to expatriate compensation for assignments to the area:[16] United Arab Emirates (12.5 percent), Bahrain (20 percent), Egypt (20 percent), Saudi Arabia (25 percent), and Israel (42.5 percent).

Additional incentives usually (or may) include housing allowances, either to ensure the expatriate lives as well as his or her foreign peers or to make the expatriate's housing comparable to what he or she had "back at home"—and to take care of his or her home in the parent country and the storage of household goods (again, the State Department provides quarterly reports of maximum housing allowances for foreign locations, see Table 5.1); settling-in allowances; education allowances for the expatriate (e.g., for language courses), his or her spouse, and any other dependents (e.g., for private schools for the expatriate's school-age children); all travel and relocation expenses necessary to go to and return from the foreign assignment; local transportation in the foreign locale; any language training expenses prior to leaving for the assignment; and special perquisites, such as club memberships in the foreign assignment and special R&R and home leaves for the expatriate and his or her family.

DETERMINING THE TYPE AND AMOUNT OF ADJUSTMENTS.   In addition to the many incentives that firms have offered to their expatriates, MNEs have also traditionally provided a number of equalization adjustments. These have included compensation for any fluctuations in exchange rates between the expatriate's parent-country currency and that of the foreign assignment; all locally mandated payments, such as payment of salary for additional days or weeks per year (in many countries, firms must pay employees for thirteen to fourteen months every year, or as in Saudi Arabia, must pay for seven days work per week, i.e., must pay for rest days as well as workdays); an agreement to adjust for decreases in the value of the expatriate's compensation due to high inflation in the foreign country; similarly, an allowance to adjust for differences in (higher) costs of living (see Tables 5.1 and 5.2, data provided by the Department of State and Runzheimer International); reimbursement for any mandatory payments into the host-country's welfare plans, such as health insurance or social security; and ensuring that the expatriate will not have to pay more in income taxes while on the foreign assignment than he or she would have to pay while at home.

Table 5.2   Living Costs as Determined by Runzheimer International*

CITY/COUNTRY	RECEIVING LOCATION EXPENDITURE	STANDARD CITY US EXPENDITURE	DIFFERENTIAL	%
Kuwait City	$59,786	$35,540	$24,246	168
Kuwait	KD 17,897			
ROE	$1.00 = KD2.9935			
Riyadh	$62,087	$35,540	$26,547	175
Saudi Arabia	SAR 234,819			
ROE	$1.00 = SAR3.7821			
Tel Aviv	$52,488	$35,540	$16,948	148
Israel	IS 140689			
ROE	$1.00 = IS2.6804			
Hong Kong S1	$103,443	$35,540	$67,903	291
Hong Kong	HK 803,018			
ROE	$1.00 = HK7.7629			
Tokyo	$167,267	$35,540	$131,727	470
Japan	Y 20,677,547			
ROE	$1.00 = y123.62			
London	$62,856	$35,540	$27,316	177
United Kingdom	L 42,882			
ROE	$1.00 = I.68223			
Brussels	$64,810	$35,540	$29,270	182
Belgium	BF 2163,617			
ROE	$1.00 = BF33.384			
Sao Paulo	$71,585	$35,540	$36,045	201
Brazil	CR 1,045,141,000			
ROE	$1.00 = CR14,600			
Mexico City	$59,519	$35,540	$23,979	167
Mexico	MP 184,819,589			
ROE	$1.00 = MP3105.2			
Toronto	$51,109	$35,540	$15,569	144
Ontario Canada	CS 64,587			
ROE	$1.00 = CS1.2637			
Madrid	$87,521	$35,540	$51,981	246
Spain	PTA 9,936,259			
ROE	$1.00 = PTA113.53			
Barcelona	$65,908	$35,540	$30,368	185
Spain	PTA 7,482,535			
ROE	$1.00 = PTA113.53			
Munich	$67,426	$35,540	$31,886	190
Germany	DM 106,998			
ROE	$1.00 = DM1.589			

The figures are based on a *family size of two, income of $60,000*, and compare expenses for a US national in Standard City US to an expatriate in 13 locations.

This table compares just three items: Housing, Goods & Services, and Transportation; income tax and savings comparisons are not included. *February 1993.

Source: Runzheimer International, Runzheimer Park, Rochester, Wisconsin, 53167. Reprinted with permission. All rights reserved.

The most common and probably significant of these adjustments is the cost-of-living adjustment (COLA). A number of consulting firms can provide data to help companies determine local costs of living around the world. Table 5.2

illustrates the type of data (in very abbreviated form and for only a few cities) that Runzheimer International can provide its MNE clients. As both the State Department and the Runzheimer tables show, costs of living vary considerably from one foreign locale to another. A number of consulting firms can provide this type of cost-of-living data for locales around the world, comparing such costs to either particular U.S. locations or some average of U.S. cities.

The purpose of the COLA is to enable expatriates to maintain as closely as possible the same standard of living in the foreign assignment that they would have had at home. The COLA is determined by calculating the costs for typical goods and services in the home location as well as in the foreign location and adjusting accordingly. Since the typical expatriate resides in a major city where costs of living tend to be quite high (particularly the costs of transportation and housing, which may not be available—except at very high cost—in forms comparable to what the expatriate family experienced at home), COLAs of 50 percent or more are common.

The ratios vary according to family size and income, and the consulting firms that provide this type of data will alter the estimates based on these factors. Fluctuating exchange rates and local rates of inflation (which are often quite high in developing countries, for example) will also alter the figures and may require frequent updating. As an example, a manager posted to Munich, Germany, with spouse (refer to Table 5.2) would receive a COLA of 90 percent above what he or she had needed to spend in his or her hometown for basic housing, goods and services, and transportation. If the dollar weakens relative to the deutsche mark, the expatriate would receive more and vice versa if the mark strengthened against the dollar.

These adjustments also vary according to the technology that the consulting firm uses to determine the cost of living in various foreign locations. At least two common techniques are used. One of these uses staff of the consulting firm that are located in the particular foreign cities to estimate the cost of living in those locations based on their surveys of costs in a standardized market basket of required goods and services. A second technique involves the surveying of existing and former expatriates of the clients of the particular consulting firm. Often this second technique—which arguably assesses the actual items that expatriates typically buy, as opposed to a theoretical market basket of goods and services—results in a lower cost of living than that arrived at by the first technique. Obviously, MNEs have an interest in trying to minimize the level of this adjustment, which as shown above can often be a significant amount of money.

Depending on the location, these incentives and adjustments typically cost the MNE more than $150,000 per expatriate relocation. This is in addition to their base salary and benefits and the costs associated with the move. For example, in Tokyo, the rent for an expatriate family often exceeds $100,000 per year.[17] It is no wonder that the cost of expatriate failure is so high or that large multinationals are beginning to reconsider their approaches to expatriate compensation.

One of the consequences of these increasing costs is that firms are increasingly looking to forms of incentive pay based on performance (either individual or organizational, even though this may be difficult to assess, as discussed in the previous chapter) for expatriates just as they are in domestic operations.[18] In order to minimize costs, firms are designing bonus deferrals, in-kind benefits, and possibly stock-based plans for expatriates as well as HCN and TCN executives (for globalized stock option and equity participation plans, see the next section), tied to achievement of long-term strategic objectives in the subsidiaries (such as growth in subsidiary revenues and profits or return on capital employed at the subsidiary level).

Localization

A relatively new approach to expatriate compensation is referred to as localization. This approach is being used to address problems of high cost and perceived inequity among staff in foreign subsidiaries. Under localization, expatriates (usually individuals who are early in their careers and who are being assigned overseas for long-term assignments) are paid comparably to local nationals. This can be relatively simple to administer, but since expatriates may come from different standards of living than experienced by local nationals, special supplements for expatriates paid under a localization approach may still have to be negotiated.

Lump sum

Another approach that some MNEs are trying, particularly in response to concern over the perception that the balance sheet intrudes too heavily into expatriates' life-style decisions, is the lump sum approach. In it the firm determines a total salary for the expatriate, and then lets the expatriate determine how to spend it, for example, on housing, transportation, travel, home visits, education, and so forth.

Cafeteria

An approach which is increasingly being used for very highly salaried expatriate executives is to provide a set of "cafeteria" choices of benefits. The advantages accrue to both the firm and to the individual and are primarily related to the tax coverage of benefits and perquisites as compared to cash income. Since the individual doesn't need more cash, this approach enables him or her to gain benefits such as a company car, insurance, company-provided housing, and the like that do not increase the expatriate's income for tax purposes.

Regional systems

For expatriates who make a commitment to job assignments within a particular region of the world, some firms are developing a regional compensation and benefits system to maintain equity within that region. This is usually seen as a complement to the other approaches. And if such individuals are later moved to another region, their pay will be transferred to one of the other systems, such as the balance sheet approach.

Once the amount of the expatriate's compensation has been determined, the firm must decide whether the expatriate will be paid in local currency or parent-country currency. Where there is limited convertibility between the parent-country currency and that of the foreign locale, or there is rapid inflation, it is probably better for the firm to take care of providing the expatriate's salary in local currency (of course, with guarantees against loss of purchasing power if there is rampant inflation).

It is typical for U.S. MNEs to pay their expatriates based on a U.S. scale plus incentives and adjustments. This is paid partly in local currency and partly in U.S. dollars (with the amount in local currency pegged to ordinary living expenses and the amount in dollars usually left in a U.S. savings account, while bonuses are paid in dollars and typically left in the United States).

Flexibility in Expatriate Compensation

Current methods for paying expatriates are being criticized for many different reasons.[19] There is concern that all of these approaches don't adequately take into account the nature of the assignment or the country of assignment and often actually discourage expatriates from assimilating into the local culture. The housing differentials frequently serve to provide host-country housing which is likely to be better than that enjoyed by their host-country counterparts. Even the continuation of home-based purchasing patterns for goods and services does not encourage the cultural awareness so critical to the expatriate's success in the host country.

In addition, critics argue, it seems as though the expatriate compensation systems ought to pay more attention to the differences in perceptions by expatriates and by host-country nationals about issues like the value of money compensation versus other types of perquisites. A flexible menu of perquisites, traditional incentives and adjustments, and tax reimbursement schedules might well meet some of the criticisms while actually reducing overall costs to the firm. Such an approach might even enable an MNE to replace the traditional cost-of-living concerns with a quality of life or a quality of career opportunity focus.

Taxes on Expatriate Income

A major determinant of an expatriate's life style abroad can be the amount of money the expatriate must pay in taxes. Employees who move from one country to another are confronted with widely disparate tax systems, philosophies, and rates. For example, a U.S. manager earning $100,000 in Canada would pay nearly $40,000 in taxes, in excess of $10,000 more than in the United States.

Thus, taxes are one of the most complicated compensation issues for IHRM. Table 5.3 shows the widely varying rates for a number of countries. For example, the marginal tax rate in Sweden is 51 percent and in the Netherlands 60 percent, while it was 31 percent in the United States (it was raised in 1993 to 33.5 percent for the highest-income levels) and only 11.5 percent in Switzerland. Expatriates (or their firms) are, of course, responsible for taxes on their (expatriates') incomes (this can mean in both their home countries *and* their host countries). Since MNE policies typically establish that the firm will cover these costs for their expatriates (at least any differential over what the expatriate would pay in only his or her home country), the use of PCNs can be very expensive. The multinational firm must therefore determine a strategy for dealing with these variances and potentially heavy costs. (In countries with lower tax rates, the expatriate's compensation is typically

Table 5.3 Maximum Marginal Federal Tax Rates*

COUNTRY	1991 MAXIMUM MARGINAL RATE	INCOME LEVEL AT WHICH REACHED IN LOCAL CURRENCY	IN U.S. DOLLARS**
Australia	47.00	A$50,000	38,948
Belgium	55.00	BF2,347,000	68,720
Brazil	25.00	Cz$288,000	708
Canada	29.00	Can$56,568	49,374
Finland	39.00	FIM275,000	68,002
France	56.80	FFr246,770	43,738
Hong Kong	25.00	HK80,000	10,294
Italy	50.00	Lit337,700,000	273,537
Japan	50.00	Y20,100,000	160,599
Taiwan	40.00	NT$3,000,000	111,390
Mexico	35.00	Ps73,839,500	24,367
Netherlands	60.00	Gld85,930	45,960
Singapore	33.00	S$400,000	231,540
Spain	56.00	Pta(,084,000	87,388
Sweden	51.00	Skr180,000	29,765
Switzerland	11.50	SFr595,200	415,063
United Kingdom	40.00	L237,000	417,983
United States	31.00	US$82,150	—
Venezuela	30.00	BS4,250,000	7,448

* Maximum marginal rates are those applicable to resident citizens as of January 1, 1991, with one exception: The rate of the U.K. reflects April 1991 change. Where different rates apply to married and single employees, the married employee rate is shown. Social security taxes are excluded.
** Based on 1991 yearly average exchange rate.

adjusted to reflect that fact, so that a manager, for example, being posted in Hong Kong—with low tax rates—would still receive comparable overall compensation to a colleague who is posted in Singapore—with higher tax rates.)

In general, MNEs follow one of four strategies: laissez faire, tax equalization, tax protection, or an *ad hoc* policy.[20] The following paragraphs describe and evaluate these alternatives.

Laissez faire

This approach is uncommon, but smaller employers and those employers just beginning to conduct international business may fall into this category with their taxation policies. In essence, the expatriate is expected to take care of his or her own taxation, even if it means tax obligations in both home and host countries.

Tax equalization

This is the most common program. Under this strategy, the firm withholds from the expatriate's income the tax obligation in the home country and then pays all the taxes in the host country. In essence, taxes are equalized between countries. This can be quite expensive if the expatriate is posted to a high-tax country, such as many European countries.

Tax protection

Under the tax protection strategy, the employee pays his or her taxes up to the amount that would be owed in the home country, with the employer paying the difference. In essence, the employer pays the expatriate any excess of foreign income tax over U.S. income tax. If the tax rate is less in the foreign assignment, then the employee receives the difference. The employer protects the expatriate against higher foreign taxes.

Ad hoc

Under this strategy, each expatriate is handled differently depending on the individual package he or she has been able to negotiate with his or her employer. In addition, the typical allowances paid to expatriates are viewed as taxable income in the United States (and often also in other countries). The resulting tax bill—in both the United States and the host country—can negate the financial incentives provided the expatriate. To compensate, companies usually reimburse their expatriates for the global tax costs in excess of the tax they would have been responsible for if they had remained in the United States (or other parent country, for non-U.S. expatriates). As with other components in the expatriate compensation package, the purpose is to keep the employee whole. Indeed, the *Price Waterhouse 1990 Survey of International Assignment Tax and Compensation Policies for U.S. Expatriates* found at least 75 percent of responding firms provided the following benefits tax-free to their employees on foreign assignment:[21]

- Tax reimbursement payments;
- International premium;
- Cost-of-living adjustment;
- Housing allowances;
- Automobile reimbursements (for business use);
- Emergency leave;
- Moving expenses; and
- Dependent education.

In addition, many firms provide a car tax-free for personal use (48.3 percent) or club memberships (62 percent).

MNEs that operate in many countries are subject to widely disparate tax rates (see Table 5.3). Because of this and the complex systems of taxation, with differing attitudes toward what is and is not taxed in various countries, MNEs must use international accounting firms for advice and for preparation of expatriate tax returns.

An additional factor involves the varying country-specific practices related to social security taxes and government-provided or -mandated social services, ranging from health care to retirement programs. These can add considerably to the foreign taxation burden.

Taxation of U.S. Expatriates

U.S. citizens are taxed on their income, regardless of where their incomes are earned or where they live.[22] Fortunately, special rules can limit the U.S. tax liability of U.S.

expatriates. As of the time of this writing, Internal Revenue rules allow U.S. employees to exclude up to $70,000 of foreign-earned income (and certain foreign housing costs above a particular amount) providing the expatriate meets one of two tests: (1) 330 days' presence in foreign countries in any consecutive 12-month period or (2) foreign residence for any period that includes an entire taxable year. The income and foreign housing exclusions are both prorated on the basis of the number of days in the year in which the expatriate qualified under one of the tests. In addition, U.S. tax laws provide a "foreign tax credit" that U.S. citizens may use to reduce their U.S. tax liabilities (limited to 90 percent for minimum tax, and only applicable to U.S. income tax on foreign income). This is a dollar for dollar reduction against U.S. taxes. The bottom line in terms of the amount of tax owed, however, is dependent on the level of tax rate in the foreign country compared to the tax rates in the United States.[23]

One thing the United States has done to simplify tax obligations for MNEs is to negotiate income tax and social security treaties with a number of America's major trading partners—referred to as totalization agreements. There are totalization agreements for income taxes with approximately thirty-five countries and for social security taxes with sixteen countries (Austria, Belgium, Canada, Finland, France, Germany, Republic of Ireland, Italy, Luxembourg, Netherlands, Norway, Portugal, Spain, Sweden, Switzerland, and United Kingdom).[24] These treaties generally provide tax exemption to residents of one treaty country on short-term assignment (typically 183 days' presence in a year) to the other country.

Because taxes on expatriate compensation coupled with provided incentives and adjustments make expatriates so expensive, firms are increasingly looking for ways to reduce these expenses without eliminating the attractions of overseas service. IHRM in Action 5.2 illustrates some of the strategies that U.S. MNEs are finding successful for reducing the costs. Because managing this area of international compensation is so complex, most MNEs have had to develop strategies that involve the use of outside assistance. IHRM in Action 5.3 describes how Physical Acoustics Corp., a computer manufacturer from New Jersey, deals with this complexity.

IHRM IN ACTION 5.2
SAVE THE GLOBAL BOTTOM LINE

Foreign governments have become more aware of loopholes, so it's getting increasingly difficult to avoid paying taxes in the host country. There are currently a number of legitimate ways to avoid paying some of the tax and reduce the cost of operation, but tax laws everywhere in the world continue to evolve. International accounting firms and human resources consultants specializing in international business can save your company money if you consult them before any action is taken.

Here are some ways to save that apply in some countries:

1. *Provide employees with assistance that doesn't show up as income.* Provide housing, rather than pay a housing allowance. Make contributions to schools or buy schol-

arships for employees' dependent children instead of paying educational allowances. Reimbursement of employees' actual home-leave expenses may be treated favorably in some countries. A loan often isn't taxable or is taxed at a lower rate. You can give your employee a bonus later with which to pay off the loan.

2. *Provide some of the income in the home country.* Some countries' tax laws allow corporations to split the payroll with the home country, as long as a certain amount is paid in local currency. You also may be able to pay for such remaining home-country expenses as benefits, pension, social security, or mortgage payments on employees' permanent residences.

3. *Provide part of the compensation before or after the assignment.* An employee may receive a large bonus before departure and another after returning home. These payments often are taxed at a lower rate because they are outside his or her period of residence in the host country.

4. *Time the assignment to take advantage of residency laws.* One company used this strategy to negotiate a savings of $170,000 in taxes for two employees, earning annual salaries of $57,000 and $48,000, who were sent to Italy. The negotiated savings applied as long as they were nonresidents and lived in the country nine months or less. In some countries residency depends on whether the expatriate is living in leased or purchased housing.

The United States has tax treaties with many countries and is negotiating such arrangements with others. U.S. citizens or residents may be exempt from taxation in those countries; for example, providing the assignment doesn't exceed a certain number of days (often 183 days in one tax year), the employer isn't a home-country company, and the income earned isn't used as a deduction in computing the profits of any home-country company. Obviously, such treaties are useful only for short-term assignments.

The assignment might be spread out over more tax periods, requiring a lower tax on partial years. For example, a two-year assignment might be spread over three tax periods, by sending the employee to the foreign country in the middle of the tax year, thereby reducing earnings on the first and last tax years. Tax years vary. In the U.K. the tax year begins April 5, but in Australia the date is June 30.

5. *Take advantage of incentives offered in the host country.* Many countries provide tax advantages to employees of industries they are trying to attract. These advantages may vary from one area to another within the same country, or there may be other strings attached. Companies that provide workers having specific skills needed in the host country often can receive tax incentives.

If your company provides a needed service, you may be able to negotiate a *tax holiday* with the host country. This may be especially true in Eastern/Central Europe or the new countries of the former Soviet Union. An accounting firm or international management firm can negotiate this for you.

It is possible in some countries to establish a foreign subsidiary that's considered a local rather than a U.S. company. This usually requires staffing the company with enough locals to give credibility as a local company.

The ways multinational corporations can save money on expatriate taxes are complex and continue to change.

Source: "Global Payroll—A Taxing Problem," by P. Stuart, PERSONNEL JOURNAL, October 1991, p. 84. Reprinted with permission of PERSONNEL JOURNAL, ACC Communications, Inc., Costa Mesa, CA. All rights reserved.

IHRM IN ACTION 5.3
HOW TO MANAGE
INTERNATIONAL TAXES

With major subsidiaries in the United Kingdom, France, Germany, and Japan, and competitors close on its heels, Physical Acoustics Corp. (PAC), a manufacturer of computers based in Lawrenceville, New Jersey, is committed to finding the best international tax strategies it can. Here is Chief Financial Officer John C. Heenan's blueprint for success:

- *Use local tax advisers.* "Every country has a different set of tax laws on everything from income taxes to duties," warns Heenan. For example, when PAC's U.S. office bills its Japanese subsidiary for consulting work, the fees are taxed by both Japan and the United States; a similar transaction with the company's U.K. subsidiary, on the other hand, is taxed only by the U.S. government. Rather than expecting his U.S. tax advisers to keep current on all international tax minutiae, Heenan uses his American contacts—including CPA and law firms, bankers, and industry sources—to help find qualified tax experts overseas.
- *Appoint a U.S. executive to coordinate international tax policy.* At PAC, Heenan is point man on international taxes, keeping the company's overall financial interests in mind while consulting regularly with local tax experts. He relies on his foreign advisers to keep him informed of key changes by telephone and written reports. Having local tax policies and updates trickle up to one U.S. office makes it easier to plan corporate activities to maximize overall tax advantages.
- *Look for tax-advantaged opportunities that don't exist in the United States.* Heenan has found especially valuable ones on the employee-benefits front: "As you get to know the tax laws of different countries, you see many ways to motivate and reward key employees that aren't permitted in the United States." PAC, for example, can give European managers trips and company cars without subjecting those employees to the tax liabilities they'd face in the States. "In the United Kingdom, if one of my managers spends enough time outside the country working on sales, he can qualify for a fairly significant income-tax break because he is seen as working to enhance the export market," Heenan says.
- *Keep international taxes in perspective.* Heenan stresses that international tax regulations should not direct a corporation's overall business activities. "International taxes are just another financial factor we have to keep in balance to achieve our most important goal, which is to manage a growing and profitable international business."

Source: "How to Manage International Taxes," by J. A. Fraser, © April 1992. Reprinted with permission of INC. Magazine. Copyright 1992 by Goldhirsh Group, Inc., 38 Commercial Wharf, Boston, MA 02110.

The Cost of an Expatriate

To illustrate in generic terms what this typically means for a firm sending an expatriate and family abroad, Table 5.4 shows why the common cost for an expatriate can exceed $300,000 in the first year. Even though some of these expenses, such as the relocation costs, will occur only the first and last years of the foreign assignment, the costs of maintaining an expatriate in a foreign operation obviously still greatly exceed those of maintaining the same person in a domestic assignment.

Table 5.4 The Cost of an Expatriate

AN EMPLOYER'S TYPICAL FIRST-YEAR EXPENSES FOR SENDING A U.S. EXECUTIVE TO LONDON, ASSUMING A $100,000 SALARY AND A FAMILY OF FOUR:

Direct Compensation Costs	
Base salary	$100,000
Foreign-service premium	15,000
Goods and Services differential	21,000
Housing costs in London	39,000*
Transfer Costs	
Relocation allowance	$5,000
Airfare to London	3,500
Moving household goods	25,000
Other Costs	
Company car	$15,000
Schooling, two children	25,000
Annual home leave (four people)	5,000
U.K. personal income tax	56,000*
Total	$309,500

Note: Additional costs often incurred are not listed above, including language training and cross-cultural training for employee and family, and costs of selling or renting home and cars in the U.S. before moving.

*Figures take into account payments by employee to company based on hypothetical U.S. income tax and housing costs.

Source: Organization Resource Counselors, Inc., reported in "Grappling With the Expatriate Issue: The Price of an Expatriate," by Joann S. Lublin, THE WALL STREET JOURNAL, Dec. 4, 1989, B1. Reprinted by permission of THE WALL

Major Problem Areas in Expatriate Compensation

It should be obvious by now that international compensation management is more complex than its domestic counterpart. This is at least partially due to the following problem areas not confronted in domestic HRM. First, the collection of data about pay rates, benefit packages, government practices, and taxation systems in different countries, and in different languages and cultures (from unknown possible sources), makes it very difficult to design comfortable pay packages for expatriates or for consistency among various overseas operations. Secondly, pay systems, particularly for expatriates, must contend with government currency controls (e.g., limiting amounts that can be taken out of the country) and constantly changing exchange rates, making it necessary to constantly adjust expatriates' incomes in local currencies. A third issue that adds to the complexity are the varying rates of inflation encountered in foreign locations, which may also require frequent reestablishment of expatriates' pay rates to counteract the effects of sometimes high inflation rates.

As IHRM in Action 5.1 hinted, it is often very difficult for MNEs to get country-specific compensation data that has much reliability. Very few governments collect or publish adequate data. And local trade associations that collect and publish such information (as is available in most developed countries) exist in very few locations. Therefore, MNEs must rely on the information provided by accounting firms with international practices, consulting firms that specialize in developing such data, U.S. State Department data, or developing their own data through local MNE "compensation clubs" that share such information. None of these options provide necessarily reliable data, particularly in less developed countries, illustrating the difficulties encountered by international HR managers as they try to develop cost- and managerially effective compensation packages for their expatriates and equitable compensation programs for their foreign subsidiaries.

An additional problem with international compensation programs involves the maintenance of payroll files on international personnel.[25] The normal (i.e., domestic) HRM information system will not be designed to handle all the additional pieces of information that are common, particularly for expatriates, such as foreign service premiums, language training expenses, education allowances for dependents, storage of household goods, currency conversion, and the like. Compounding the problems associated with maintaining these files is that typically the compensation package for each expatriate is unique, developed specifically for that expatriate and his or her family. And, of course, tax and withholding requirements are different in every country as well. Keeping these files up-to-date and using the information in them for employee decision making, such as pay increases or adjustments or career and job-assignment decisions, gets even more difficult as many countries maintain laws against the transfer of "private" employee information out-of-country. There are no easy answers to these problems, short of specifically designing a computer program to handle the problems of your international employees or hiring a firm to handle them for you, but for sure they must be considered when tackling the issue of creating and managing a compensation program for an international work force.[26]

One last area of concern for the development of international compensation systems involves MNEs' attempts to include IHR issues in the strategic management of their firms. International compensation systems are affected at a number of points, including the following: Efforts to downsize often include expatriates because of the high expense, but then it becomes more difficult to convince new people to accept foreign assignments; pressuring IHRM to control costs; fitting IHR compensation systems into the firm's efforts to localize while globalizing; trying to simplify the design and administration of the international compensation system; coping with the new types of expatriates, particularly dual-career couples; and figuring out the legal necessity to apply U.S. discrimination laws, such as those that "protect" the disabled, employees over forty years old, and employees on the basis of their religion, gender, race, or national origin.

The Special Problem of "Bandits"

Many mature MNEs have a special problem with expatriates who have stayed overseas for many years and continue to receive many or all of the special incentives and adjustments that they received when they went abroad initially.[27] Often these individuals occupy important positions within the foreign operations of the firm, are located in highly desirable locations, such as Switzerland, and refuse to be reclassified as locals. Obviously this can be very expensive for the MNE and, thus, must be dealt with in a way that hopefully holds on to the expertise of the employee while reducing costs. Many firms are now establishing a policy that requires such "bandits" to reclassify after some periods of years, say, six or eight, to local status.

Benchmarking International Compensation Practices

Many firms are now trying to determine what successful MNEs are doing in terms of design and implementation of their international compensation systems. This attempt at benchmarking the best practices may be an exercise in the "codification of ignorance."[28] Surveys of practices of MNEs may be doing nothing more than identifying what is currently being done. But as the above discussion indicates, many practices have evolved over time, without much knowledge or research to indicate which practices are best and under what circumstances. Over time this may result in many firms following what are totally wrong, costly, or inappropriate practices. There is clearly a need for more and better research on international compensation and benefits practices.

Compensation by Foreign Multinationals in the United States

Just as American firms have recognized the need to pay their expatriate executives at least as well as their local colleagues (in countries where the locals make more than their U.S. counterparts), such is also true for foreign firms that operate in the United States. Foreign owners of U.S. companies are realizing that they must match U.S. executive compensation practices to stay competitive and to retain their U.S. executives.[29]

In most countries, executive compensation is not a subject that receives much attention, either outside firms or within them. This is clearly not the case in the United States. Besides, overall executive salaries tend to be much higher (with maybe fewer perquisites) in the United States. Thus, foreign firms with operations in the United States, particularly those that have acquired U.S. firms, have had to adapt their policies to fit the U.S. practices. For example, foreign firms have relied more heavily on high base salaries and less on annual and long-term incentives than is common in the United States.[30] Since this can lead to problems with retention of their U.S. executives, foreign-owned firms in the United States are increasingly adapting their compensation practices.

Compensation and Taxation of Foreign Nationals Working in the United States

A last issue of concern to compensation for expatriates involves compensation and taxation for foreign nationals on assignment to the United States (these employees are increasingly referred to as inpatriates). A discussion of the treatment of immigrants into the United States is beyond the purposes of this text. U.S. immigration and tax laws are both very complex (see Chapter 3 for a discussion of the immigration laws). So, what is provided here is only a summary statement about this issue.[31]

First, U.S. MNEs that bring inpatriates into the United States are increasingly realizing that they need to adapt these employees' compensation programs just as they must do for their expatriates that are sent abroad from the United

States.[32] At a minimum, trying to keep inpatriates in as many of their home-country benefit programs as possible and pegging their compensation to their home-country structures appear to help minimize many of the problems discussed at the beginning of the chapter. As with U.S. expatriates, such foreign employees in the United States can typically be removed from extra premiums and adjustments after they have been in the United States for a period of time, such as after four or five years.

For U.S. tax purposes, foreign individuals living and working in the United States may be considered either "resident aliens" or "nonresident aliens." The U.S. resident is subject to U.S. tax on all worldwide income, in the same manner as a U.S. citizen, while the nonresident generally is taxed only on certain income connected with a U.S. business or from U.S. sources. Other variables adding complexity to the classification of foreign nationals' concerns are whether they are entering the United States on immigrant or nonimmigrant visas and whether their country of origin has negotiated a tax-equalization treaty with the U.S. As U.S.-based MNEs (U.S. or foreign owned) expand their use of foreign staff in their U.S. operations, considerations such as the tax treatment of these employees become just as important as the tax treatment of U.S. expatriates sent abroad.

DESIGNING A COMPENSATION STRATEGY FOR MULTINATIONALS

In addition to the problems associated with compensation and benefit packages for expatriates, sooner or later the MNE must begin to examine its compensation and benefit programs among its foreign employees at each and all of its foreign operations. The greater the number of foreign subsidiaries and joint ventures and the greater the number of countries within which the MNE operates, the greater will be the problems associated with establishing, monitoring, and controlling compensation programs on a worldwide basis.

The stage of the MNC's evolution or development makes a big difference in how it handles compensation of PCNs and TCNs/HCNs. If it is still in stage 1 (export) or 2 (sales subsidiaries), it will differentiate between PCNs and HCNs/TCNs, and most HRM attention will be given to compensation packages for expatriates (PCNs) from headquarters. Later, when in stage 3 (international), 4 (multinational), or 5 (global) (i.e., becoming more global in emphasis and attention), the compensation package will be more likely to be designed for all employees worldwide.

A number of different options for establishing a worldwide compensation system have been used by varying MNEs. These include basing global employees' compensation on:

- *Headquarters scale.* A worldwide scale based on salary levels in the parent company with differentials established for each affiliate according to their differing cost of living.
- *Citizenship.* A scale based on employees' countries of citizenship.
- *Global.* Determining a global base per position for everyone (possibly with affiliate differentials). This, then, becomes a form of equal pay for equal work on a worldwide basis. The global approach is usually followed only for employees above a particular job or salary classification.

One major problem that arises is the establishment of host-country nationals' salaries on some form of consistent yet global basis. The solution often is to create two classifications—local and international. All local nationals above a certain classification level are placed on the headquarters scale, with salaries that are then performance-based. And yet, even here, practices can vary enough so as to make this strategy difficult to implement. In the United States (and most developed countries), there is typically a fairly constant differential between job classifications (i.e., about a 15 percent increase in salary from job class to job class), and this tends to be the case across all job classifications. In many developing countries, where there tend to be many people with low levels of education and training and few with high levels of education, it is common to have low pay at all of the lower job classifications, with very little differential among them and then a major jump in compensation only at the upper few classifications. This creates a situation where there can be a much greater ratio between top management and lower-level employees, such as between the top manager and his or her secretary, than would be the case in the typical U.S.-based, parent-country MNE workforce.

Not only is there great disparity between wage rates and salary levels in different countries, but it is also difficult to get reliable data on what those rates and levels are. In some regions of the world where such data collection may be easier and where many firms operate in most countries, such as within Europe, the use of salary surveys is quite common.[33] But it is much more difficult in other regions.

Nevertheless, international banks (e.g., the Union Bank of Switzerland), consulting firms (e.g., Hay International), and the U.S. Department of Labor research and publish comparative wage rate data on at least some common locations for MNEs (see Table 5.5). These data show, for example, that hourly manufacturing pay rates in 1991 ranged from $2.17 in Mexico and $4.32 in Korea to $15.45 in the United States and $22.26 in Norway.

Another important aspect of this problem of comparisons of salaries among various countries concerns pay at different levels, particularly when related to relevant costs of living. Figure 5.2 shows the result of a recent analysis by Organization Resources Counselors for *Fortune* magazine of typical salaries for upper-middle managers earning $125,000 in the United States and equivalent salaries in Japan, Germany, and Great Britain. The salary is higher in Japan and Germany, but as the analysis shows, expenditures for taxes, savings, cars and commuting, and so on vary considerably from country to country. All of these need to be taken into consideration when trying to determine appropriate salary structures for staff in foreign subsidiaries.

Figure 5.3 shows the data from another major consulting firm, Hay International Compensation. This analysis illustrates, for a number of countries and for firms with $500 million to $800 million in yearly sales, the typical level of CEO pay as compared to entry-level professionals, which varies from a multiple of 7.5 in France to 13.6 in the United States. It is particularly obvious from all of these studies how important accurate data is when developing compensation strategy as

Table 5.5 Hourly Compensation Costs in U.S. Dollars for Production Workers in Manufacturing for Selected Countries

COUNTRY	1975	1991
United States	$6.36	$15.45
Australia	5.54	13.35
Austria	4.34	17.47
Belgium	6.41	19.41
Brazil	.87	2.55
Canada	5.79	17.31
Denmark	6.28	18.05
Finland	4.61	20.57
France	4.52	15.26
Germany	6.35	22.17
Greece	1.69	6.72 (1990)*
Hong Kong	.76	3.58
Israel	2.25	8.55 (1990)*
Ireland	3.03	11.90
Italy	4.65	17.18
Japan	3.05	14.41
Korea	.33	4.32
Luxembourg	6.35	16.64 (1990)*
Mexico	N/A	2.17
Netherlands	6.58	18.55
New Zealand	3.21	8.35
Norway	6.78	22.26
Portugal	1.58	4.21
Singapore	.84	4.38
Spain	2.59	12.65
Sri Lanka	.28	.31 (1989)*
Sweden	7.18	22.07
Switzerland	6.09	21.79
Taiwan	.40	4.42
United Kingdom	3.32	13.42

* Last Date Available.

Source: Bureau of Labor Statistics, U.S. Department of Labor, "International Comparisons of Hourly Compensation Costs for Production Workers in Manufacturing, 1991," Report 825, June 1992.

well as how complex the development of this strategy is for today's multinational firms.

Compensation of Third-Country Nationals

As the number of TCNs in MNEs increases, their compensation often approaches that of their expatriate colleagues. However, firms have problems in defining TCNs for compensation purposes as it is difficult to decide which base to use to determine their salaries. In the past they were defined in terms of their home countries, but as they move around, this makes less and less sense. The increasing trend is to define them in terms of a region of the world, usually tied to their parent language and culture. Many multinationals establish cultural zones. For example, Western

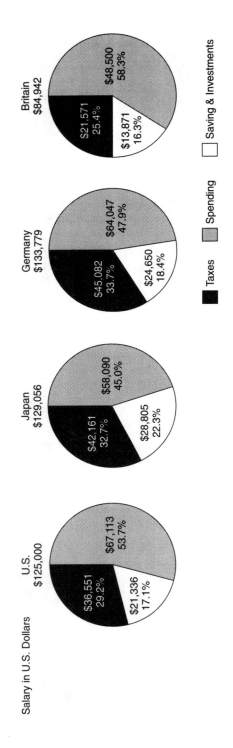

Salary in U.S. Dollars

U.S.
$125,000
- $36,551 29.2%
- $67,113 53.7%
- $21,336 17.1%

Japan
$129,056
- $42,161 32.7%
- $58,090 45.0%
- $28,805 22.3%

Germany
$133,779
- $45,082 33.7%
- $64,047 47.9%
- $24,650 18.4%

Britain
$84,942
- $21,571 25.4%
- $48,500 58.3%
- $13,871 16.3%

■ Taxes   ▨ Spending   ☐ Saving & Investments

Percentage of after-tax income spent, etc.

	U.S.	Japan	Germany	Britain
Alcohol & tobacco	1.8	1.2	1.7	5.3
Cars & commuting	10.0	4.3	8.6	9.8
Clothing	6.0	8.1	7.3	7.3
Food at home	8.0	17.3	10.3	11.7
Food away from home	5.5	3.8	4.2	3.7
Furnishings & household operations	6.3	1.3	8.6	6.2
Housing	17.2	10.0	13.2	16.0
Medical care	2.3	2.3	1.4	0.6

To construct these budgets, Organization Resources Counselors sampled jobs paying $125,000 in the U.S. and compared them with foreign salaries for similar positions. All numbers reflect current exchange rates, taxes, and prices. For the spending breakdown, ORC used its database to capture national differences. Housing takes the biggest bite in the U.S. because homes are much larger. Clothing and groceries cost more abroad, where dining out is both more expensive and less common (fewer wives work). America's gas is cheap, but nowhere else do people own so many cars or drive them so far.

Figure 5.2. Compensation for the Typical Upper-Middle Manager in Select Countries

Source: Analysis by Organization Resources Counselors, reported in "Where People Live Best," by S. Tully. Reprinted with permission of FORTUNE, © 1991 Time, Inc. All rights reserved.

Europe might be considered one zone, with Africa considered to be another, and so on. Other firms use a combination of geographic and language zones. Thus, a manager might be defined as a national as long as he or she is within his or her parent region. This manager is treated as a traditional TCN only when he or she moves to a different zone.

International Benefits and Related Taxes

The design of a comprehensive compensation program for all worldwide employees must include nonsalary benefits. MNEs' major concern for designing their benefit packages is the widely varying approaches to employee benefits as approached by each country. The problems this creates cannot be overstated. In the United States, for example, benefits make up a significant portion of the cost of payroll, averaging about 38 percent of payroll expenses in 1992. In the United States, many benefits that in other countries are provided by the government and paid for through employer taxes or are mandated by the government, are provided on a private and voluntary basis by each firm. This includes significant benefits such as health care, retirement pensions, vacations, and holidays.

An important example involves the handling of health care. In some countries, such as the United States, health care is basically a private system paid for by either individuals or their employers. In most other countries, though, such as Canada and West Germany, health care is provided by a tax-supported system of government-controlled medicine. In yet other countries, such as Great Britain and Mexico, in addition to the government-sponsored, tax-supported system of health care, there is a competing private medical system mostly paid for by in-

	NO. OF FILMS	ENTRY-LEVEL PROFESSIONALS	CEOs	PAY MULTIPLE
U.S.	530	$35,300	$481,000	13.6
Japan	60	28,400	371,000	13.1
Germany	195	49,500	767,500	12.3
U.K.	584	28,500	351,100	12.3
Italy	400	29,600	357,300	12.1
France	243	34,300	258,300	7.5
Average (w/o U.S.)		$34,060	$420,820	12.4

Figure 5.3 CEO Pay Multiples in Select Countries

Source: Hay International Compensation, reported in "HRM Update," by C. Pasternak, HR MAGAZINE, April 1992, p. 19. Reprinted with permission of Hay International. All rights reserved.

surance, with premiums paid by some employers, particularly for higher-level managers.

In every area of benefits, the variance from country to country in terms of what is normally provided, what is paid by the government from tax revenues, and what employees expect of their employers, is quite wide. The benefits manager in the MNE is faced with such tremendous complexity that it is very difficult for any such manager to be knowledgeable about more than a few countries. As with taxes, the MNE must typically seek advice and assistance from international accounting and HR consulting firms.

Vacation Requirements

Figure 5.4 illustrates an example of the variances among countries in a benefit that is mandated in some countries and voluntarily provided in others. It shows the va-

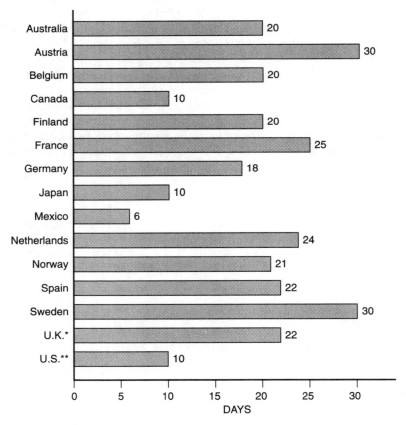

Figure 5.4   Worldwide Vacation Requirements (for employees with one year of service)

Source: Hewitt Associates, reported in HR FOCUS, May 1992, p. 7. Reprinted with permission of Hewitt Associates. All rights reserved.

cation requirements in a number of different countries. Among the countries listed, vacation provisions range from six days for employees with one year of service in Mexico to thirty days for such employees in Austria and Sweden.

A U.S. worker must often stay at a job for thirty years to match the level of paid vacation time commonly provided to beginning workers in many European countries.[34] The United States, Canada, New Zealand, and Japan are the developed countries that provide the shortest paid vacation time for employees—each granting an average of only ten to fifteen days a year.

In the United States, paid vacation time is left to the discretion of each company, a situation which is true for most benefits. Most base the amount of time provided on the employee's length of service. The average received by American employees in their first years at a firm is eleven days. After five years of service, they earn fifteen days, on the average. Ten years of service results in seventeen days, and thirty years earns employees twenty-four days of paid vacation.

In contrast most European countries (and others as well) mandate paid vacation for workers. Sweden and Austria require companies to give their employees thirty days of vacation; France requires five weeks; and Germany requires eighteen days. In addition, most European employers actually extend employee vacation time to six weeks. Even in the U.K., which doesn't mandate any paid vacations, employees average twenty-two days off with pay.

Because of these widely varying practices, corporate policy on establishing and changing benefits must be monitored in such a way as to minimize unnecessary differences among subsidiaries while maintaining parent-company concern for costs, competitiveness, and comparability from locale to locale.[35] Since a foreign subsidiary's benefits program may be more difficult to monitor or control than the parent-company's domestic counterpart, it often makes sense to appoint an effective local manager in each country to act as that country's benefits coordinator, responsible for coordination and liaison with headquarters. And yet there must be global or at least regional coordination as well. When managers transfer from one country to another, they will expect to at least retain benefits, such as vacation time, comparable to that from their home country. For expatriates moving from countries with relatively low levels of such benefits, this will not create a problem. But for managers moving in the other direction, this can be the source of significant concerns.

Pension Plans

Pension plans provided by MNEs create their own special set of complexities. For example, when Johnson & Johnson examined its pension system a couple of years ago, it "discovered" that it not only had a U.S.-defined benefit pension plan covering some 20,000 participants with $1.2 billion in assets but also had another 15 plans with 15,000 participants worldwide and another $700 million in assets.[36] IHRM in Action 5.4 show how complex managing this pension program is. And this is only one of the many benefit programs with which MNEs must concern themselves.

In 1988, Johnson & Johnson formed a task force to look at its U.S. pension plan's actuarial assumptions and funding strategy. After completing the study for the domestic plan, the task force turned to an examination of the international companies and their pension plans. There were a lot of questions: What were the foreign subsidiaries doing with their investments of pension funds and what were their funding patterns? Why were they funded in a particular way? Why did they use certain assumptions? Was there any special tax or regulatory item that would impact funding or investments? The study examined all Johnson & Johnson major international plans, ranging in asset size from $2 million up to $250 million.

The first task was to gather information that was not at that time available at corporate headquarters, in New Brunswick, New Jersey, such as: How's their asset management doing? What are the returns? How are the funds invested? Who manages the funds? What was found was a lot of money sitting "out there" and no consistently applied philosophy as to why it was there in those amounts and what should be done with it. There was one exception; as on the domestic side, the philosophy that was handed down (from the parent firm) was to fund generously. What this study achieved was to let Johnson & Johnson begin to question that philosophy in light of the current environment.

There were a few countries where the firm didn't fund a pension plan because it didn't make sense, due to government-provided social security pensions and other country-specific regulations: Germany, Italy, and France. For example, in Germany there is not only a benefit to not funding, it costs to fund a private pension plan. In Italy, there is a major obligation to pay severance of any type and no vehicle was in place to fund it. On the other hand, Johnson & Johnson had funded pension plans in 13 other countries, typically with more than one company in each country and usually more than four. Some countries had two plans; some had countrywide arrangements; in some countries, every company in the country had its own plan. Every country was different.

In each location, the study first determined who the key pension contact was and then tried to figure out who else was on the local pension committee. Thus one of the results of the study was to create a living document on who all the players were—something that hadn't existed in New Brunswick previously.

Country by country the results of the study were fascinating. At the end of the study, results fell into certain categories: first, everyone finally understood that the requirement was to fund adequately, not generously, and they understood the dangers of overfunding. Second, increased coordination between local and corporate people was established. And third, professional staff from headquarters were now directly involved with foreign subsidiaries in advising on pension investments in order to improve what had been spotty investment performance.

The study took longer than expected; but now, according to Johnson & Johnson, all objectives have been met. Wherever possible, plans have been combined, proper funding targets have been established, and employee contributions have been reviewed for separation from employer funds. In addition, investment results have been improved and better worldwide coordination has been achieved. Johnson & Johnson continues to look for ways to improve the management of its benefit plans, especially in anticipation of major changes in benefits as a result of the European Community. As yet, many of the EC directives are not yet drafted, but important changes will continue to be made into the foreseeable future.

Source: Johnson & Johnson, Inc., New Brunswick, New Jersey. Reprinted with permission of Johnson & Johnson.

Stock Options, Equity Participation Plans, and Employee Ownership

In recent years the trend in global firms has been to look for ways to internationalize their employee equity participation schemes.[37] In particular, this has included experimenting with ways to grant stock options and restricted stock to their overseas employees.[38] And since U.S. companies have developed the most sophisticated structures for providing equity (shares of stock) to employees in various forms of pay-for-performance and employee ownership schemes, many global firms have looked to U.S. MNEs for concepts and techniques for achieving the objective of improving the ability of their global workforces—particularly their managers—to share in the success and rewards of their global efforts. Of particular interest has been the use of U.S.-style stock-based executive compensation programs. As stated by William M. Mercer International and Arthur Andersen & Co.:

> These plans are seen as a means of more closely identifying executives with their companies' business objectives. Such plans focus executive attention on the company's long-term growth and profitability, and align the financial interests of executives with those of the stockholders. And they can provide a mechanism for setting performance standards and rewarding their achievement.[39]

But the design of such programs is not easy. Every country has its own laws and regulations related to the use of such practices and their tax treatment. And not all foreign employees understand the concept of firm ownership or necessarily agree with it when they do.

IHRM in Action 5.5 illustrates the difficult experiences of some American MNEs as they have tried to extend their employee stock ownership plans overseas. Now the American Financial Accounting Standards Board (FASB) is considering changes in the accounting treatment of employee share-acquisition plans, which may have a dampening effect on the extension or continuing use of these plans.[40] Both U.S. firms (using these plans overseas) and foreign firms operating in the United States with such plans for their American employees will be affected by such accounting changes. Even though there are many difficulties, however, in establishing these stock sharing schemes, at least one international consulting firm has found ". . . how great the welcome has been by local management in a number of countries for an ability to participate in a share option or share scheme providing parent company shares."[41]

IHRM IN ACTION 5.5
EMPLOYEE STOCK PLANS RUN
INTO FOREIGN SNAGS

Unexpected hurdles arise as U.S. companies begin offering stock plans to many staff members worldwide. Such programs, designed to increase loyalty and productivity, sometimes run into problems because share ownership is unknown or restricted in numerous foreign countries. In July 1989, PepsiCo rolled out a stock-option plan called SharePower for about 140,000 of its 308,000 employees. But 21 percent of those eligible have yet to receive options, worth 10 percent of annual compensation.

"We had to develop a customized approach" to employee training "in every country we operate in," says Charles Rogers, Pepsi vice president, compensation and benefits. In certain locales, such as Greece, poorly educated staffers didn't even know what stock was. In Mexico, Brazil, and Japan, Pepsi had to switch from large-scale videotape presentations to flip charts for small groups because "videotapes are a relatively foreign form of communication" for businesses there, Rogers adds.

Du Pont, while planning a similar program unveiled last February, discovered that it couldn't give stock options in twenty-five of fifty-three nations—primarily because laws ban stock options or limit ownership of foreign shares. The chemical concern substituted stock-appreciation rights, giving cash for any appreciation in its stock price without enlarging the pool of employee shareholders. Legal hurdles kept Du Pont from giving either stock options or appreciation rights in Ecuador.

To avoid such stumbling blocks, Reader's Digest Association and Colgate-Palmolive are designing global stock programs country by country. Reader's Digest employees in the United States have been able to buy shares at a 10 percent discount since January, but a United Kingdom unit uses a modified stock-option arrangement instead. "It would be almost impossible to have a plain-vanilla plan that would apply in all countries," says Joseph Grecky, vice president, human resources.

Colgate wants to extend its U.S. stock grants to permanent employees worldwide, starting with Britain next spring. Tailoring plans for all sixty-two countries where it operates "will take a long time," says Reuben Mark, chairman and chief executive.

Source: "Employee Stock Plans Run Into Foreign Snags," by J. S. Lublin, THE WALL STREET JOURNAL, Sept. 16, 1991, B1. Reprinted by permission of THE WALL STREET JOURNAL, copyright © 1991, Dow Jones & Company, Inc. All rights reserved worldwide.

Nevertheless, it probably does not make sense to extend an employee share ownership scheme overseas unless certain conditions exist. These conditions include a strong commitment to employee ownership in foreign operations by senior management, belief by management that the firm is truly a global company with a strong commitment to the development of foreign employees, stability in the foreign workforce, a large enough foreign workforce in enough countries to warrant the start-up and administrative costs, and enough maturity in the firm's business to ensure its stability in its foreign operations.[42]

Employee share ownership plans (ESOPs)

In a major variant on this theme of providing equity (ownership shares) to employees on a global basis, many multinational firms are examining the American approach to what is described as "employee share ownership plans," or ESOPS. The primary focus here is to provide employees with a significant percentage of ownership in the firm.

The concept of employee ownership is not new nor is it a concept limited to a few countries. Over the years, numerous approaches to employee ownership have been tried in various countries with differing degrees of success.[43] Now, newly democratizing and newly industrializing countries are looking afresh at the idea of employee ownership as one approach to converting their state-owned enterprises to privately owned firms. Since a number of different approaches have been tried, multinational firms with an interest in providing employee ownership can follow patterns that have evolved in the countries of their foreign subsidiaries or they can export concepts from their home countries to the extent that local laws allow such innovations.

In the United States, tax law provides incentives to employers to establish employee stock ownership plans (ESOPs). Money used to purchase shares in a firm that are distributed to employees is tax deductible. By 1990, over 10,000 firms had ESOPs in the United States, covering over 10,000,000 employees. Many American multinational firms have ESOPs in the United States and would like to extend this opportunity to their foreign employees. But the tax laws in most countries do not provide any incentive to do so.

The following is a short summary of the employee-ownership practices in a number of countries.

CENTRAL AMERICA.   Firms in Latin America are primarily owned by foreign companies, governments, or wealthy families. Nevertheless, there has been some experimentation with employee ownership. Approximately 20 percent of LAC-SA, the national airline of Costa Rica is owned by employees. And about 30 percent of La Gloria (a large chain of department stores) is owned by its employees. In both cases the firms are selling stock to employee associations that are distributing the shares to employees. In Guatemala there are now about fifty firms with employee associations that are purchasing shares for their members.

EUROPE.   There are no tax-advantaged, U.S.-style ESOPs in Europe except in the United Kingdom. Many countries have developed various approaches to employee share ownership, and many are now examining the U.S. experience to see if it might be adopted there. In the U.K., there have been forms of employee ownership since the nineteenth century. Recent examples include the John Lewis Partnership with an employee trust that owns all shares in the company and distributes profits to employees as bonuses, and Imperial Chemical (ICI), which allows employees to buy shares on preferential terms and has a profit-sharing scheme that distributes shares of stock to employees. In 1989, the U.K. parliament passed legislation providing tax deductibility for employer contributions to U.S.-style employee share ownership plans.

In most other countries in Europe, the tax laws provide tax deductions (usually limited in scope) to individuals for income used to purchase shares in their employers' firms; for example, this is true in France, Sweden, Belgium, Denmark, and Switzerland. In other countries, such as Germany, Italy, and the Netherlands, shares distributed to employees by the firms are not counted by the tax authorities as income. In Spain, the Mondragon group has provided experience with worker-owned cooperatives for many years. Included in this group are now more than 160 individual cooperatives with over 20,000 members and US$1 billion in sales with exports of more than US$230,000,000.

Even with these limited advantages for employee share ownership, European MNEs are looking for ways to provide this opportunity throughout their operations. For example, Asea Brown Boveri (ABB) recently put shares in the company worth over US$600 million on offer to its employees in over twenty-five countries, available in some twenty local currencies.

JAPAN.   As is generally the case, the interest within any particular country in employee ownership is based on local factors. In Japan, there is increasing interest in employee share ownership as an additional strategy for helping to deal with problems associated with a rapidly aging population in a country with no private or public retirement income support. ESOPs are seen as a possible way to provide a source of economic relief (to provide income after retirement and to enhance employee motivation—for higher productivity, which will increase the values of their firms and thus their shares). At present, these schemes in Japan are essentially employee savings plans contributed to by both employees and employers.

AUSTRALIA.   Australia has a long history of interest in worker ownership, originally as an alternative to classical capitalism, or, more recently, as a way to establish economic democracy. That is, there were political reasons to pursue worker ownership. This primarily took the form of cooperatives. But now there are a number of firms with employee ownership as well, but still often founded out of religious, paternalistic, or egalitarian motives.

The trend in Australia has been that when certain firms became quite successful, they were converted into cooperatives or employee-owned ventures. In addition, a number of smaller firms were converted to employee ownership upon the death or retirement of the founder or owner. And many firms which are today owned by the employees were originally cooperatives that were restructured, often because of financial problems.

There is now some limited support in the tax system for ESOP-style share ownership. But Australian legislators continue to be concerned over the economic, political, and social effects of ESOPs. Thus there is a strong feeling that they need to know more about providing additional tax incentives to encourage the establishment of U.S.-style ESOPs.

EGYPT.   Even in countries such as Egypt, firms are experimenting with employee ownership. A new tire company has been formed in Cairo with a major portion of its initial capitalization coming from an employee shareholders' association. This ESA was created to substitute for a legal trust, a device which does not exist currently in Egyptian law. This ESA borrows the money to purchase shares for the 750 employees. This loan is repaid out of the dividends on the shares. No employee payroll deductions are required. And the workers' shares are pledged as the only source of security for the loan.

CENTRAL AND EASTERN EUROPE. Most of the countries in the former Soviet bloc are examining the use of various forms of employee ownership as one way to privatize enterprises that were formerly all state-owned. Sometimes employees must purchase the shares, in other situations they are receiving the shares in a "free" distribution from the state, or they receive vouchers that can be turned in for shares, and so on. Philosophically, the idea of employee (worker) ownership fits the social values of many people in these countries. But practically, there is no experience anywhere in the world for converting economies from state-owned and -operated to market-based and private ownership on these scales. Only time and experimentation will provide evidence of what will work in these economies.

Insurance

Insurance is another area of benefits that can add complexity to the design of compensation programs for expatriates or foreign subsidiaries. Most big firms provide their managers and senior technicians with life insurance as part of their employees' benefit packages. But many life insurance policies have clauses that in case of declared or undeclared war the insurance is null and void (which may be more likely to happen in a foreign subsidiary for local hires or expatriates). Thus the firm may need to purchase special coverage for expatriates while they are overseas and negotiate special programs for foreign subsidiaries.

In addition, the typical travel coverage (such as that provided when buying airline tickets through a credit card) may not be valid for employees if going to foreign assignments for an extended period of time. Again, the firm may want to consider purchasing special travel insurance for its expatriates and their families and its other international travelers.

Depending on the location of the overseas assignment, the firm may also have to provide special "work risk" insurance for more dangerous or remote locations and possibly other forms of special insurance, for example, kidnapping insurance (discussed in the next chapter).

Maternity and Family Leave

An area of employee benefits that has been receiving increasing attention from state and federal legislators in the United States involves the provision of leave for reasons related to family need (e.g., maternity leave, paternity leave, family leave, with or without pay, with guarantee of getting one's job back at the end of the leave). Almost immediately after Bill Clinton became President in January 1993, the U.S. Congress passed a family leave bill, providing unpaid leave for employees who need to take care of family emergencies, a bill which the new President signed (it had

Table 5.6 Maternity Leave in the European Community

COUNTRY	MATERNITY LEAVE	PAY
Belgium	14 weeks (6 before birth)	100% for 1–4 weeks, thereafter 80%
Denmark	28 weeks (4 before birth)	90% of salary
FRG (Germany)	14 weeks (6 before birth)	100% of salary or fixed sum
Greece	15 weeks (6 before birth)	100% of salary
Spain	16 weeks	75% of salary
France	16 weeks (6 before birth)	84% of salary
Ireland	14 weeks (6 before birth)	70% of salary
Italy	20 weeks (8 before birth)	80% of salary
Luxembourg	16 weeks (8 before birth)	100% of salary
Netherlands	12 weeks (6 before birth)	100% of salary
Portugal	90 days (6 weeks before birth)	100% of salary
UK	40 weeks	6 weeks at 90% of salary and 12 weeks at a fixed reduced sum

Source: National Women's Health Network, Protection at Work for Pregnant Women and Women Who Have Recently Given Birth—A Proposal for a Directive from the European Commission, Annex 1 Maternity Leave," THE NETWORK NEWS, July/August 1992.

been previously vetoed by President Bush). A number of states have passed similar legislation.

Most other countries appear to be further advanced on the provision of this particular benefit. Approximately two-thirds of all nations, including most industrialized countries, have provisions for paid and job-protected maternity leaves of four to twelve months prenatal and three to twenty-nine months postnatal.[44] The leave may be paid by the employer or by the government, or both. In some countries, including Norway, the Netherlands, Belgium, and Germany, up to 100 percent of salary is reimbursed during maternity leave. Leave in Sweden is available to either parent at 90 percent wages during the first twelve months and less thereafter. Table 5.6 illustrates the maternity leave provided in the twelve countries of the European Community (as of 1994, called the European Union or the EU). Even though the EU is trying to develop common practices on these types of social policies, Table 5.6 shows the diversity that exists even within these close-proximity countries.

Flexible Benefits

In this last, short section of the chapter, consideration is given to what is referred to as "flexible benefits" in the United States. Flexible benefits are the approach to benefits in an increasing number of American organizations. In essence, employees are typically given choices, up to a certain dollar limit, among a series of options for their benefits, including such things as pension contributions, health insurance options, dental insurance, life insurance, and so forth.

MNEs are beginning to examine flexible benefits for their global operations, designing global flexible benefit plans similar to what has been tried within the United States.[45] This is happening because:

1. Flexible benefits have been successful in the United States, so employers in other countries are beginning to take a look at the idea.
2. MNEs need to attract and retain more diversified workforces (in terms of age, marital status, family situation); thus they are looking at flexible benefits as a way to attract workers with diverse benefit needs.
3. Foreign firms are investing in American health-care companies and are thus being exposed to how important flexible benefits are in the United States for controlling rising health-care costs.
4. The increased aging of the labor force around the world is leading MNEs to look at flexible benefits as a way to provide diverse benefits to all workers with a single benefits program.

Issues such as tax treatment of benefits, private versus state health care, employee expectations and culture, nonstandardized social benefits from country to country, and varying company structures will need to be addressed in order to design flexible benefit packages that might be used throughout an MNE. Nevertheless, such an approach may help simplify worldwide complete compensation systems for multinational firms.

SUMMARY

This chapter presented IHRM practices related to the development of compensation and benefit programs among MNEs. The discussion followed three primary foci: compensation for expatriates; compensation and benefit programs for MNEs in the multiple locations of their overseas workforces, i.e., at their various subsidiaries; and issues related to the wide diversity of approaches to compensation and benefits in various countries around the world.

The chapter described six alternative approaches to compensation for expatriates, with extensive discussion of the balance sheet approach, which adds numerous incentives and adjustments to a parent-country base and is the most commonly-used method for paying expatriates. But the complexity of the balance sheet approach and the necessity of firms to get deeply involved with their expatriates' lives when using this approach (as well as the high cost of expatriate compensation) has led many firms to begin experimenting with one of the other possible approaches.

The issue which adds most of the complexity to the compensation of expatriates involves taxation practices and taxation rates in different countries. In an effort to ensure that their expatriates don't need to pay double taxation (for both their countries of origin and their countries of residence while expatriates), MNEs use one of three methods: laissez faire, tax equalization, or tax protection. In all cases, the purpose is to limit the tax liabilities of the expatriate. Compensation and taxation issues are also discussed for foreign multinationals operating in the U. S.

Lastly, the chapter described and discussed many of the various approaches taken to compensation and benefits, such as vacation and pension practices, in a number of different countries. For MNEs that operate in multiple countries with local subsidiary workforces in those countries, having an understanding of these country-specific variances becomes critical to designing rational HRM practices for the total firm.

The design and management of compensation programs for expatriates and for multiple workforces around the world is indeed a complex and difficult function. This chapter demonstrated why compensation and benefits absorb the bulk of the typical international HR manager's time and energy.

ENDNOTES

1. Reynolds, C., "Are You Ready to Make IHR a Global Function?" *HR News: International HR,* February 1992, pp. C1–C3.
2. See, for example, Crandall, L. P. and M. I. Phelps, "Pay for a Global Work Force," *Personnel Journal,* February 1991, pp. 28–33; Czinkota, R. M., P. Rivoli, and I. A. Ronkainen, *International Business* Ch. 20, "International Human Resource Management" (Chicago: Dryden Press, 1989); Green, W. E., and G. D. Walls, "Human Resources: Hiring Internationally," *Personnel Administrator,* July 1984, pp. 61–64, 66; Gross, R. E., and D. Kujawa, *International Business Theory and Managerial Applications,* 2nd ed., Ch. 18, "Personnel Management" (Homewood, IL: Richard D. Irwin, 1992); Mesdag, L. M., "Are You Underpaid?" *Fortune,* March 19, 1984, pp. 20–25; and Stuart, P., "Global Payroll—A Taxing Problem," *Personnel Journal,* October 1991, pp. 80–90.
3. See, for example, Gajek, M., and M. M. Sabo, "Flexible Compensation Plans: A New International Model for Attracting and Retaining World-Class Talent," *International Business,* November 1993, pp. 26+; Overman, S., "The Right Package," *HR Magazine,* July 1992, pp. 71–74; Senko, J. P., "Controlling Expatriate Execs' Costs," *Management Review,* March 1991, pp. 38–39.
4. Black, J. S., "Returning Expatriates Feel Foreign in Their Native Land," *Personnel,* August 1991, p. 17.
5. For a good discussion of these issues, refer to Dessler, G., *Personnel/Human Resource Management,* 5th ed., Appendix, "International Issues in Human Resource Management" (Englewood Cliffs, NJ: Prentice Hall, 1991).
6. Stone, R. J., "Compensation: Pay and Perks for Overseas Executives," *Personnel Journal,* January 1986, pp. 64–69.
7. Czinkota, M. R., P. Rovoli, and I. A. Ronkainen, *International Business* (New York: Dryden Press, 1989), p. 580; Stone, "Compensation: Pay and Perks for Overseas Executives."
8. This framework for expatriate compensation is adapted from Reynolds, C., *Compensation Basics for North American Expatriates: Developing an Effective Program for Employees Working Abroad* (Scottsdale, AZ: American Compensation Association, 1994); and Reynolds, C., "Advanced Compensation for International Human Resource Management," preconference workshop at the Sixth Global Congress for Personnel Management, San Francisco, February 28, 1994.
9. Crandall and Phelps, "Pay for a Global Work Force."
10. Society for Human Resource Management/Commerce Clearing House, *1992 SHRM/CCH Survey on International HR Practices* (Chicago: Commerce Clearing House, 1992).
11. Overman, "The Right Package."
12. Reprinted in "Perspectives," *Personnel Journal,* March 1991, p. 24.
13. Senko, J. P., "The Foreign Service Premium & Hardship Differential," *Mobility,* May 1990, pp. 10–12.
14. Ibid.
15. Ibid.
16. Runzheimer International (consulting firm headquartered in Rochester, WI), reproduced in *HR Focus,* September 1991, p. 8.
17. Senko, J. P., "Controlling Expatriate Execs' Costs," *Management Review,* March 1991, pp. 38–39.

18. See, for example, Bishko, M. J., "Compensating Your Overseas Executives, Part 1: Strategies for the 1990s," *Compensation and Benefits Review,* May–June 1990, pp. 33–43; Brooks, B. J., "Long-Term Incentives: International Executives," *Personnel,* August 1988, pp. 40–42; Brooks, B. J., "Trends in International Executive Compensation," *Personnel,* May 1987, pp. 67–70.

19. Bennett, A., "What's an Expatriate?" *The Wall Street Journal,* April 21, 1993, p. R5; Harvey, M., "Empirical Evidence of Recurring International Compensation Problems," *Journal of International Business Studies,* Fourth Quarter, 1993, pp. 785–799; Harvey, M., "Designing a Global Compensation System: The Logic and a Model," *Columbia Journal of World Business,* December 1993, pp. 56–70; Gajek and Sabo, "Flexible Compensation Plans."

20. See, for example, Stuart, "Global Payroll—A Taxing Problem."

21. Presented in Ibid., p. 81.

22. Holleman, W. J., "Taxation of Expatriate Executives," *The International Executive,* May–June 1991, pp. 30–33; Stuart, "Global Payroll—A Taxing Problem." A number of accounting firms also publish guides to taxes for expatriates. For example, see Coopers & Lybrand, *U.S. Nationals Working Abroad: Tax and Other Matters* (New York and Regional Offices: Authors, 1992).

23. Ibid.

24. Powell, B. L., "U.S. International Social Security Agreements," *Benefits & Compensation International,* June 1993, pp. 6–10.

25. Crandall, L. P., "Getting Through the Global Payroll Maze," *Personnel Journal,* August 1992, pp. 76–77; Dowling, P. J., "Hot Issues Overseas," *Personnel Administrator,* January 1989, pp. 66–72.

26. Ibid.

27. Overman, "The Right Package"; Andre, R., "High Technology, Incorporated: The International Benefits Problem," in *International Human Resource Management,* eds. M. Mendenhall and G. Oddou (Boston: PWS-Kent, 1991).

28. Thanks to Cal Reynolds, ORC., New York, for this phrase.

29. Nemerov, D. S., "How Foreign-Owned Companies Pay Their U.S. Executives," *Journal of International Compensation & Benefits,* January–February 1994, pp. 9–14.

30. Ibid.

31. For additional information, refer to Benson, D. M., T. St. G. Bissell, D. P. Bork, and E. J. Reavey, *Taxation of Foreign Nationals Working in the United States* (New York: Coopers & Lybrand, 1989).

32. Carey, B. P., "Why Inpatriates Need Special Remuneration Packages," *The Journal of European Business,* May–June 1993, pp. 46–49.

33. See, for example, Howes, P., "Companies Labor to Level the Paying Field," *The Journal of European Business,* September–October, 1993, pp. 18–21.

34. Data from a survey by Wyatt Co., reported in "Vacations Are Brief for American Workers," *Personnel Journal,* December 1992, p. 19.

35. Krupp, N. B., "Managing Benefits in Multinational Organizations," *Personnel,* September 1986, pp. 76–78; Murdock, B. A., and B. Ramamurthy, "Containing Benefits Costs for Multinational Corporations," *Personnel Journal,* May 1986, pp. 80–85.

36. DiLeonardi, F. A., "Money Makes the World Go 'Round," interview with Eugene Barron, assistant treasurer of Johnson & Johnson, *The Wyatt Communicator,* Spring 1991, pp. 15–19.

37. Carey, B. P., "Share Tactics," *The Journal of European Business,* July–August, 1993, pp. 14–16; William M. Mercer International and Arthur Andersen & Co., *Globalizing Compensation: Extending Stock Option and Equity Participation Plans Abroad,* Authors, 1990.

38. Hewitt Associates, *Granting Stock Options and Restricted Stock to Overseas Employees* (New York: Authors, 1993).

39. Ibid., p. 1.

40. Boylan, C. J., "Editor's Comments: New Limits of Global Employee Stock Ownership?" *Journal of International Compensation & Benefits,* January–February 1993, pp. 7–8; Cambron, B., "International Newsletter: United States," *Journal of International Compensation & Benefits,* January–February 1993, p. 6.

41. William M. Mercer Fraser, Ltd. (London, "Options in a Shrinking World," *The Mercer Fraser Quarterly Review,* 89 (Autumn 1990), 3.

42. Carey, "Share Tactics."

43. This section is based on Briscoe, D. R., "Employee Share Ownership Plans: An International Comparison with Application to Newly Industrializing Economies," presented to the 1991 National Conference, Association for Global Business, Atlanta, Georgia, November 6–9, 1991.

44. Reported in "Most Nations Require Employers to Provide Maternity Leave, Meeting Told," *BNA's Employee Relations Weekly,* April 2, 1990, p. 433.

45. Johnson, R. E., "Flexible Benefit Programs: International Style," *Employee Benefits Journal,* 16(3), September 1991, pp. 22–25.

6

Union and Employee Relations for Multinational Firms and International Employee Health and Safety

This chapter considers two aspects of traditional HRM responsibility set in the international context: employee and union relations and employee health and safety, both of which might be considered to be concerns in the governance of employees. This chapter demonstrates that labor relations receives more attention from the international HR manager than do health and safety concerns.

With respect to union and labor relations, many issues confront multinational HR managers. As with all international HR responsibilities, the diversity of approaches taken by different countries also plays a major role. In this chapter, two issues related to labor or employee relations are discussed: the problems that MNEs encounter when they interact with labor unions in multiple countries and the wide variety of employee relations practices they encounter around the world.

Multinational enterprises typically must deal with many union and employee relations issues in their foreign operations that differ drastically from what they are familiar with at home. In some countries, workplaces and employees may not be unionized at all, although there may still be extensive government regulation of the employment relationship; while in other countries it may be that employees who can't or don't unionize in the home country of the parent firm are unionized. In addition, whether a union is present or not, practices related to the management and governance of workforces around the globe vary dramatically in workplace decision-making processes, layoff and termination practices, and other concerns related to discipline and grievance problems and procedures.

HR managers with responsibility for labor relations issues in MNEs typically approach these issues in one or more of the following ways:[1]

1. *Understanding international regulations* applying to labor relations, such as those developed by the European Community (EC), the International Labour Organization (ILO, a body of the United Nations), or the Organization for Economic Cooperation and Development (OECD, an agency established by twenty-four major industrial powers to develop common trade policies);
2. *Analyzing labor relations issues that are common to all MNEs;* and
3. *Conducting an analysis of the labor relations laws and practices in each of the countries* within which the MNE operates.

Obviously these approaches overlap. And the typical IHR manager will try to understand international labor relations from all three perspectives. Accordingly, the labor relations section of this chapter is also organized around these three approaches.

HR managers, in most of their responsibilities, enjoy relative autonomy to develop policy and make decisions that can be applied in all countries. But this is not so true for labor relations. Firms must share decision-making power with unions (or other representatives of employees, for example, works councils) to greater or lesser degrees throughout the world but almost always to some degree. And because many businesses, particularly American businesses, do not like dealing with unions, they often behave as if they would prefer to not deal with labor relations issues in the international arena at all.

Of course, this isn't possible. So, responsibility for labor relations is frequently left to the local subsidiary. MNEs typically develop worldwide approaches to issues such as executive compensation, but such a worldwide approach to labor relations is quite rare. Thus, IHR departments within MNEs typically follow one of these approaches to labor relations in a global context:

1. *Hands off* (by headquarters of the parent firm). In this approach, responsibility for labor relations is left in the hands of local managers.
2. *Monitor.* In this approach, headquarters HR managers will try to forestall major problems for the parent company by asking intelligent and insightful questions about labor relations responsibilities and activities at each of their foreign locations. But primary responsibility still stays in the hands of local managers.
3. *Guide and advise.* This approach is a step beyond mere monitoring. Here IHR managers from headquarters will provide ongoing advice and guidance to subsidiary managers on how to conduct labor relations. Of course, this requires a higher degree of knowledge about local labor relations regulations and practices. Still, overall control stays in the hands of the local staff.
4. *Strategic planning.* At this level of involvement, international labor relations issues are fully incorporated into the MNE's strategic planning. Management of all aspects of the global firm, including labor relations, are integrated into a centralized program, particularly for policy purposes. Local control may still exist, but all labor relations practices will follow this global strategy.
5. *Set limits and approve exceptions.* MNEs that follow this approach to their international labor relations provide even more specific centralized control over lo-

cal practices. Subsidiaries are allowed freedom of action only within quite narrowly defined limits, and any efforts to try different approaches must be approved by headquarters.
   6. *Manage totally from headquarters.* In this scenario, local subsidiary staffs have no
      freedom of policy or practice in their labor relations activities. Indeed, all labor
      relations actions are directed by staff from headquarters.
   7. *Interface of headquarters IHR and line management in the field.* In this final ap-
      proach, labor relations in the field, as managed by the local HR and manage-
      ment staff, are fully integrated with HR assistance from headquarters.

Firms at the level of using option 5, 6, or 7 tend to be American firms that have
strong antiunion approaches to labor relations and are trying to follow this approach as much as possible in their overseas operations. Of course, in many countries (e.g., where there are works councils) even these firms must deal with third
parties, whether they want to or not. For example, IBM, which is a nonunion firm
in the United States, must deal with unions extensively in its French subsidiary,
where if even a single employee claims to represent one of the unions, the firm must
negotiate with that union. Indeed, IBM France even has its own "company union"
so that the firm negotiates with six different unions. Still, much autonomy is usually possible, even when the law requires dealing with third parties, such as the
unions or other representatives of employees. And because each country is different in its evolution of labor relations law and practice, leaving primary responsibility for labor relations to the local level is often the only workable approach
(maybe with certain overlying strategic objectives providing some guidance).

THE GLOBAL ENVIRONMENT AND INTERNATIONAL LABOR REGULATIONS

The newly global economy places new stresses on industrial relations. Multinational enterprises (with operations largely decentralized to operate as local actors
in many countries around the world) and transnational, or global, firms (with operations throughout the world and decisions made about employees, sourcing, fi-
nancing, technology, and location of manufacturing and services without regard to
international boundaries) tend to dwarf the power and influence of labor unions.
        Unions mostly exist only at local, firm, regional (within a country), or national
level, even though a few have the term *international* in their names. There has been
very little cooperation between unions across national borders, and there is no union
structure similar to that of the multinational firm, so that, for example, an international union might be able to negotiate a global agreement with an MNE that would
apply to all of its operations around the world. Gradually, however, unions are beginning to develop regional offices to try to deal with regional issues that are arising
because of the development of regional trading blocks. The regional issues include
EC-wide works councils, with representatives from all components of a particular
firm throughout Europe, as a response to the development of the European Community, and offices established by the United Automobile Workers to deal with cross-
border issues between the United States and Canada in the auto industry. Indeed,
unions in Europe have developed some fifty industry-based Europe-wide committees, but thus far national and multinational firms have not agreed to meet with them.

Because of the nature of MNEs, unions tend to be very concerned about their lack of relative power. MNEs operate in many countries and often in many industries. In contrast, unions almost always have membership in only *one* country and normally in only *one* industry. Thus MNEs are seen as a threat by unions. Unions can typically bring pressure to bear on only a small segment of an MNE— one industry (or even one firm within one industry) within one country.

> Union leaders see the following characteristics of an MNC as the bases for the threat to union bargaining power: formidable financial resources; alternative sources of supply; ability to move productive facilities to other countries; superior knowledge and expertise in labor relations; a remote locus of authority; and production facilities in many industries.[2]

In practical terms, what this means is that unions view MNEs as being able to:[3]

- Force workers in one country, faced by competition from workers in other countries, to "bid down" their wages and benefits in order to keep their jobs (for an example, see IHRM in Action 6.1, the story of Hyster Company in Europe);
- Take advantage of differences in legally required benefits for workers by manipulating the operations in countries where the costs of adjustments are lowest and thus forcing excessive dislocation burdens on workers in these low-benefit countries; and
- Outlast workers in the event of a strike in one country because cash inflows to the MNE are at least partially maintained by operations in countries where there are no strikes.

IHRM IN ACTION 6.1
POWER TACTICS IN
MULTINATIONAL UNION-
MANAGEMENT RELATIONS

On arriving for work on Valentine's Day, the 500 employees of Hyster Company's forklift truck factory in Irvine, Scotland, were taken to a meeting run by Hyster's chief executive, William Kilkenny. He was fresh in from the head offices in Portland, Oregon, bearing big new plans for Irvine. With a British government grant, he disclosed, Hyster was set to invest $60 million in the plant. Hyster was prepared to reorganize and expand. It was willing to close two production lines at its Dutch factory and move them to Scotland. Irvine would gain 1,000 jobs. In return, Hyster wanted a sacrifice. Workers would have to take a pay cut of 14 percent, managers 18 percent. They had, Kilkenny told them, forty-eight hours to decide.

On the following morning, each employee received a letter from the company. "Hyster," it said, "is not convinced at this time that Irvine is the best of the many alternatives open to it. It has not made up its mind. The location of the plant to lead Europe is still open."

At the bottom of the page there was a ballot. A yes or a no was called for. Only eleven people voted no.

Workers complained that they had no warning, no consultation. Said one, "It was industrial rape—do or else." Hyster's workers in Irvine have no union, but the vote might have been no different if they had. The most powerful union in Europe is no match for a company run out of Portland, Oregon, U.S.A. A union is concerned with the workers in its country; a multinational corporation knows no bounds.

MNCs rarely tell scattered workers everything. But workers of different nationalities rarely tell each other anything. In an age when information is power, they lack both.

A day after its Scottish staff accepted a pay cut, Hyster telexed the news to its plant manager in Holland. It was the Dutch manager's first official word of Hyster's "decision," which turned out to include the firing of a number of Dutch workers and his own early retirement.

Dutch law calls for consultation about such things, and the plant union took Hyster to court. There, a judge ordered Hyster to discuss its strategy with members of the factory works council. It did, revealing the sliver of its corporate plan that applied to them. The union did not like it and went to court again.

A long legal battle could have cost dearly, so Hyster struck a deal: The workers would drop the suit, and the company would not transfer production for three years. Now the Scottish workforce is off balance again, despite Hyster's assurance that its expansion will go through.

COMPANY'S VIEW

Hyster's managing director in Europe is an American. But he is fighting a different war. "We're battling the Japanese," he says. "They've captured an alarmingly large share of the European market. To counter them, we have to produce a cost-effective forklift truck, and to do that, we've implemented a worldwide restructuring program. That required some very tough decisions. Given the circumstances, we've made every effort to communicate effectively with our employees."

UNION VIEW

Said one union leader, "What they call decentralized industrial relations means isolation for us. Without a multinational union you're at the mercy of a company like this." International unions have set up about 50 worker groups representing the car makers, the electronics companies, and the oil and chemical industries. Their aim is to collect and exchange information. To date, however, not one MNC has agreed to meet with any of them. The MNCs are playing "hardball," and they wield considerable power in international labor relations.

Thus unions around the world are trying to establish international federations and trade secretariats to provide assistance to national unions in dealing with MNEs. Their ultimate goal is to develop transnational bargaining. In addition, these international federations are working within both national legislatures and regional and international bodies such as the European Community, the United Nations, the Organization for Economic Cooperation and Development (OECD), and the International Labour Organization (ILO), to pass legislation and regulations—or at least guidelines—that will guide the labor relations practices of MNEs whose home countries are members of these various organizations. In particular, international directives have been established by the ILO and guidelines by OECD to at least suggest that multinational firms abide by the industrial relations statutes in force in each of the countries in which they operate.

Nevertheless, these guidelines are only as effective as individual firms and governments are willing to allow them to be.[4] Adherence to them is essentially voluntary. In a well-known case, the Badger Company, a subsidiary of Raytheon, a U.S. MNE, closed its Belgian subsidiary without paying required termination payments for displaced workers. Badger (Belgium) NV had declared bankruptcy, but Belgian labor unions argued that Raytheon should assume the subsidiary's financial obligations. Raytheon initially refused, but under intense pressure from the Belgian government and American and Belgian labor unions—and a "finding" by the OECD that their guidelines implied a shared responsibility by subsidiaries and their parents—Badger executives and Belgian officials eventually agreed to a scaled-down settlement.[5] Even though the eventual outcome supported the intent of the OECD guidelines, it also made pretty clear that the guidelines are only as effective as the pressure from unions and governments can make them.

The most active of the international union organizations has been the International Confederation of Free Trade Unions (ICFTU), which has its headquarters in Brussels. Cooperating with ICFTU are some twenty International Trade Secretariats (ITSs), which are really international federations of national trade unions operating within the same or related industries. The significance of the ITSs from management's point of view lies in the fact that behind local unions may be the expertise and resources of an ITS. Even so, as discussed above, it seems that the power and resources of MNEs greatly exceed those of unions, particularly in the international arena.

The following two situations illustrate the difficulties that unions encounter in this regard. In a situation mentioned earlier, El Al Israel Airlines in the 1980s refused to negotiate a contract with its New York employees, who subsequently went out on strike.[6] El Al proceeded to bring in employees from Israel, demanding that their American union employees accept major concessions or the firm would move to another North American city. Because the U.S. government was not willing to intervene or to provide an administrative hearing of the union's charges of unfair labor practices (and, maybe, because the union was unable to bring any pressure to bear on El Al in Israel, where the airline is government-owned and without any unions), this impasse has never been settled.

A second case involves international firms ignoring local union/LIR practices, as in Korea in recent years where there have been a number of illegal plant closings by foreign-owned subsidiaries of MNEs without the legally required notice and without their paying owed wages and other required compensation in case of plant closures.[7] There were thirty-two such closings in 1989 and the trend has been upward. Unless unions can get federal governments to support them in opposing these types of action, or the international bodies find ways to enforce their regulations, the MNEs will continue to wield greater power than do the unions representing the interests of employees and these types of abuses will probably continue.

IHRM in Action 6.1 describes a situation in which an American MNE—Hyster Company, a forklift manufacturer headquartered in Portland, Oregon—made global strategic decisions that affected the workforces in a number of countries and to which the affected local workforces and unions were basically unable to respond effectively. This case also illustrates the workings of different labor relations systems and how MNEs can operate seemingly autonomously from individual national systems.

In addition to the barriers to multinational bargaining based on the power of MNEs and the fractured nature of labor unions, a number of other obstacles remain which will need to be overcome in order for more rapid progress to occur there toward multinational bargaining:

1. The widely varying industrial relations laws and practices among different countries;
2. Major economic and cultural differences among different countries;
3. Employer opposition;
4. Union reluctance at the national level, because the national leadership often fears that multinational bargaining will transfer power from them to an international leadership;
5. Absence of a central union decision-making authority;
6. Lack of coordination of activities across national boundaries;
7. Differing national priorities; and
8. Employee unwillingness to subordinate local concerns to concerns of workers in other countries.[8]

LABOR RELATIONS ISSUES COMMON TO ALL MNEs

In general, the phenomenon of industrial relations throughout the various countries of the world may be more alike than different when comparing one country with another. Yet every country has its own unique approach to the development of the play among the industrial relations actors—labor, management, government, and the public—and their various representing organizations. While the laws and practices may be tightly and specifically stated in some countries, other countries provide ample opportunity for improvisation. Even the percentage of the workforce and the nature of the employees who belong to unions varies dramatically from country to country (see Table 6.1), though this may not indicate the power of unions within their respective countries. For example, even though a relatively low percentage of workers belong to unions in France (about 12 percent), the unions play a very important role in determining government policy toward workers and toward general industrial policy, and employers are required by law to negotiate with any union present (represented by as few as one employee) and to implement national policies on wage rates, and so on. In fact, about 85 percent of all workers in France are covered by the contract provisions negotiated by unions.

In addition, making comparisons of union density among countries is somewhat imprecise due to inconsistencies in how measures are derived (e.g., retired workers are still union members in most Scandinavian countries but not usually elsewhere and professionals such as teachers and members of employee

Table 6.1 Union Representation in Various Countries

PERCENTAGE OF WAGE AND SALARY WORKERS WHO ARE UNION MEMBERS			
COUNTRY	DENSITY (%)	COUNTRY	DENSITY (%)
Australia	41	Luxembourg	49.7
Austria	61	Mexico	26
Belgium	53	Netherlands	25
Canada	35	Norway	65
Denmark	73.2	Poland	40
France	12	Portugal	30
Germany	35	Singapore	16.5
Greece	25	Spain	16
India	28	Sweden	85.3
Ireland	52.4	Taiwan	28
Italy	40	United Kingdom	42
Japan	25	United States	12
S. Korea	18	Venezuela	25
Lebanon	20		

Source: M. Rothman, D. Briscoe, and R. CD Nacamulli, eds., INDUSTRIAL RELATIONS AROUND THE WORLD (Berlin: Walter de Gruyter, 1993); J. Visser, "Trade Unionism in W. Europe: Present Situation and Prospects," LABOUR AND SOCIETY, 13(2), 1988, 125–182; OECD, EMPLOYMENT OUTLOOK, Paris 1991; and U.S. Department of Labor, Bureau of Labor Statistics.

associations such as engineers are sometimes included and sometimes not). Changes in labor relations are also occurring so rapidly in many countries that data only a few years old can be out-of-date by significant amounts. Nevertheless, relative differences remain quite obvious.

One more factor that makes these comparisons complex concerns the number of workers in any particular country that are covered by collectively bargained union contracts. Table 6.2 lists these figures for a number of important countries. In many countries, even if there are relatively low levels of unionization, negotiated settlements can still cover a very high percentage of the labor force, as mentioned above for France.

Table 6.2 Percentage of Labor Force Covered by Collective Bargaining Agreements Negotiated in Select Countries

COUNTRY	% LABOR FORCE IN UNIONS	% COVERED BY CB AGREEMENTS
United States	12	18
Canada	35	45
Japan	25	60
Belgium	53	75
France	12	85
Germany	35	75
Italy	40	65
Netherlands	25	85
Spain	16	50
United Kingdom	42	60

Source: M. Rothman, D. Briscoe, and R. CD Nacamulli, eds., INDUSTRIAL RELATIONS AROUND THE WORLD (Berlin: Walter de Gruyter, 1993); OECD, EMPLOYMENT OUTLOOK, Paris 1991.

In terms of the patterns of labor relations practice themselves, some countries have developed industrial relations systems patterned after the laws and traditions of other countries. Many others have pursued relatively unique avenues to labor relations. Nevertheless, within this milieu, each country has developed a tradition and legal framework that reflects its own special history and political experience. As a consequence, firms that conduct business on a multinational or transnational basis must understand and cope with a great deal of diversity in the performance of industrial relations around the world. This typically leads to decentralizing the labor relations function (much as is also true of the general HRM function), providing subsidiaries with considerable autonomy in managing employee relations.

George McCullough, industrial relations executive at Exxon Corporation, illustrates this point with the following statement about Exxon's view of local autonomy for labor relations:[9]

> My company operates in 137 countries. The variations in our labor relations processes, the manner in which we go about collective bargaining, and the differences in items included in collective agreements are staggering. Even in two countries like Holland and Belgium, where the proximity between Rotterdam and Antwerp has caused us to consolidate some management functions, the labor relations processes are totally independent of each other and the contracts bear little resemblance.

In some countries (e.g., Canada, the United States, Germany, and Japan), union activity is basically economic. That is to say, unions involve themselves primarily with economic issues of concern to their members, such as wage rates, hours of work, and job security; and this is usually manifested through some form of union-management collective bargaining. In other countries, particularly England, France, Italy, and those in Latin America, unions tend to be very political and often try to achieve their objectives through political action rather than through direct collective bargaining. In some countries, union activity is focused on industry-wide or even national bargaining while in other countries union relations are very decentralized, taking place almost exclusively at the local firm level. Thus, even in industrialized countries, major differences in labor relations can be found relative to issues such as (1) the level at which bargaining takes place (national, regional, industry, or workplace); (2) centralization of union-management relations; (3) the scope of bargaining, that is, the topics which are usually included; (4) the degree to which the government is involved or can intervene; and (5) the degree of unionization. In order to be effective in labor relations throughout the operations of an MNC, IHR managers need to understand these issues in each of the countries in which they conduct business.

In addition to diversity, the other common theme in industrial relations around the globe at this time in history—the first half of the 1990s—is drastic and pervasive change. In most countries, particularly the United States and most European countries, the union scene is changing rather dramatically.[10] For example,

> Europe's trade unions are facing a decline unprecedented in the postwar period. As in the U.S., the shrinkage of smokestack industries such as autos and steel is

leaving European unions hard pressed to deliver job security. The resulting decline in union membership is weakening labor's traditionally active role in government policy-making in many countries. . . . [T]he nationwide and industrywide bargaining that has given union negotiators strong leverage in Europe is breaking down [and] employers are winning efficient work rules.[11]

This rapidly changing nature of labor relations practice around the world plus the diversity inherent in country- and culture-specific laws and traditions, has made it even more important for HRM managers in multinational/transnational firms to have a thorough understanding of the basics of the industrial relations systems in the countries in which they operate. They must also develop an understanding of the concerns and approaches of labor unions to coping with large multinational or global firms. The intent of this chapter is to provide some of that understanding.

The American multinational may face an even more difficult problem, for American labor relations are quite different in many respects from those practiced in other countries. The primary features of the American labor relations scene include the following:

- Only nonsupervisorial and nonmanagerial employees have the right to organize or join unions;
- Typically, professional and technical employees also do not form or join unions;
- The only employees who belong to unions work for employers where a majority of those employees have voted in free but secret elections for union representation;
- Contracts between such unions and employers are negotiated primarily at the local level between a single union and a single employer;
- Such collectively bargained contracts are legally enforceable and typically last for three years;
- The only mandatory subjects for bargaining are wages, hours, and working conditions;
- Both unions and employers are restricted in their behaviors toward each other by a considerable amount of regulation; and
- Disagreements over the meanings of contracts are handled through established grievance procedures, settled by union and management acting together and settled in the case of impasse by a privately hired, neutral arbitrator.

This highly decentralized, "business" unionism (although extensively regulated) is significantly different than the form of unionism present in most other countries of the world (which is often referred to as "political" unionism).[12] In most countries, labor relations practices are typically very different, even opposite, to these characteristics. Thus the American multinational firm may have even more difficulty coping with this diversity in labor relations practices, because its experience and familiarity may well not provide adequate guidance in other countries.

In particular, the American MNE will need to answer the following questions regarding the practice of labor relations in each of the countries within which it operates:

1. What are the nature and role of the employers' associations in each country? Because there is very little multiemployer bargaining in the United States, American MNEs will need to learn much about these associations in their for-

eign locales. These associations provide the primary vehicle through which bargaining is conducted in most other countries. Sometimes the multiemployer bargaining is regional (within an industry), sometimes industry-wide, and sometimes national, covering all or most industries. The questions the MNE needs to address relative to employers' associations include: Which associations exist? Should the MNE belong (why, why not)? What does membership entail, do most employers join, and can the firm avoid joining? Even with the weakening of unions as is occurring in many European countries, industry and/or national agreements are still being negotiated that apply to all or most employers and employees.

2. What are the nature of the unions in each particular country? Are they associated with political parties and if so, which ones? Are they related to the Church? How are they organized: by firm, region, industry, national? Who belongs? Who is covered by the contracts?

3. Is it possible to operate union-free? (It is often impossible.)

4. Is there multiunionism within firms, so that the MNE must negotiate with multiple, often competing unions, within the same subsidiary?

5. Are there closed-shop requirements or practice? That is, is the situation such that employees must belong to the union(s)?

6. Is there white-collar unionization? Do managers belong to unions, such as the *dirigenti* in Italy?

7. What is the nature of the plant or site-level role of unions? Are there shop stewards? Are there works councils that are essentially arms of the unions?

8. What is the nature of contracts or agreements with unions? Are the contracts enforceable? Are they breakable for any reasons? For what reasons can and do unions go on strike? What topics are contained in the contracts?

All of these questions illustrate potentially significant differences between labor relations practices in other countries and in the United States, with which American IHR managers are more likely to be familiar.

Grievances, Discipline, and Terminations

One specific area in which the practices in countries around the world typically differ significantly from those in the United States is in their procedures for handling grievances, discipline, and terminations. In most countries, legislation regulates what firms can do in terms of discipline and provides major avenues for employee participation that lessens the need for any type of grievance procedure, as would be considered in the typical American firm.

A major example of the differences in these areas is provided by the requirements of notice and severance pay for terminated or laid-off employees that are mandated in most countries. Indeed, as is explained in Chapter 8, it is very difficult to terminate any employee for any reason in many countries. But when it is possible and done, to do so usually requires significant compensation. Such compensation often is required even for termination of employees for disciplinary and for performance problems as well as for the normal reasons of economic necessity.[13] In most countries, the amount of severance pay is pro-rated by the employee's age, years of service, and level of salary, so that, for example, a terminated forty-five-year-old employee with twenty years' service and a salary of US$50,000 in Belgium would be owed US$94,000 in severance pay.[14] A similar employee terminated in Ire-

---

IHRM IN ACTION 6.2
UNFAIR DISMISSAL PROTECTION
IN EUROPE

Most U.S. employees are not protected from unjust dismissal by law. This is not the case for employees in Great Britain, France, Germany, or Italy. In Britain, for example, the Employment Protection Consolidation Act of 1978 and the Redundancy [the term used in Europe for economic layoffs] Payments Act of 1965 provide specific rights to employees who are fired. The 1978 law requires that employers give workers up to twelve weeks' notice of dismissal depending upon the length of service of the employee. The Redundancy Act requires employers to give lump-sum payments to workers with two years' service or more who are dismissed as part of reductions in force. In Britain, workers may complain to industrial tribunals if they believe they have been unjustly dismissed. Employers may be asked to provide written reasons for the dismissals.

In France, a law passed in 1973 states that an "employer may dismiss employees at any time" but only for a "genuine and serious cause and by following a specified procedure."Genuine and serious causes must relate directly to the ability of the employee to perform his or her job. These causes might include incompetence, loss of physical ability to do the job, offensive behavior, repeated unexcused absences or lateness, and so on. The dismissal procedure involves a variety of steps, some which must be carried out within a specific time period after the precipitating incident. These include summoning the employee by registered mail that he or she will be dismissed. The employee may ask for a written explanation of the reasons for dismissal and may sue for wrongful dismissal. If the employee wins, he or she may be reinstated or receive not less than six months' pay.

In Germany, the Civil Code, the Act on Protection Against Unfair Dismissals (APAUD), and the Work Council Act protect employees from arbitrary firing. The Civil Code and APAUD require that notice be given prior to dismissal, with the amount of notice varying according to length of service. These laws also define circumstances under which dismissal is justifiable, such as disability, misconduct, and economic reasons. The Work Council Act established worker councils to represent employees in organizations. These councils must review dismissal cases before firing can occur. Labor courts handle disputes concerning unjust dismissals.

In Italy, the Civil Code requires that notice or payment of an equivalent amount of wages must be given prior to dismissal. The Code also requires that dismissed workers receive a special dismissal payment based on seniority. Laws that require written explanations for dismissal and define justifiable reasons for dismissal were passed in 1966 and 1970.

Original sources: Hepple, B. A., "Unfair Dismissals Legislation in Great Britain"; Rojot, J., "Protection Against Unfair Dismissals in France"; Weiss, M., "Protection Against Unfair Dismissals in West Germany"; and Treu, T., "Protection Against Unfair Discharge in Italy"; all in *Protecting Unorganized Employees Against Unjust Discharge*, eds. J. Stieber and J. Blackburn (East Lansing, MI: School of Labor and Industrial Relations, Michigan State University, 1983); and Blanpain, R., ed., "Restructuring Labour in the Enterprise: Law and Practice in France, F.R. of Germany, Italy, Sweden, and the United Kingdom," *Bulletin of Comparative Labour Relations*, 15, (1986).

land would be owed US$13,000 and in Venezuela US$106,000. It is not unusual for termination pay for longer-term employees to equal as much as eighteen months' pay.

In some countries, employers will find it difficult to terminate employees at all. In Portugal, for example, all terminations are legal actions defended in court, while in countries such as Germany terminations are topics for consultation with employee works councils. IHRM in Action 6.2 provides some detail on the regulations governing dismissals in a number of European countries.

COMPARATIVE LABOR RELATIONS—A COUNTRY-BY-COUNTRY ANALYSIS

Due to the complexities of comparing labor relations systems country by country and to space limitations within this text, this section can provide only a few simple basics in contrasting practices in a few countries. Additional coverage of comparative IHRM practices (which often overlap considerably with labor relations as discussed here) is in Chapter 8.

Europe

European labor relations are very different than those practiced in the United States.[15] The primary differences lie in the politization of labor relations in most European countries, the greater class separation between workers and management or ownership, and the more direct role of the government in both regulating the relationship between labor and management and in taking responsibility for social security concerns of workers. In addition, due to the longer history of unions in most European countries, unions have a much higher degree of acceptance and integration into the economy. In particular:

1. In Europe, firms typically negotiate their agreements with unions at the national level through employer associations representing their particular industries, even when there is local, within-company negotiations as well. This national agreement establishes certain minimum conditions of employment which frequently are augmented through bargaining with the union at the firm or local level.

2. Unions in many European countries have more political power than those in the United States, with the result that when employers deal with their union(s) they are, in effect, often dealing directly or indirectly with the government. Unions are often allied with a particular political party—generally referred to as the labor party, although in some countries these alliances are more complex; for example, a number of different political parties, each supported and primarily identified with a particular union or set of unions.

3. There is a greater tendency in Europe for salaried employees, including those at managerial levels, to be unionized, often in a union of their own (such as the *dirigenti*, in Italy).

4. Unions in most European countries have been in existence longer than those in the United States. Consequently, they occupy a more accepted position in society and need be less concerned about gaining approval.

In Great Britain, the country with the earliest developed industrial economy, there are more than three times as many labor unions as there are in the United

States.[16] Large manufacturing firms typically negotiate with about seven different unions. Even though unions have been present in Great Britain for a long time, there is little formal labor law. Instead, unions there have opted for more freedom of action, seek many of their objectives through the national Labour party, wildcat strikes, class struggle against private firm ownership, and direct government involvement in guaranteeing worker security. Throughout the 1980s, the government was in the hands of the conservative Tories, effectively limiting the role of unions in the national economy. At least partially because the economy faired quite well during this period, union membership has been on the deadline in Great Britain as almost everywhere else, declining from 54 percent in 1979 to about 40 percent in 1990.

In France, as well as in Great Britain, there is also a great deal of government intervention in the collective bargaining process. This is particularly true in industries where there is a high degree of government ownership. For example, at Renault, the French government-owned automobile manufacturer, unions make use of political pressures in their bargaining with managers, who are in effect government employees. The resulting terms of agreement then become standards for other firms. As in the U.K., French firms typically negotiate with five or six unions, even if only a few employees belong to each one. But the results then apply to all employees. And, as in Germany, the Netherlands, and elsewhere, French firms also must consult with works councils, the elected memberships of which normally consist of primarily union members. (For more information about works councils, refer to comparative HRM practices in Chapter 8.)

In some European countries, unions are even given the right to participate in the boards of directors of firms. In Sweden, for example, unions have the right to choose two members of certain companies' boards. In addition, in Sweden, as in many other European countries, unions participate in operating management decisions through works councils. In Germany, unions also have access to membership on boards of directors through a process called *co-determination*. In German steel and coal firms, unions select five board members, stockholders select five members, and these ten select an eleventh member. Outside the steel and coal industries, the number of union members of boards depends on a firm's size. Unions get one-third the membership in firms with 500 to 2,000 employees and equal representation with stockholders in firms with 2,000 and more employees. German unions also get a role in operating management in steel and coal firms because they have the right to approve the chairmanship of the management board that makes daily management decisions.

In the European Community itself,[17] the elimination of trade barriers by the end of 1992—the phenomenon referred to as "EC 1992"—is having a major effect on labor and employee relations. Over the years, most European countries have written into their federal laws protection for most employee rights, rights that are more often negotiated in collective bargaining in the United States. As a way to recognize these rights after the merger of the European economies, a social charter of worker rights was negotiated in late 1989 and agreed to by all members of the EC except Great Britain, which has maintained a more individualistic approach to labor relations. Under this social charter, which has not yet been approved by all the participant countries, workers are guaranteed a number of rights: the right to organize, to participate in company decisions, to work in a safe environment, to be paid equitable wages, to have access to vocational training, to have equal opportunities for women, and to have protection for children, seniors, and the disabled.[18] Recession and political conflicts in 1993 have shifted the focus in many EC countries to internal problems and away from integration issues such that EC-wide agreement on these social issues appears to be further away than was initially projected.

Section 7 of the Social Charter deals with "Freedom of Association and Collective Bargaining." As indicated earlier in this chapter, unions express concern that multinational firms have an unfair advantage in negotiation with employee unions. The Social Charter affirms the rights of employers and workers of the European Community to free association in order to constitute professional organizations or trade unions of their choice for the defense of their economic and social interests. This right is already encoded in the laws of each of the member states. But the EC is now expressing interest in encouraging EC-wide dialogue between "the two sides of industry," which may, "if the parties deem it desirable, result in contractual relations. . . ." Indeed, the European Commission (the executive and administrative body of the European Community) has developed an ongoing dialogue procedure associating the leaders of the employers' organizations and the trade unions in the Community.

France

There are five major national unions in France with most large employers also having a "company union." The unions are organized at the national level but do not require representation elections within firms. If any employee claims to represent any one of the unions, the employer must negotiate with that union. The result is that most employers negotiate with six unions (the five national unions and their own company union). Even though union membership is only about 12 percent, the agreements they negotiate cover almost all employees, managers included. By law, large employers deal with three different employee bodies: personnel delegates (elected by employees—but nominated by the unions—to discuss employee grievances), works councils (elected by employees—but nominated by the unions—for consultation on major business issues such as reorganization, new technology, and employment issues), and union delegates (appointed by the unions for negotiation of salaries, working time, and working rules). Thus the unions have a major influence that is greater than their membership would suggest.

Agreements are negotiated (both at the national or industry level and within the firm) with one or more of the unions that then apply to all employees. These agreements then determine the conditions under which employees sign their individual contracts with their employers.

Italy

Italy, as is true in most European countries, has relatively low union membership, at about 40 percent, with much higher employee coverage for agreements, about 65 percent. Italian unions are closely aligned with political parties, but in recent years employers (both private and public sector) have seemed to have the upper hand in negotiations. Union activity tends to be concentrated in the period prior to negotiations, usually every three years. As already mentioned, one special aspect of labor relations in Italy concerns the negotiations for (and by) managers (the *dirigenti*).

Germany

Union membership in Germany equals about 35 percent of the labor force. Unions are organized primarily by industry with negotiations on a national level. Even though the trade union movement is quite strong, unions in Germany tend not to be very militant, with respect for labor agreements and infrequent strikes, at least partially because many issues of concern to workers have been institutionalized in federal law.

The Netherlands

Dutch labor relations are characterized by major emphasis on mutual consultation and cooperation at all levels.[19] On a national level, employers' federations and trade unions meet in various institutions, with or without government representatives and individual members. At this level, discussion primarily concerns macroeconomic issues such as labor markets and employment policy and social security. Resulting from these discussions are recommendations to the central government as well as to the various employers' federations and unions.

The influence of unions at the firm level is relatively small in Holland. Unions play their most important role at the industry or sector level. At this level, employers' federations and unions meet primarily to negotiate collective agreements per sector. The main foci of these agreements are the terms of employment, including salaries, working times, holidays, safety, and vocational training. The agreements contain a general set of agreed-upon regulations which have to be taken into account when establishing individual labor contracts at the company level.

On the firm level, the number of agreements, replacing (or supplementing) the broader industry-wide agreements, is growing. All employers with more than thirty-five employees must have a works council, with members elected by employees. Works councils must be consulted on decisions or plans relating to restructuring, major investments, major changes in firm activities, and firm-activity relocations. Firms must also seek approval from works councils regarding decisions about pension schemes, working time, holidays, compensation and job classification systems, and policies pertaining to recruitment, training, performance appraisal, group work discussions, and grievances.

When these issues are dealt with in collective agreements, the firm does not need to seek advice from the works councils. But because works councils are more likely to be sympathetic with business concerns, firms increasingly prefer to deal on these issues with the works councils. Unions tend to remain primarily oriented to national and sector-level concerns with the general relations between employers and employees. Nevertheless, as is usually the case throughout European works councils, most of the members are also union members (or, at least, nominated by the unions) and sympathetic to their concerns.

Japan

The Japanese labor relations situation is quite different from that present in European countries. There are about 33,750 unions, which are primarily company unions. That is, unions are organized only at the firm level, although large national firms do have a union that covers all of their operations within Japan. Many of the personnel practices credited with being responsible for Japan's economic miracle, such as lifetime employment, seniority-based promotions, and firm-performance-based bonuses, were developed as a response to a very militant union action after the end of World War II. Largely because of their successes, today's Japanese unions tend to be quite responsible in negotiations, they abide by their contracts, and strikes are quite rare. (When strikes occur, they tend to be short—typically one day or less—and primarily for the purpose of showing employee solidarity to management.)

Canada

Canadian labor relations are a combination of the British system and the U.S. system. In addition, many industrial unions are either affiliated with or actual components of their U.S. counterparts or parent unions. Majority representation is necessary for unions to gain certification, which is required for mandatory collective bargaining. Contracts are legally binding for the duration of the contract (with strikes generally prohibited). Contracts almost universally include grievance and arbitration machinery.

Central and South America

In most Latin American countries, there is a close relationship between the unions and the government, with the result that many rights and benefits for workers have been codified in law. Even though only about one quarter of the labor forces tend to be represented by unions, industry and regional agreements negotiated by unions cover a much greater percentage of employees. In Mexico, unions need only twenty employees to force negotiations with an employer. Agreements on wages are negotiated on an annual basis while the rest of the contract typically lasts for two years. Depending on the location within Mexico, unions can be relatively militant, but the strike record is fairly moderate overall, with the state and federal governments likely to intervene in labor conflicts if they are seen to pose problems for the general economy.

Africa

In general, unions are undeveloped in Africa, as are the economies in most countries. There is some national confederation of unions, but most union activity in

Africa takes place at the firm level. Union activity is closely aligned with political activity.

EMPLOYEE HEALTH AND SAFETY IN THE INTERNATIONAL ARENA

This is one of the most difficult topics to write about in IHRM. There has been very little written about this issue (or any of the specific aspects of it) in either the popular press or the academic or practitioner press. Nevertheless, a number of specific aspects of this topic can be conceptualized. These include the establishment of health and safety policies on a global basis for all employees of the MNC, coping with health and safety practices and regulations that vary from country to country, dealing with specific health and safety concerns of expatriates and their families as they are posted to foreign assignments, and the very specific—although possibly overdramatized—threat of kidnapping and/or terrorist acts against foreign operations and expatriates and their families. Given the lack of information on these concerns, the following tries to at least introduce some of the factors that the HR manager in an MNC might need to consider when dealing with international health and safety issues.

Employee Health and Safety

In most large firms, even though responsibility for employee health and safety resides in the HR department, the HR manager responsible for international HR in the typical MNC does not often deal with health and safety issues among subsidiaries. Responsibility for health and safety issues is normally left to the local subsidiary within the constraints of local custom, culture, and regulation. Attention to these concerns clearly varies dramatically from country to country.

It is even difficult to compare business health and safety statistics across countries in order to assess the results of the varying practices.[20] For example, different countries follow different reporting standards regarding what constitutes an injury and whether it must be reported. Even for workplace fatalities, variation in methods makes cross-national comparisons difficult. For instance, some countries but not all include deaths that occur when an employee is traveling to or from work, whereas others exclude deaths from occupational disease.

In the United States, occupational fatalities are reported in relation to the number of person-hours worked. In 1987, the rate was .027 deaths per million person-hours. Japan uses the same method and reports a fatality rate of .010.

Most other countries report fatalities per 1,000 people employed per year. Data for a sample of these countries from 1987 are shown below. (Remember that these data are not directly comparable to the rates for the United States and Japan.)

Austria	.097
Canada	.075
Cuba	.112
Denmark	.030
Egypt	.160
France	.075
Greece	.058

Hong Kong	.075
New Zealand	.072
Norway	.040
Poland	.107
Spain	.120
United Kingdom	0.17

(Given the range and disparity of these figures, it is likely that even these data are not exactly comparable.)

Rates vary widely for a number of reasons, including the mix of industries present in each country. Some industries are inherently more dangerous than others. For instance, the mining and quarrying industries tend to have the highest fatality rates in most countries, while construction, transportation, utilities, and agriculture have moderately high rates. The retail trade, banking, and social service industries generally have far fewer fatalities. Thus those countries with a mix of industries that favors those with lower fatalities will have more favorable country-wide statistics.

A country's occupational health and safety laws and enforcement procedures may also influence fatality rates. A comparative study in 1986 of five European countries and the United States concluded that the United States is the weakest in terms of law enforcement mechanisms. Sweden, the former East Germany, and Finland were the highest-ranked (although with what is now known about the levels of pollution, the age and maintenance of equipment, and the poor quality of labor and health statistics in many former East German factories and factory towns, the conclusions about the former East Germany might well be called into question), followed by the former West Germany and the United Kingdom. The study concluded that a strong national union movement facilitated the passage and active implementation of effective health and safety measures. In Sweden, union-run safety committees may order production stopped if they believe a hazard exists and may keep it stopped until the hazard is remedied. These committees also have a great deal of control over the hiring and firing of industrial physicians and safety engineers. Because these types of practices and emphases vary so much from country to country, it is important for HR managers in MNEs to be sensitive to these differences as they develop health and safety policies and react to various health and safety actions by employees and unions throughout their firms' global operations.

It can be anticipated that with the development of better communications worldwide, employees and unions will become more aware of how employer and industrial safety practices vary from country to country. Along with this awareness will probably come increased pressure in all countries to emulate the best and safest practices everywhere.

In general, unions and the philosophy of industrial democracy are stronger in Europe (and Australia) than in the United States. In recent years, these factors have led to the passage of laws giving European employees or their elected worker representatives (in works councils) a stronger role in monitoring and enforcing workplace safety. Legally mandated works councils or workers' safety committees in the Netherlands, Luxembourg, France, Belgium, and Denmark give workers substantially more control over occupational safety than U.S. workers have. (U.S. workers, under the Occupational Safety and Health Act, do have considerable protection of their workplace health and safety. But the approach in the United States has been to place primary emphasis on the setting of health and safety standards and to provide government mechanisms of inspection and fines for enforcement, rather than to rely on employee committees.)

The European Community has adopted a common framework for setting occupational health and safety standards, and as the EC expands its membership, additional countries will come under this framework. Pursuant to this framework, member nations are modifying their workplace safety laws to achieve common standards, with some resistance from countries such as Great Britain that have traditions of greater independence of their firms. The intent is to retain the high safety standards set in the more progressive countries, while minimizing the competitive advantage that might otherwise flow to nations with less stringent standards. (Refer to IHRM in Action 8.1 in Chapter 8 for a discussion of ethical issues in IHRM as they might apply to a concern about MNEs establishing operations in foreign countries that might have less stringent health and safety standards and less effective enforcement of such regulations.)

At the opposite end of the spectrum, the setting and enforcement of occupational safety standards in developing countries—and in Central and Eastern Europe (to say nothing of the more difficult to define and monitor occupational health standards)—often leaves much to be desired. Most developing countries have only rudimentary employment safety laws on the books and very limited funds for enforcing such laws. Concern over this issue became one of the stumbling blocks in congressional approval of a North American Free Trade Agreement (NAFTA) with Mexico, such that "side agreements" dealing with environmental and labor issues were negotiated prior to final approval. Many people were concerned that American firms were moving operations to Mexico to capitalize on cost advantages due to lower health and safety standards and lax enforcement of existing laws. Even though many of the *maquiladoras* (twin-plant operations, typically assembling products from parts manufactured in the United States or elsewhere and then exported under favorable tariff conditions to the United States) maintain facilities and operations as clean and safe as their counterparts in the United States, American unionists and environmentalists sustained a concern that American firms not take advantage of Mexico's limited resources for enforcement of health and safety regulations.

Efforts by developing countries to attract foreign investment are often enhanced by offering a business environment relatively free of government regulation. Unions typically are weak or are primarily focused on issues such as politics, wages, and fair treatment of employees, so they aren't focused on workplace safety concerns. In addition, the tendency to rely on labor-intensive enterprises, the preponderance of dated equipment, the pressure for production and jobs, and the lack of safety training for specialists as well as for workers, in general, also contribute to the poor safety records in many developing countries. The point of this for MNEs (typically from countries with more highly developed health and safety concerns) is whether or not to export these concerns, standards, and internal monitoring and enforcement, to their foreign subsidiaries, and, if so, how to do that in an environment where such has not been the practice.

Additional areas of concern to multinational IHR managers within this topic of employee safety include the differences in medical systems in various countries (both in the form and quality of the delivery of medical services and in access to high-quality health care); the coverage of the health-care system in different countries and who pays for health care; and the form and level of support systems for various forms of disabilities. (Chapter 8 discusses some aspects of the various health-care delivery systems in a number of countries as a part of a presentation of comparative IHRM practices.) All of the above issues will have an impact on employment practices for both expatriates and local nationals. Attention to fitness, employee stress, use of drugs, awareness of problems with major health issues such as AIDS, and problems with inadequate nutrition all are issues that can also influence IHR practices in foreign locations.

Health and Safety for Expatriates

Many of the above issues overlap with concerns for the health and safety of expatriates and their families. Some are standard concerns for employees while traveling and some are for employees after arrival at their new assignments. Under any circumstance, these concerns are usually left up to the IHR department to worry about and resolve. Expatriates need to be briefed on and prepared to deal with problems of safety while traveling, orientation to the different medical system in their new countries, how to take care of prescriptions and any special medical conditions, the identification of doctors and hospitals to provide for health care in their new locations, and usually the acquisition of medical evacuation insurance to cover possible contingencies.

The following paragraphs discuss a few specific concerns relating to safety for expatriates.

Terrorism

One aspect of the topic of health and safety for IHRM that has received a small amount of attention but is probably the least important (unless, of course, it happens to you!) is the problem of terrorism and/or kidnapping.[21] International terrorists have at times targeted the facilities and executives of MNEs (and/or their families).[22] Even though the news media attention to these acts makes it seem as though they happen all the time, everywhere, to all expatriates and their families, the frequency of and danger involved with terrorist acts demonstrates that people are more likely to drown in their own bathtubs than to be killed by terrorists![23] This is not to say that expatriates and their families don't need to be briefed on such concerns and oriented to a constant awareness of the potential risks. The incidence of terrorist acts against MNEs and their personnel did indeed increase regularly throughout the 1980s.[24]

Of course, some countries present greater risks than others. And when expatriates are being asked to serve in locales of greater risk, greater precautions need to be taken. Various corporate reactions have ranged from essentially trying to ignore such terrorism to abandoning certain markets where such terrorism is seen as more likely. Some firms have tried to protect their managers and their families in various ways, such as fortifying their homes, providing trained chauffeurs and guards, and using local-sounding names for their subsidiaries to try to hide the identities of the MNE parents of their local operations. In addition, some firms have purchased kidnap and other kinds of insurance to cover their key executives; of course, information about the extent and amounts of this are not typically made public.

In total, fewer than 50 percent of MNEs have any formal program to deal with real or potential terrorist actions. And among those firms that did have any type of antiterrorist program, they were more likely to spend their money on security equipment and the protection of assets than on the training of expatriates or their families.[25]

Crime

Actually, the biggest threat to international travelers is not terrorism but old-fashioned crime, such as theft and pickpocketing.[26] In addition, the arrest and incarceration of traveling employees who either knowingly or innocently break local laws can be a major concern. "Travelers have been thrown in jail for exceeding a credit card limit, buying artifacts from an unlicensed dealer, entering an Islamic country with alcohol, or failing to meet a contract deadline."[27] Indeed, in some countries, false arrest of American personnel can be a problem, particularly where this is a practice of local, low-paid government officials or police as a means to earn extra income.

Traumatic events

Other kinds of emergencies while traveling abroad are much more likely to occur than terrorism. These include sudden illnesses, serious accidents, major problems with transportation (such as bad weather or a strike on the traveler's airline), hotel fires, and natural disasters (such as floods or volcanic eruptions). The trauma experienced by such problems when in another country can be greatly compounded due to distance from home and normal support systems, language difficulties, cultural misunderstandings, and different laws and different medical or criminal justice systems.

Under all circumstances, business travelers and expatriates need to be briefed as to what to expect and how to react when confronted with any health or safety problem. In addition, many firms find it important to retain one or more of the travelers' assistance programs or insurance programs that can provide help when the firm's overseas travelers or expatriates and their families experience difficulties.

IHRM in Action 6.3 provides a glimpse at the types of services that one of these companies (MEDEX Assistance Corporation—which provides prompt access to medical and related services for clients anywhere in the world) can provide when a traveler (or expatriate) faces a medical problem. Such assistance would be of most help to travelers and expatriates when in remote locations and/or third-world countries.

IHRM IN ACTION 6.3
INTERNATIONAL MEDICAL
EMERGENCY ASSISTANCE

On December 22, MEDEX was informed that a man had been hospitalized in a tiny clinic in the small village of Zinder in the Niger Republic in West Africa. The man—a Dr. Shaw—had suffered serious leg injury when the vehicle he was riding in overturned during a Young Europe for Africa expedition. Because the clinic lacked the necessary facilities and personnel to treat Dr. Shaw, MEDEX personnel immediately arranged a light aircraft to transport him to Niamey, some 1,000 kilometers away.

After assessing Dr. Shaw's injuries—torn leg tendons and a fractured left radius—the treating physician in Niamey stated that he could not perform the operation. He added, however, that if an operation was not performed within a very few days, the tendons and nerves may retract to the point that a successful operation could not be performed.

When it became evident that the first available seat on a scheduled flight would not be available for about five days, MEDEX arranged for Dr. Shaw to be flown—in the early hours of Christmas morning—to University College Hospital in London. The following day, the broken radius was corrected, the severed tendons were reconnected, and a knee wound was cleaned and closed. Dr. Shaw was released from the hospital on January 4.

In a lengthy letter of praise to MEDEX, Dr. Shaw wrote, "I owe a huge debt of gratitude to your organization. I could have been trapped in Zinder for days, with a septic arthritis and in danger of losing my leg. It was a situation where each delay made the risks greater. Your ability to get me out within four days of the accident was remarkable. The French doctors and diplomats were very impressed. I am very thankful.

"On a more personal level, I and my family were touched by the care you took to keep us informed of developments. . . . My parents were delighted to be told in separate phone calls that the plane had left, that it was ahead of schedule, and that it had arrived safely."

Source: "MEDEX Assistance Case History," MEDEX ASSISTANCE CORPORATION brochure, Baltimore, MD, 1992. Reprinted with permission. All rights reserved.

SUMMARY

This chapter discussed two topics of importance to the international HR manager: labor relations and employee health and safety. Often, because labor relations practices differ so much from country to country, responsibility for union and employee relations are left in the hands of subsidiary (i.e., local) HR managers. Nevertheless, MNEs typically express some concern about designing common practices throughout their overseas operations and unions are interested in trying to develop collective bargaining practices on an international level. In addition, MNEs are confronted with a number of directives on labor relations practices from international political bodies, such as the Organization for Economic Cooperation and Development and the European Union. But the widely varying practices in different countries and strategic business decisions by MNEs often lead to labor relations practices that vary from country to country.

In addition to discussing these types of issues, this chapter described the systems of labor relations practices in a number of countries so that MNE HR managers can manage their union and employee relations more effectively.

One specific aspect of employee relations discussed in the chapter involves employee health and safety around the globe. The variety of health and safety experience and practices in various countries have been described as were health and safety concerns, such as terrorism and crime, for expatriates and their families.

ENDNOTES

1. Much of the framework for this chapter is based on a presentation on "Comparative Labor Relations" by Geoff Latta, Organizational Resources Corporation, New York, at "Building Global Partnerships: The HR Challenge," sixteenth annual meeting of the Institute for International Human Resources, New Orleans, March 27, 1993.

2. Kennedy, T., *European Labor Relations* (Lexington, MA: Lexington Books, 1980).

3. Adapted from R. Grosse and D. Kujawa, *International Business*, 2nd ed., Homewood, IL: Irwin, 1992.

4. Liebhaberg, B., *Industrial Relations and Multinational Corporations in Europe* (London: Gower, 1980).

5. Blanpain, R., *The Badger Case and the OECD Guidelines for Multinational Enterprises* (Deventer, Netherlands: Kluwer, 1977); Blanpain, R., *The OECD Guidelines for Multinational Enterprises and Labour Relations, 1976–1979: Experience and Review* (Deventer, Netherlands: Kluwer, 1979); Campbell, D. C., and R. L. Rowan, *Multinational Enterprises and the OECD Industrial Relations Guidelines* (Philadelphia: Industrial Relations Research Unit of the Wharton School, University of Pennsylvania, 1983); Jain, H. C., "Disinvestment and the Multinational Employer—A Case History from Belgium," *Personnel Journal*, 59(3), 1980, 201–205.

6. Reichel, A., and J. F. Preble, "The El Al Strike in New York," *Journal of Management Case Studies*, 3 (1987), 270–276.

7. Lee, M. B., "Industrial Relations in Korea," in Rothman, M., D. R. Briscoe, and R. C. D. Nacamulli, *Industrial Relations Around the World* (Berlin: Walter de Gruyter, 1993).

8. Rothman, Briscoe, and Nacamulli, *Industrial Relations Around the World*; Levinson, D. L., Jr., and R. C. Maddox, "Multinational Corporations and Labor Relations: Changes in the Wind?" *Personnel*, May–June 1982, pp. 70–77.

9. McCullough, G. B., "Comment," in *Multinationals, Unions, and Labor Relations in Industrialized Countries*, eds. R. F. Banks and J. Stieber (Ithaca, NY: New York State School of Industrial and Labor Relations, Cornell University, 1977), p. 150; quoted in Grosse and Kujawa, *International Business*, p. 475.

10. See, for example, Atkinson, K., "State of the Unions," *Personnel Administrator*, September 1986, pp. 55–59; Northrup, H. R., D. C. Campbell, and B. J. Slowinski (1988) "Multinational Union-Management Consultation in Europe: Resurgence in the 1980s?" *International Labour Review*, 127 (5), 525–534; Rothman, Briscoe, and Nacamulli, *Industrial Relations Around the World*; Dowling, P. J., and R. S. Schuler, *International Dimensions of Human Resource Management* (Boston: PWS-Kent, 1990); and Tigner, B., "The Looming Labour Crunch," *International Management*, February 1989, pp. 26–31.

11. Melcher, R., J. Templeman, J. Rossant, S. Dryden, and B. Arnold, "Europe's Unions Are Losing Their Grip," *Business Week*, November 26, 1984, pp. 80–88.

12. Rothman, Briscoe, and Nacamulli, *Industrial Relations Around the World*.

13. Dowling and Schuler, *International Dimensions of Human Resource Management*; "Employee Dismissals Can Prove Costly for Companies in Europe," *HR Focus*, August 1992, p. 18.

14. "Employee Dismissals Can Prove Costly for Companies in Europe."

15. See, for example, Rothman, Briscoe, and Nacamulli, *Industrial Relations Around the World*; Baglioni, G., and C. Crouch, eds., *European Industrial Relations* (London: Sage, 1990); Bamber, G., and R. Lansbury, *International and Comparative Industrial Relations*, rev. ed. (London: Routledge, 1993); and Johnson, T., and M. O'Culachain, eds., *Employment Law in Europe* (Coopers & Lybrand, Aldershot, England: Gower Publishing, 1992).

16. Ivancevich, J. M. *Human Resource Management*, 5th ed., Homewood, IL: Irwin, 1992, pp. 646–649.

17. Baglioni and Crouch, eds., *European Industrial Relations*; Coopers & Lybrand, *Employment Law in Europe* (Hants, England: Gower Publishing, 1992); Rothman, Briscoe, and Nacamulli, *Industrial Relations Around the World*.

18. In 1992 the European Community began publishing a series of volumes explaining progress on the key components of the common market. Volume 6 of this series describes the *Community Social Policy*. It is the EC's intent to regularly reissue and update these volumes. This first edition includes over 300 pages of description of the "Community Charter of the Fundamental Social Rights of Workers."

19. This is adapted from Schuler, R., and E. Van Sluijs, "Davidson-Marley BV: Establishing and Operating an International Joint Venture," *European Management Journal*, 10(4), December 1992, 428–437.

20. Much of this section is based on a discussion in C. D. Fisher, L. F. Schoenfeldt, and J. B. Shaw, *Managing Human Resources*. 2nd ed., Boston: Houghton Mifflin, 1992. Their discussion is based on these references: the forty-ninth issue of the *Yearbook of Labour Statistics* (Geneva: International Labour Organization, 1989–1990), pp. 982–995; Elling, R. H., *The Struggle for Workers' Health: A Study of Six Industrialized Countries* (Farmingdale, NY: Baywood Publishing, 1986), pp. 427–450; Gevers, J. K. M., "Worker Participation in Health and Safety in the EEC: The Role of Representative Institutions," *International Labour Review*, July–August 1983, pp. 411–428; Chew, D. C. E., "Effective Occupational Safety Activities: Findings in Three Asian Developing Countries," *International Labour Review*, 1988, pp. 111–124; Bixby, M. B., "Emerging Occupational Safety Issues in the United States, Europe, and Japan," *Proceedings of the Third Conference on International Personnel and Human Resource Management*, Vol. 1, Berkhamsted, England, July 1992. Also, refer to Wokutch, R. E., and J. S. McLaughlin, "The U.S. and Japanese Work Injury and Illness Experience," *Monthly Labor Review*, April 1992, pp. 2–11.

21. See, for example, Copeland, L., "Traveling Abroad Safely: Some Tips to Give Employees," *Personnel*, February 1987, pp. 18–24; and Ronkainen, S. A., "International Human Resource Management," Ch. 20 in Czintoka, M. R., P. Rivoli, and I. A. Ronkainen, *International Business* (New York: Dryden Press, 1989).

22. Harvey, M. G. "A Survey of Corporate Programs for Managing Terrorist Threats," *Journal of International Business Studies*, Third Quarter, 1993, pp. 465–478.

23. Griggs L. and L. Copeland, *Going International: How to Make Friends and Deal Effectively in the Global Marketplace*, New York: Random House, 1985.

24. Harvey, "A Survey of Corporate Programs for Managing Terrorist Threats."

25. Ibid.

26. Copeland, "Traveling Abroad Safely."

27. Ibid.

7

International HRM Support Services and Special International Services

This chapter discusses two aspects of IHRM that have received even less attention in the professional and academic literature on HRM than the other topics in this text, many of which have also received only limited attention from writers. These two areas of responsibility are (1) the support services that HR departments develop (primarily in larger firms) to adequately perform the core responsibilities which have been presented in Chapters 3 through 6: staffing, training and development, compensation and benefits, labor/employee relations, and health and safety; and (2) the many special services with which HR departments are normally asked to help their expatriate workforces and other employees and managers who travel internationally for the firm.

IHRM SUPPORT SERVICES

In the typical HR department in a large firm, a number of activities are performed that generally support the core responsibilities. These include the HR information system (including records on employees), human resource planning (including employee forecasts, career plans for managers, and succession planning for executives), job analysis and the writing of job descriptions (for recruiting and training purposes and the setting of performance expectations), job evaluation and wage surveys and the development of job classifications and wage rates, labor market analysis to determine the availability and abilities of potential employees, the development of performance appraisal systems, and personnel/HRM research.

Regrettably, there is essentially no writing on these topics in an international context, except as reflected in the limited references to these subjects throughout this text and a very limited amount of literature on how these responsibilities are handled in a few other major countries, such as Japan. In addition, there is almost no literature on how large multinational firms extend these activities to their international operations. Within the purely domestic operations for large firms (particularly in the United States, Europe, and Japan), these issues receive considerable attention.[1] They probably receive a lot of attention within the domestic operations (meaning in the parent-company operations) of the typical large MNE. But little seems to be done with them in extension to their foreign subsidiaries, except possibly where the subsidiaries have become major "local" firms in their own right; for example, Ford, IBM, and GM (Opel) in Europe, Unilever in the United States (Lever Bros.), and Honda in the United States. But in these types of cases, the foreign operations of these firms are for all practical purposes domestic firms in the countries where they have major manufacturing, sales, and research and development activities. And in these major countries these support services are well-developed in most major firms.

The following discusses two of these support services: IHRM research and IHRM information systems.

IHRM Research

A major HR support activity in many large firms is personnel (or HRM) research. However, there appear to be few resources devoted to research on an international basis for IHRM issues. As was discussed in Chapter 1, cross-national research is quite difficult and expensive to conduct. Thus, many issues that have been raised in this text, for example, determining which hiring practice, job classification system, or compensation system works best in which national context for which type of international employee, have not been researched.

Such research still needs to be done. Because of the lack of such research (and probably because of the relative newness of much international business), MNEs often extend policies to the international level that have been established by experience or by research conducted within the operations of the parent firm (and, thus, within the culture of the parent country). As an example of one such extension, IBM has established a policy not to use graphology (the use of handwriting analysis to help in the screening of potential employees) anywhere in the world, based on evidence (and attitudes) developed in the United States pertaining to its limited usefulness. This prohibition applies even to France, where it is a commonly used technique. Research in multiple countries might verify whether this is a practice that has acceptance and/or usefulness in some countries. Obviously, IHRM research could be fruitfully applied to most areas of IHRM responsibility.

IHRM Information Systems

As firms internationalize their business operations, they eventually reach the point where they also want to internationalize their information systems. This will include the human resource information system (HRIS). But, because the formats and purposes of the HRIS were established to service only HRM in the domestic operations (and, if the firm is large enough and has been overseas long enough, it probably also has at least some HR information systems established in its subsidiaries to service only those operations), internationalizing the HRIS is a very complex and difficult activity.[2]

Increasingly, when management in the multinational firm wants information on employees, they want it on all the employees, from all the foreign locations, as well as from the parent company. This means they want information on employees from, of course, XYZ Inc., but also on employees from XYZ PLC in London, XYZ Gmbh in Munich, XYZ FrOres in Marseilles, and XYZ SLA in Buenos Aires.

But systems from multiple countries are rarely compatible. And the HRIS established in the parent company is rarely capable of handling variances in data form and format from other countries. Thus, field lengths must be adjusted for various postal codes, formats must be changed to reflect different preferences for stating the date (dd-mm-yy versus mm-dd-yy), name fields must be adapted to longer names, hyphenated names, and two middle initials, and so forth. In addition, representing differing educational systems, certification traditions, multiple languages (or at least some nontraditional English letters, such as enyes), and many other issues all must be accommodated.

And all of this must be done within the context of understanding the approaches taken to the use of employee information in the cultures of the firm's various foreign subsidiaries. In some countries, attitudes toward authority will create differing attitudes toward the use of personnel data. In other countries, information about employees may be used very informally such that there is no local use for a computerized or formal HRIS. And in still other countries, only managers from the "right" schools may be given access to such information, making it difficult to keep the HRIS up-to-date and limiting the usefulness of the information in the HRIS. Thus getting cooperation from managers in the foreign subsidiaries may not always be easy. They will need to see the value of the international HRIS efforts for them. And without their support, it will remain impossible to develop a viable international HRIS.

Even when everyone at headquarters and out in the field understands and agrees to the importance and value of the international HRIS, its development will still be a slow process. Many issues will have to be analyzed, understood, and addressed before final implementation of an international HRIS can be achieved. These issues will include legal concerns, type of data to be included, language of the data, cultural values related to the capture and use of the data, documentation procedures, training in the use and maintenance of the system, who will have access to the data and how such access will be protected, and conversion from the existing system to the new, internationalized one.

Specific problems with the portion of the HRIS that deals with an MNE's international compensation programs were discussed in Chapter 5. In particular, that discussion involved the maintenance of payroll files on international personnel.[3] As stated above, the normal (i.e., domestic) HRM information system is not designed to handle all the additional pieces of information commonly required for international employees, such as foreign service premiums, language training expenses, education allowances for dependents, storage of household goods, currency conversion, and the like. Nor is the HRIS usually flexible enough to handle the *ad hoc* nature of most expatriate compensation packages or the country-by-country tax and benefit programs. Keeping these files up-to-date and using the information in them for employee decision making, such as pay increases or adjustments or career and job-assignment decisions, gets even more difficult as many countries maintain laws against the transfer of "private" employee information out-of-country, at least to certain countries.[4]

SPECIAL INTERNATIONAL SERVICES

One of the areas of responsibility for IHRM that goes beyond the activities normally delegated to the domestic HR manager involves all the international support services that IHRM must provide. These are particularly for expatriates, repatriates, and inpatriates and their families but are also typically for other technical employees and managers who travel to foreign operations for the firm.

Special international personnel services can be divided into two general categories: services related to relocation and orientation for expatriates and repatriates and those that might be labeled "administrative services."

Relocation and Orientation

This area of service can consume much time from HR managers given international responsibilities. Because of that, and to ensure that employees being sent abroad receive the best possible attention to the very personal concerns of relocating to another country, most of these services are usually hired from firms that specialize in the provision of these services for expatriates, repatriates, and inpatriates. Alternatively, many large MNEs are starting to combine their domestic and international relocation activities. The relocation function evolved out of firms' needs beginning in the 1960s to help their relocating employees with problems such as the selling of houses, the shipment of household goods, the location of temporary living quarters, the purchase of a new house, the control of family in-transit time, and the control of overall relocation costs.[5] These essential relocation activities turn out to be essentially the same for domestic as for international relocations (although the international transfer tends to be much more intense, particularly for spouses and families).

The following provides an introduction to a number of key aspects of the services related to an international relocation.

TAX AND FINANCIAL ADVICE.   This is one of the first services provided by the IHRM department to employees being sent overseas. Personal income tax preparation becomes quite complicated. And the overall handling of finances, in circumstances in which income is likely to increase dramatically as well as to involve multiple currencies, new banking systems, varying exchange rates, and so on, is likely to require assistance for the new expatriate and his or her family. This is generally coordinated by the IHRM department.

VISAS AND WORK PERMITS.   It usually falls on the IHRM department to obtain the necessary visas for the expatriate (and his or her family) as well as to arrange for whatever work permits are required. Normally, this involves maintaining the personal relations with foreign government officials that are necessary to get these documents in a timely manner (since individuals often have limited time to make such preparations after the firm makes the decision to send them abroad). This becomes particularly complex if the firm tries to find employment for the trailing spouse or other family members.

INTERNATIONAL MOVING.   There are many complexities in arranging and managing successful international moves for expatriates and their families. Needless to say, this is also typically one of the most stressful aspects of moving abroad for most employees and their families. Again, the IHRM department usually has responsibility to assure that the employee's move takes place in a smooth, problem-free way.

After a myriad of relocation considerations, the actual physical move overseas of expatriate, family, and household is often the last item to get "handled."[6] Nevertheless, it is one of the more important considerations in guaranteeing a successful expatriate experience. At a minimum, managing the overseas move involves the following:

- Making all necessary travel arrangements, including arranging accommodations for when the family initially arrives as well as their permanent housing in the new location.
- Retaining the services of the best possible mover.
- Developing overseas moving policy. Ideally, a firm sending employees overseas has developed a policy to deal with the major issues confronted in such moves. Overseas movers look for some basic elements in the overseas moving policy. First is the use of an authorization letter, confirming to both the mover and the employee the basic details of the move. Both the mover and the employee need to know what quantity of goods can be shipped (both outgoing and returning, since most expatriates acquire additional goods while overseas). In addition, the policy should address restrictions on such items as second pickups or deliveries of household goods, use of American carriers, and what items are defined as household goods. Such policies help movers and employees avoid problems and make the move go smoothly.
- Determining the proper timing of the move (from the points of view of both the firm and the family).
- Arranging for local housing; either prior to arrival of the expatriate or inpatriate or after his or her arrival and with his or her involvement.
- Arranging for and ensuring the smooth shipment (and storage) of household goods. Given the importance of personal effects on the emotional well-being of an expatriate, selection of a mover is critical. The mover must be willing to commit the necessary personnel and resources to ensure that the move is made with the least possible difficulty and with the best possible end results. For the most part, the type and quantity of goods moved is determined by the destination.

Weather, local infrastructure, accommodations, customs regulations, and transportation resources all influence how, how much, and what type of goods should be shipped.

MEDICAL EXAMS FOR PARTICULAR FOREIGN LOCATIONS.   Where medical services may not be up to the parent-country standards, the firm will want to ensure that it isn't going to face any unnecessary health complications.

TRAINING   (about the country, culture, and language of the new assignment for the expatriate or inpatriate and his or her family). This was discussed in Chapter 4.

EDUCATION AND SCHOOLING FOR THE EXPATRIATE/INPATRIATE'S FAMILY WHILE IN THE FOREIGN ASSIGNMENT.   Sometimes, adequate schools for the expatriate/inpatriate's children are not available locally, and the firm must pay for the children to be schooled elsewhere (e.g., in boarding schools), which will also entail extra expense for children to return home periodically or for the parents to visit them. The HR department will be expected to assist the expatriate/inpatriate family to locate acceptable schooling.

Administrative Services

Most of these services could potentially be provided elsewhere in the firm, but they generally are delegated to the HR department. All of them are, at least initially, established to ease the process of transferring employees from one country to another. Then because the HR department has found ways to resolve the availability of these services, they are often extended to other needs of the firm yet stay within the responsibility of the HR department.

- *Travel arrangements* (as discussed above—and for everyone in the firm that travels internationally). This can involve acquiring necessary visas, making all necessary travel arrangements (airplane tickets, etc.), and buying travel insurance.
- *Housing in the foreign locale* (for all international travelers for the firm). This can involve negotiating contracts, signing rental agreements, finding hotel rooms, apartments, and so forth.
- *Determining the availability and operation of transportation in the foreign locale,* including rental cars, chauffeurs, metro, bus, and rail systems.
- *Office services,* such as translation and translators, for business contracts, housing and rental agreements, business letters, and business negotiations.
- *Currency conversion.* New expatriates may not have experience with or an understanding of living in another country and having to deal with conversion of their home-country currency into that of the host country. The IHRM department is normally tasked with ensuring that the expatriate understands whatever complications might arise as pay arrangements are worked out to accommodate varying exchange rates and varying local-currency inflation rates.
- *Local bank accounts.* Since banking systems vary dramatically from country to country, the expatriate often needs assistance in establishing a local bank account (if indeed that is possible) as well as in understanding how the banking system operates in his or her new country of residence. In many developing countries, the banking system is quite underdeveloped (particularly in relation to what the typical manager from the United States or Western Europe is used to), such that, for example, there may not be an established checking system for paying bills. The expatriate will need to be oriented to these realities.
- *Government relations.* This will initially include familiarity with the proper offices to get visas and work permits but may eventually extend also to local government offices for business services such as telephones and business licenses.

The IHRM department may find these many services cumbersome and complex, but the successful MNE must have access to them. It makes sense that they be provided by the IHRM staff. And they do serve to keep the HR department closely involved with the firm's international activity.

SUMMARY

This chapter introduced two aspects of support services that IHRM departments often provide for their firms. These include traditional support activities, such as research and information systems services, that help IHRM implement their core responsibilities. And it included discussion of a number of administrative services that IHRM departments in many MNEs are asked to provide for the firm's international activities, such as relocation and translation services.

Neither of these kinds of services has received much space in the HRM literature, even though they both are important to the success of MNEs.

ENDNOTES

1. Refer to any major HRM textbook, such as Cascio, W. F., *Managing Human Resources,* 3rd ed. (New York: McGraw-Hill, 1992); Mathis, R. L., and J. H. Jackson, *Human Resource Management,* 7th ed. (Minneapolis/St. Paul, MN: West, 1994); Fisher, C. D., L. F. Schoenfeldt, and J. B. Shaw, *Human Resource Management,* 2nd ed. (Boston: Houghton Mifflin, 1993); and Sherman, A. W., Jr., and G. W. Bohlander, *Managing Human Resources,* 9th ed. (Cincinnati, OH: South-Western, 1992).

2. Briscoe, A. F., F. Silverman, and T. Noyes, "Internationalizing Your HRIS," *The HRSP Review,* October–November 1993, pp. 10–14; Stambaugh, R., "Bridging the Gap: Global Systems and Multi-Domestic Corporations," *The HRSP Review,* October–November 1993, pp. 16–21.

3. Crandall, L. P., "Getting Through the Global Payroll Maze," *Personnel Journal,* August 1992, pp. 76–77; Dowling, P. J., "Hot Issues Overseas," *Personnel Administrator,* January 1989, pp. 66–72.

4. Ibid.

5. Loewe, G. M., "Evolution of the Relocation Function," *Journal of International Compensation & Benefits,* January–February 1994, pp. 43–46.

6. Siemens, B., "International Moving—Beyond the Twilight Zone," *HR News: International HR,* February 1992, C8.

8

HRM Practices
in Other Countries

An important aspect of IHRM, one that has been touched on in almost every chapter, concerns the need of IHR managers in multinational firms to understand the HR practices in the countries in which their firms operate. This chapter provides an introduction to the HRM practices in a number of countries. By necessity—both due to the limited availability of such information and to the space constraints of this book—this can be only a limited introduction to the HR practices in a limited number of countries. The attempt has been made to describe some of the practices which would be of most interest to a multinational or global firm.

Providing information about comparative HR practices in multiple countries is a difficult and complex process. Large accounting, law, and consulting firms with practices in many countries have the staffs to study these practices and to provide such information to their client MNEs. In addition, large MNEs have local staffs in the countries in which they operate that can provide such comparative information to these firms' headquarters. But as with international safety and health issues, what has been written in easily accessible locations, such as practitioner journals, is quite limited.

Even so, IHR managers need knowledge about HR practices in the other countries in which they operate (or are thinking about operating) for at least three reasons:

1.   To understand and therefore operate more effectively in the global economy within which their firms operate (and so they can provide effective advice and decisions related to the HR aspects of that global business);

2. For professional development; that is, to learn about innovative (or, just different and maybe better) ways to perform HRM responsibilities; and

3. To be better able to evaluate whether home-country and parent-company practices will or won't work better in foreign locales.

Therefore this chapter provides a basic introduction to HRM practices in a relatively small set of countries (although these are many of the most important for international business). Nevertheless, HR managers in MNEs need to learn as much as they can about the HR practices and regulations in the countries in which they operate and must continually assess the degree to which they want to, can, or should export policies and practices from their parent firms and countries to their foreign subsidiaries. IHRM in Action 8.1 discusses some of the ethical issues involved with trying to resolve these types of questions.

IHRM IN ACTION 8.1
THE ETHICS OF HR DECISION
MAKING IN FOREIGN
OPERATIONS

The basic ethical dilemma for human resource management in a multinational firm involves what the international HR manager should do when an employment practice that is illegal or viewed as wrong in the home country is legal and acceptable in the host country. Examples might include sex or race discrimination in hiring, job placement, or compensation; use of child labor; or providing unsafe working conditions.

Ethicists present two opposing approaches to questions of this type. One approach is ethical relativism, which suggests that what is right is what a society defines as right. If a society says that virgins shall be sacrificed at every full moon or that women shall not be paid the same as men for the same work, those rules are right for that society at that point in time. There can be no external frame of reference for judging that one society's set of rules is better than another's. IHR managers who try to impose their values on human resource practices in a host country are guilty of ethical imperialism. Under the philosophy of ethical relativism, it is entirely appropriate to follow local practices regarding the treatment of employees. Though appearing on the surface to be a liberal, open-minded approach, this view may result in actions that home-country constituencies (at least from the Western industrialized countries) would find entirely unacceptable, such as child labor or gross inequality.

The opposite position is called ethical absolutism. This is the view that there is a single set of universal ethical principles, which apply at all times and to all cultures. This approach might be very useful to an IHR manager, as it would suggest which local practices—though they be quite different from those of the parent country—are morally acceptable because they do not violate universal principles and which are not morally acceptable and must not be followed. The problem with this view is specifying what the universal principles are and developing a logical case for why these, and only these, principles are truly universal. In adopting the values of a single culture or religion as universal one again runs the risk of ethical imperialism.

Thus both of these philosophies create potential problems for the IHR manager and for expatriates being posted to foreign subsidiaries. At least one author, Thomas Donaldson, therefore, has tried to provide a framework for decision making in a multinational environment that tries to resolve these possible ethical dilemmas. He states that the task is to "tolerate cultural diversity while drawing the line at moral recklessness" (Donaldson, 1989, p. 103). In some ways, his approach is absolutist because it relies on a statement of ten fundamental international rights (which have been recognized by international bodies, such as the United Nations): freedom of physical movement; ownership of property; freedom from torture; right to a fair trial; nondiscriminatory treatment; physical security; freedom of speech and association; right to a minimal education; political participation; and subsistance. Organizations need to avoid depriving individuals of these rights wherever they do business.

However, these rights alone are not sufficient guidelines. When IHR managers are trying to decide if their corporation can follow a practice that is legal and morally acceptable in the host country but not in the parent country, Donaldson suggests that they ask themselves a series of questions. First, ask *why* the practice is acceptable in the host country but not at home. Answers to this question fall into two categories: (1) because of the host country's relative level of economic development or (2) for reasons unrelated to economic development. If the answer is (1), the next question is whether the parent country would have accepted the practice when (or if) it was at the same level of economic development. If it would have, the practice is permissible. An example might be the building of a fertilizer plant that provides a product necessary for the feeding of the poor population of the country, despite the fact that there is a risk of occupational disease for employees working in the plant. If the parent firm were willing to accept this risk (or the parent country) for itself under similar circumstances, then the building of such a plant would be all right within Donaldson's framework.

The second answer, that the difference is not based on economic considerations, requires a more complicated decision process. The manager must ask two additional questions: (1) Is it possible to conduct business successfully in the host country without undertaking the practice? and (2) Is the practice a clear violation of a fundamental right? (Donaldson, 1989, p. 104). The practice is permissible *only if* the answer to both questions is no. That is, the practice is acceptable if it is critical to doing business in the country *and* it does not violate a fundamental right. Otherwise, the organization should refuse to follow the local practice.

For example, in Singapore it is common to see help-wanted ads for "Chinese women, age 21–28." This type of advertisement violates U.S. laws and mores regarding age, sex, and ethnic discrimination. Would it be permissible for a U.S. subsidiary in Singapore to run an ad like that? According to Donaldson, the answer is no because the discrimination is not tied to the level of economic development, is not necessary for doing business in Singapore, and violates fundamental international rights to nondiscriminatory treatment (a right which is codified in the resolutions of a number of international bodies, such as the United Nations and the International Labour Organization).

Source: Adapted from Cynthia D. Fisher, Lyle F. Shoenfeldt, and James B. Shaw, HUMAN RESOURCE MANAGEMENT, 2nd ed., copyright 1993 by Houghton Mifflin Co. Used with permission. All rights reserved.

Original sources: W. T. Stace, "Ethical Relativity and Ethical Absolutism," in T. Donaldson and P. H. Werhane, eds., ETHICAL ISSUES IN BUSINESS (Englewood Cliffs, NJ: Prentice Hall, 1988), pp. 27–34; W. Shaw and V. Barry, MORAL ISSUES IN BUSINESS (Belmont, CA: Wadsworth, 1989), pp. 11–13; and T. Donaldson, THE ETHICS OF INTERNATIONAL BUSINESS (New York: Oxford University Press, 1989).

COMPARATIVE DATA

First this chapter provides some comparative data on selected countries in order to illustrate some of the very basic differences that exist in terms of certain issues of importance to IHRM. Then descriptions of IHRM practices in a number of countries are provided.

Figure 8.1 provides data on the size of the civilian labor force in ten countries plus the United States. Although this might not be the first issue of concern to a multinational firm seeking locations for foreign operations, it might be important to know the relative sizes of various countries' labor forces in order to staff certain types of operations. These data also illustrate that many countries that receive a lot of attention in the business and political press are significantly smaller than one might otherwise assume.

Figure 8.2 shows the participation rates (the percentage of the adult population that is in the labor force) for the same nine countries (minus Mexico) plus the United States, again using definitions similar to those in use by the U.S. Bureau of Labor Statistics. Again, there is considerable difference between, say Italy, with a participation rate of slightly over 44 percent, and the United States, with a participation rate of over 61 percent. The differences are largely due to the participation rate of women in the various countries and illustrate possible cultural differences with possible potential for labor force growth.

The amount and nature of work available in any given country is also related to the normal numbers of hours of work. Table 8.1 illustrates the average work years and weeks, the number of annual vacation days (as also reported in Chapter

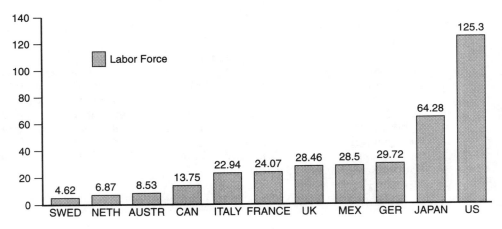

* In millions, approximating U.S. concepts

Figure 8.1   Civilian Labor Force*

Source: Bureau of Labor Statistics, U.S. Department of Labor.

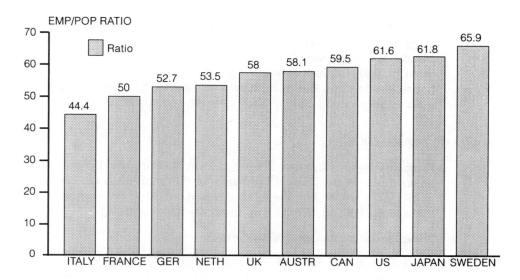

* 1991 Employment—Population Ratio: 10 Countries Approximating U.S. Concepts (as % of civilian working-age population).

Figure 8.2   Labor Force Participation Rates*

Source: Bureau of Labor Statistics, U.S. Department of Labor.

Table 8.1 Hours of Negotiated Scheduled Work: An International Comparison*

	AVG. WORK YEAR (HRS)	AVG. WORK WEEK (HRS)	ANNUAL VAC. IN DAYS	HOLIDAYS
Japan	2,143	44	NA	14
Portugal	1,980	44	22	14
U.S.	1,904	40	12	11
Switzerland	1,873	40.8	23.5	8
Spain	1,800	40	22	14
Italy	1,776	40	31	8
U.K.	1,769	38.8	25	8
France	1,755	39	25	11
Belgium	1,748	38	20	11
Netherlands	1,732	39	32	7
Germany	1,648	37.7	30	12.5

* As of Oct 1, 1990; negotiated hours.

Source: Bureau of Labor Statistics, U.S. Department of Labor.

5), and the number of holidays. Of course, these latter two factors also relate to the number of hours during which employees are available for work in the various countries. One impact of this type of information has been that, for example, Germany, with the highest annual wages in the world and the lowest number of work hours, has been examining both its wage and vacation/holiday policies in order to make changes that will help keep Germany competitive in world markets.

COMPARATIVE HR PRACTICES

First, this section describes HR practices in the European Economic Community as an economic unity. Then HR practices within individual countries in the EEC (or, as generally referred to, the EC) are examined. Last, this section provides descriptions of the HR practices in a number of other countries.[1]

The European Community (European Union)

By the end of 1992, the twelve countries of the European Community (see Table 8.2) were well on their way to completion of the removal of internal barriers to trade, a process that had been given the label "EC '92." At the beginning of 1994, the name was changed to the European Union (EU). This process of integration included policies that impacted the movement of goods, services, capital, and people among the member states.

A number of components of the treaties defined the conditions for EC '92 that involve people in these twelve countries in their roles as employees. These include acceptance by each country of one another's educational and training requirements so as to facilitate the movement of labor from country to country, common regulations on issues such as discrimination and the treatment of women, the participation of employees in the management of their firms, common HR practices for programs like pensions, and a wide range of issues contained under what is referred to as the "Social Contract." Most of the trade issues within EC '92 had been adopted by the various countries by the end of 1992 (the original target date and thus the name given to the process), but agreement on the Social Contract will take longer, partially because there is more disagreement in this area of policy and more variance in practices from country to country.[2]

Table 8.2 summarizes a few of the country-specific practices as they existed in 1989–1990, illustrating some of the significant differences. Elsewhere in this book, other aspects of these differences have also been presented, for example, variances in family leave practices and differing income tax practices. Additional countries are interested in EC membership—such as the European Free Trade Agreement countries (with first preference being given by the EC to Sweden, Norway, and Austria), Turkey, Cyprus, and the countries of Central and Eastern Europe. As a partial requirement for membership, they are beginning to develop similar employment policies and practices in order to qualify. Eventually, as these countries realize common HR practices, multinational firms from elsewhere in the world will have to understand and utilize these practices—definitely in their European operations but possibly in other countries as well. The European trading block is already the largest in the world, and as it adds additional countries it will become even larger and wield even greater influence over non-European MNEs.

Pensions

One of the IHR concerns that illustrates the new realities within the EC involves policies relative to employee pension plans. The European Court of Justice ruled in 1990 that firms with employer-sponsored pension plans throughout the twelve member nations of the European Community cannot set different ages for receiving pension payments for men and women. The decision in the case of *Barber v. Guardian Royal Assurance Exchange Group* took effect May 17, 1990, and was immediately binding on all EC member states.[3]

Germany

Germany is the largest country in the EC and with the addition of the former Eastern Germany became an even more important economic and political factor within Europe. Germany is also one of the largest exporting countries in the world, even the largest at times. Its workers are recognized as among the best trained and most highly skilled in the world (and, importantly, among the most highly paid with some of the most extensive benefits, including the most extensive list of official holidays, extensive vacation periods, and the shortest official workweek among industrial countries).

One of the German HR practices that receives a lot of attention is co-determination. Co-determination involves a series of laws that gives employees varying levels of rights to participate in the economic decision making of their employers, particularly as those decisions impact employees. At the lowest level of participation, workers are elected to workers councils that employers must inform and consult on most economic decisions. Certain decisions, however, such as employee dismissals, work procedures, and workplace design, require more than just informing or consulting with the council. These require work council participation in any relevant decisions. At an even deeper level of participation, work councils have approval rights over decisions such as working hours, training programs, and safety regulations. In addition, under related laws, workers (and/or union representatives) also have the right to sit on boards of directors of firms over certain sizes. (This was described in more detail in Chapter 7 on labor relations.)

Even though Germany receives essentially all of the attention for worker council rights, a number of other European countries have similar legislation, for example, France, the Netherlands, and Sweden.

France

France is the second-largest coun°try in the EC and wields economic and political influence consistent with its size. Indeed, French individuals were (and are) the primary forces behind the EC's development. France has one of the lower

Table 8.2 Current Employment Policies and Practices Among EC Countries

COUNTRY	EMPLOYMENT FORMALITIES	MINIMUM PAY	MAX. HOURS (INCLUDING OVERTIME)	MINIMUM ANNUAL HOLIDAY	MINIMUM NOTICE TO BE GIVEN BY EMPLOYER	TERMINATION FORMALITIES	EMPLOYEE PARTICIPATION
Belgium	Certain terms must be in writing	Yes	8 per day; 40 per week	4 weeks	Workers: 14–28 days. Others: 3 months for up to 5 years' service + 3 mos: for every 5 years' service. Higher paid employees notice period agreed on when notice given or decided by Court.	Can terminate without notice for gross misconduct (but this does not include all instances of incompetence). Redundancy payments.	Work councils.
Denmark	Contracts usually oral.	No, but must conform to one of 2 compulsory wages systems.	Depends on collective agreement.	2 1/2 days per month.	Workers: depends on collective agreement. Others: 1–6 months.	Can terminate without notice for misconduct; unfair dismissal and redundancy payments.	Employee representatives on board of directors where there are more than 30 employees.
France	Contracts in writing. Collective agreements may be generally binding.	Yes	10 per day; 39 per week.	2 1/2 days per month (includes 5 Saturdays).	1 month after 6 months' service; 2 months after 2 years' service.	Unfair dismissal. Redundancy payments. Authorization of redundancies required.	Employee and union representatives. Works councils.
Germany	Fixed-term agreements restricted; collective agreements may be generally binding	No, but if a collective agreement, this must make provision.	8 per day; 48 per week	18 days.	Workers: 2 weeks to 3 months. Others: 6 weeks to 6 months from end of calendar-year quarter.	Unfair dismissal. Prior consultation on redundancies or dismissals with works council and in some cases the labor authorities.	Works councils

Greece	No substantial formalities.	Yes	48 per week.	4 weeks (after 1 year's employment).	Workers: none. Others: 1 month to 2 years.	Severance payments of 5–52 days' pay for workers or 1–24 months' pay for other employees. If notice given, only 1/2 payable.	Employee committees.
Ireland	Employees may require employees to supply written statements of terms of employment.	No.	No generally applicable statutory maximum.	3 weeks.	1–8 weeks.	Unfair dismissal. Redundancy payments.	No formal requirements.
Italy	Contracts in writing. National collective agreements.	Collective agreement.	48 per week; 8 per day	Collective agreement.	Collective agreement.	Severance payments. Can dismiss only for redundancy or good cause.	No formal requirements.
Luxembourg	Written contracts must be provided. Agreements may be binding on a sector.	Yes.	40 per week; 8 per day.	25 working days (5 days' holiday equals one week).	4 weeks to 6 months, depending on category of worker and length of service.	Severance payments, 1–12 months. Prior notification of redundancy and redundancy payments.	Employees' representatives. Joint works councils. Employee directors.
The Netherlands	No substantial formalities.	Yes.	48 per week; 8 1/2 per day; 5 1/2 days per week.	4 weeks.	Interval of payment (usually 2 weeks or 1 month) or a period of up to 13 weeks (26 weeks for older employees) based on length of service, whichever is longer.	Authorization of labor office usually required to dismiss with notice. May need to go to the Court; either procedure can take several months.	Works councils in undertakings with 35 or more employees.

Table 8.2 Current Employment Policies and Practices Among EC Countries (cont.)

COUNTRY	EMPLOY-MENT FOR-MALITIES	MINIMUM PAY	MAX. HOURS (IN-CLUDING OVERTIME)	MINIMUM ANNUAL HOLIDAY	MINIMUM NOTICE TO BE GIVEN BY EM-PLOYER	TERMINATION FOR-MALITIES	EMPLOYEE PARTICIPATION
Portugal	Fixed-term contracts must be in writing.	Yes	Office workers: 42 hours per week. Others: 48 per week; 8 per day.	Not less than 21 days nor more than 30 days.	Redundancy-notice period fixed when conditions of redundancy established.	Can dismiss only for "just cause" or redundancy. Prior notification of redundancies.	Workers' commissions and registered trade unions.
Spain	No substantial formalities.	Yes.	40 per week; 9 per day.	2 1/2 days per month.	1 month after 1 year's service; 3 months after 2 years.	Only for specified causes. Dismissal for other causes: compensation to 45 days pay per year of service.	Employee delegates and committees, employee directors.
United Kingdom	Written statement of terms of employment.	No.	No.	No.	1–13 weeks.	Unfair dismissal. Redundancy payments. Prior notification of redundancies.	No formal requirements.

Source: R. Sedel, "Europe in 1992: HR Implications of the European Unification," PERSONNEL, October 1989, p. 22 (reprinted with permission of the publisher from PERSONNEL TODAY, April 4, 1989).

levels of unionization in Europe (about 12 percent), but these unions wield extensive influence, with their negotiated settlements covering most of the work force (at least 85 percent). In addition, French workers have works councils (called enterprise committees and with which employers must meet on a monthly basis) and extensive benefits—including a state pension plan, required profit sharing, and extensive employee termination regulations. Except in cases of serious wrongdoing, dismissal gives rise to severance payments and required notice. Health and safety regulations are strict, with possible fines and even criminal charges for injury or death due to unsafe working conditions. It is also typical for firms to pay a thirteenth month bonus at year's end and a similar payment prior to the annual vacation.

United Kingdom[4]

Union membership in the U.K. is about three times that in the United States. Historically unions have played very important economic and political roles in the U.K. In recent years, however, while England has had a Conservative government (first under Margaret Thatcher and then under John Majors), the unions in the U.K. have wielded less influence and exhibited less militancy. British law is much less constraining than in the United States, with British unions preferring to achieve their objectives through political pressures brought to bear at the national level rather than through economics-dominated bargaining at the firm level. British labor contracts are not enforceable and can be pressured for renegotiation at any time.

Many employment conditions are outlined in laws such as the Contracts of Employment Act of 1972 and the Employment Protection Act of 1975. The Contracts of Employment Act requires an employer to give employees written information on their terms and conditions of employment, the disciplinary rules applicable to them, and the procedures available when they have a grievance about their employment or are dissatisfied with any disciplinary actions relating to them. This law also establishes the necessity for employers to provide minimum periods of notice when employment is to be terminated. Employees with a minimum period of service of 104 weeks (two years) are entitled to lump-sum redundancy payments if their jobs cease to exist (for example, because of technological improvements or because of a fall in revenues) and their employers cannot provide alternative work. The act also offers protection by providing machinery under which employees can complain against their employers for unfair dismissal and seek reinstatement, another job, or compensation.

The Employment Protection Act introduces maternity rights for women employees, which include protection against dismissal because of pregnancy, maternity pay, and the right to return to work after delivery. Many individual employee rights were consolidated in the Employment Protection (Consolidation) Act of 1978.

In terms of employee benefits, since April 1978 all persons in employment come within the scope of the Society Security Pensions Act of 1975 and are entitled to earnings-related retirement benefits. Most large industrial enterprises provide a free or subsidized midday meal. In addition, in the U.K. it is common practice to provide fully expensed cars for management and senior staff and, therefore, could represent a sizable cost of establishing a business in the United Kingdom.

There is no legal requirement (apart from eight national holidays) to grant a paid vacation period. However, at least four weeks' paid vacation is now customary in most industries and receives a degree of legal recognition as a standard condition of employment. Discrimination on the basis of color, race, nationality, ethnicity, or national origin is illegal. And health and safety of employees is protected as well.

Although the labor force in the U.K. generally is highly skilled, there are shortages of skilled labor in certain regions, especially in southeast England. This could influence where a multinational firm might want to locate.

British industry has always prided itself on its independence, so even though England is a member of the EC, Britain has regularly resisted EC initiatives, particularly in the social area (as described above).

Italy

Italy is also one of the original six members of the EC and one of the four larger members. As with other European countries, Italy has developed in unique directions. Also similar to other countries, Italy has a north-south split in its industrialization, with the north more similar to its industrial neighbors to the north and the south remaining more rural and agricultural.

Italy has also developed significant employment regulation. For example, various regulations prohibit the audio-visual checking of employees, checking employees' physical fitness, surveying employee opinions, and transferring or demoting any employee without extensive documentation of the reasons.

One of Italy's labor relations peculiarities is that its high-paid and high-status employees (high-level professionals and executives—referred to as the *dirigenti*) belong to their own union, negotiate their own employment contracts (pay and benefits), are specially protected by law, and are accorded special supplemental pay and benefits.

Belgium

Belgium has one of the most strictly defined systems of labor laws and employment regulations. This ranges from having the highest percentage of union membership of industrial countries to extensive regulations dealing with issues like hours of work, employee pay levels, and employer payroll taxes (such as 1.5 percent tax for hiring long-term unemployed and younger workers), to the most refined system of works councils in Europe, to one of the most extensive social security systems in Europe. Belgian HR practices include one of the highest levels of employee compensation in the world, a mandatory, annual "thirteenth month" payment to all employees, extensive employee termination requirements in terms of both notification and pay, coverage under Belgian law of expatriates and TCNs, consultation with the works council on all major business and HR decisions, significant government involvement in staffing levels to combat unemployment, and committees for safety and hygiene that have major responsibility for working conditions and the work environment.

Spain

Regulations as a rule are less restrictive and labor costs are lower in Spain than in other major EC countries. Minimum wages are set by labor-management agreement and vary from industry to industry. Fringe benefits are still usually rudimentary and not a major employment consideration (although with rationalization throughout the EC and the adoption of the EC social charter, this will begin to change). Social security requirements are under constant revision, with the major contribution coming from employers.

Unionization is still quite low and only the north of the country and the areas around Madrid and Barcelona exhibit productivity levels and work habits similar to those found elsewhere in Western Europe. Even so, there are fifteen national holidays, with the major urban centers and regions of the country adding their own fiestas which are local holidays.

The Netherlands

In the Netherlands, as in other Western European countries, works councils play an important role. Any firm with more than thirty-five employees must establish a works council and seek the advice of that council for mergers, plant closures, relocation or transfer of work, and all major reorganizations. If the firm has one hundred or more employees, the jurisdiction of the works council includes major new investments in the firm; the establishment of new credit sources; establishing, acquiring, or disposing of an enterprise; and the assigning of an advisory expert from the outside. In areas of importance to HR, these councils must be consulted for consent on pension, insurance, and profit sharing or savings plans; work time and holidays; merit systems; safety, health, and welfare programs; discharge and promotion policies; training and appraisal programs; complaint and grievance handling procedures; and the position of young people in the firm. In addition, works council members are provided protection from normal dismissal.

Most social security benefits are provided by the government, but other employee benefits are voluntary and thus differ from company to company. These often include subsidized canteens, savings plans and mortgages, private pension plans to supplement social security; private health-care insurance to supplement the national health insurance; a company car; a thirteenth month of salary, usually paid at Christmas time. Vacation time is a minimum of twenty days. Employment law also provides extensive job protection. Dismissal requires prior regional labor office approval, with formal notice to the employee required from one to sixteen weeks prior to termination, depending on the employee's age and length of employment. Required severance pay is also based on age and service and varies from six months to two to three years of salary.

Other Western European Countries

The following provides a short overview of HR practices in a number of other Western Europen countries.

Austria

Austria has regulated its employment practices in detail. However, there is no unified code and particularly in individual labor law there are many different statutes. The majority of employees and employers are governed by collective agreements on pay issues, which specify the minimums that employers must pay. Entitlement to vacation time is thirty working days for employees with up to twenty-five years of service and after that thirty-six working days. Employees have the right to payment if they are prepared to work but are prevented from doing so by circumstances on the employer's side, with no time limits on such continuation of payment. Employers never have the right to lay off blue-collar or white-collar employees without pay. Notice for dismissal must be filed from one to five months prior to termination, with redundancy payments ranging from two to twelve months' salary. Employers must belong to employer associations within their particular industries, which negotiate binding agreements with their union.

Firms with more than five employees must form works councils and, if there are more than five of each blue-collar and white-collar employees, then there must be appointed a works council for each group. These works councils have the right to monitor the employer's compliance with compulsory laws safeguarding the interests of employees. The most important area of co-determination for works councils involves dismissals. National social security provides both health insurance and pensions, although early retirement is quite widespread for males at sixty and for females at fifty-five. In 1993, the EC extended its first step for future membership to Austria, which has been a member of EFTA, the European Free Trade Association.

Sweden

In Sweden, the trade unions and employer's associations have tried to regulate their relationship by means of agreements in order to avoid government intervention. However, in recent years this relationship has increasingly been regulated by law. The Employment Security Act stipulates that employment shall be permanent unless otherwise agreed (with a couple of exceptions, such as probationary periods, work of a "stand-in" nature, and after retirement). The statutory holiday (vacation) entitlement is five weeks with employees able to accumulate some vacation time so that after five years employees could have ten consecutive weeks' holiday. Employers have relative freedom to terminate for cause and to lay off employees for economic reasons.

Employers and employees have pretty much absolute rights to take collective action and to negotiate agreements that determine the nature of the employment relationship. For employers with at least 25 employees, employees are entitled to appoint two members to the board of directors and two managing deputies of the firm. In firms with more than 1,000 employees and operating different lines of business, employees are entitled to appoint three directors and three deputies. Social security obligations in Sweden are paid solely by employers, with some firms negotiating limited contribution from employees for supplemental pension and health insurance.

Switzerland

The employment relationship is probably less regulated in Switzerland than anywhere else in Europe. Even so, the cost of living and labor costs are higher there than elsewhere. Approximately 32 percent of the labor force is unionized, but union membership is entirely voluntary. There is no requirement for employee participation or co-determination in Switzerland. And termination notice (up to three months) and indemnity (up to eight months' pay) are relatively reasonable.

Central and Eastern Europe

Everything is "in transition" in Central and Eastern Europe (the now independent countries of the former Soviet Union). Under communism, firms (enterprises) performed most of the functions that would normally be the responsibility of the state, such as day-care centers, schools, retirement homes, special stores for employee shopping, vacation retreat centers, even housing. In contrast, many of the tasks that are performed by firms outside of Communist economies, such as hiring, placement of employees in firms, compensation levels and pay practices, and discipline and grievance management, were handled outside the enterprise or not at all.

All this is now reversing as enterprises move toward operating as firms do in free-market economies. Thus, start-up operations can often establish "traditional" human resource practices from the beginning, while joint ventures and newly privatized firms often experience considerable difficulty in making the transition from the former system to the new free-market procedures.[5]

Latin America

Many countries in Latin America are major trading partners with the United States, including some of significant size, such as Brazil, Mexico, and Argentina. The following provides an overview of HR issues and practices in two important countries in Latin America.

Brazil

Brazil is the world's fifth largest country (with a population of 155 million) and it has the tenth largest economy. It is a country with vast resources, many of which are undeveloped yet provide significant opportunity. There is significant employment regulation but relatively limited enforcement. For example, the law requires employers with more than 200 employees to have works councils; but, in practice, few employers provide such opportunities for worker participation. Probably the most significant issue for conducting business in Brazil involves its hyperinflation. Wages must be regularly adjusted, which has led to wide ranges of salaries from the highest to the lowest remunerated employees. A thirteen month of salary is required by law. The government provides very limited social security (health care and pension) and employers typically don't provide much more. Vacation entitlements provide for thirty calendar days paid at 130 percent or, if not taken, paid at 200 percent. Employers are required to contribute to a savings fund (8 percent of payroll) to compensate employees who are terminated and is also made available when firms close, employees retire or die, and can be withdrawn by employees to purchase a primary residence.

Mexico

Mexico has long been one of the United States' major trading partners. Many American firms have maintained major manufacturing facilities in Mexico for a number of years. In addition, with the expansion of the *maquiladora* "industry" in Mexico, many more firms have opened assembly and manufacturing facilities, primarily along Mexico's northern border with the United States, in order to take advantage of Mexico's skilled but low-wage labor force. One result of this has been that more Americans are working in these *maquiladora* plants and more American firms are involved with business operations in Mexico. In the fall of 1993, the United States, Canada, and Mexico gave final approval to a North American Free Trade agreement. Even though the initial treaty concept involved only purely trade issues such as tariffs, additional side agreements were negotiated to deal with labor and environmental concerns, primarily to meet the concerns of various American interest groups.

The following provides a short introduction to HR issues for doing business in Mexico.

The Mexican Federal Labor Law governs all labor matters in Mexico. This law favors employees in all relations with employers. Unionization is the norm. The Federal Labor Board has authority over conflicts involving industries holding federal charters or federal concessions, or operating within federal zones. The state labor boards hear disputes arising within the individual states and/or involving industries that are not federal in nature. The boards are composed of representatives from government, labor, and management. This law requires certain minimum fringe benefits for all permanent employees, including a minimum of six days' paid vacation annually (increasing at a rate of two days of each year of service beyond the first), in addition to a 25 percent vacation pay premium; thirteen paid federal holidays; a profit-sharing plan; and an employer-paid payroll tax that funds employee day-care centers and housing. Employees are also paid fifteen days' salary as a Christmas bonus each year. After one year of employment, a Mexican worker is considered tenured and can be dismissed only for causes specifically set out in the Mexican Federal Labor Law. Many aspects of this labor law are more stringent than those covering similar employment issues in the United States.[6]

Only twenty employees are required to form a union, thus a high percentage of employees in Mexico belong to unions and a firm might well have to deal with multiple unions. If the officially recognized labor union declares a strike, all personnel, including management, must leave the facility. Red and black flags stand at each of the locked entrances to provide notice that the facility is on strike. Workers receive pay for all the time they are out on a legal strike.

All employment contracts in Mexico must be in writing and normally run for an indefinite period of time. If an employer fails to give written notice of a firing along with complete documentation of the offenses resulting in the termination, it is invalid. Because a violation of Mexican Federal Labor Law can result in heavy fines, and jail sentences are imposed for failure to pay the minimum wage, many U.S. businesses work closely with union representatives to assure that dismissals are valid and work closely with local consultants, attorneys, and accounting firms to ensure that all aspects of Mexican labor law are complied with. Employers generally make a severance payment to dismissed employees in lieu of making a case to labor authorities. It is usually three months' salary plus twenty days' wages for each year of service. Permanent employees who are being terminated for any cause are entitled to "seniority premiums" equal to twelve days' salary for each year of service. The same compensation is payable upon the death of an employee.

Employers are responsible for almost two-thirds of their employees' social security premiums, employees for 25 percent (and the federal government contributes the remainder). Employers are wholly responsible for paying premiums for "occupational risks." In addition, the Constitution stipulates that employers must provide adequate housing for their employees. Employers generally fulfill this obligation by contributing 5 percent of payroll to the National Workers' Housing Fund Institute (INFONAVIT).

Asia

Because of the post–World War II success stories of Asian countries such as Japan, South Korea, Hong Kong, Taiwan, and Singapore, the size of the populations and markets of many Asian countries, and the more recent rapid development of Asian countries such as China, Indonesia, Malaysia, Thailand, and India, many people think the economic center of gravity for the world is shifting toward Asia and the Asian Pacific rim. This section provides an outline of the HRM practices in a number of Asian countries.

Australia

Australia, even though it has a relatively small population, is the fourteenth largest trading nation. It is also the sixteenth largest market for U.S. goods and has the twelfth highest standard of living, third to Japan and Korea in the Far East. From its earliest history, Australians have had a strong interest in employee ownership and control of firms, although it is not common to find among major employers any form of extensive worker participation. In terms of benefits, Australians enjoy paid sick leave, an extensive "non-contributory" national system of health care and pensions, a minimum annual vacation of four weeks at regular pay, a bonus of 17.5 percent every year, eight weeks leave at regular pay after fifteen years with one employer and thereafter three months leave for each additional ten years, and extensive perks such as entertainment, car, and telephone allowances, loans, and meal allowances. In addition, many firms also provide company-sponsored pension plans and fairly liberal termination awards, with the general practice being two to three weeks' pay per year of service.

Fifty-six percent of the total labor force (including managers and professional/technical employees) belong to unions, and there are 304 unions so that many firms have 5 or 6 different unions. However, Australia is unique in that bargaining impasses are required to be submitted to compulsory conciliation and ultimately arbitration if necessary. In spite of this, Australia also has one of the worst strike records in the world, especially in terms of short-term strikes (approximately 45 percent of strikes last less than two days and 20 percent last longer than ten days). However, this record has improved considerably in recent years, with a reduction in workdays lost to strikes from about 4,200 per 1,000 employees in 1981 to under 1,300 per 1,000 employees today.

China

What is happening in Central and Eastern Europe is also happening in China, although, as with most things, with a decidedly Chinese twist. In China, the employment relationship has been referred to as the "iron rice bowl." That is, employees' job situation was akin to an iron rice bowl—indestructible (better even than the Japanese promise of life-time employment). Jobs were essentially permanent, employees could not be fired for any reason (so there was no pressure to perform), they always received their pay, and firms provided benefits from birth to grave. Now all that is changing as China, too, tries to bring the benefits of a free-market economy to its people, starting primarily in its major urban centers and the geographic area near Hong Kong.

The iron rice bowl is beginning to rust, with firms laying off unproductive employees and beginning to tie compensation to individual and organizational performance. Even so, the economic reforms being tried within the Chinese economy are often being implemented within the framework of tradition, such as using pressure from family and neighbors to deal with poor performance and absenteeism. The lack of training in free-market procedures compounds the problems with efforts to reform this largest of socialist economies.

The following IHRM in Action 8.2 describes an example of the kinds of issues a manager can confront when trying to bring Western-style standards of quality and customer service to a culture such as China's where employee and management practices have precluded the possibility of the types of actions taken by this American manager in a new Chinese tourist hotel.

IHRM IN ACTION 8.2
CHINESE INN'S NO HOLIDAY
FOR U.S. MANAGER

The Chung King Hotel opened in February 1987 in the city of Chongqing, which many foreign tourists use as a starting point for their trips on the Yangtze River. The higher-class hotel was intended to encourage tourists to spend more than the usual one night in the city. To succeed, the hotel required management and personnel of the same caliber as the physical plant. The manager chosen was Percival

Darby, an American who had previously turned the Shenzen Hotel in South China into an efficient operation with profits of $1 million in 1986.

Even in China's hotel business, which has been open to foreign investment and contracts for some time, success requires extraordinary persistence and hard work. The challenges include cooks who can sing better than they can saute, waitresses who giggle as they spill juice, chief housekeepers who think that getting rooms "almost clean" is enough, and a waitress who served a hamburger announcing: "Here's your mushroom omelette with hot cakes, sir. Enjoy your meal." Some foreign managers have become so frustrated with their work and that of their Chinese employees that they have not survived second tours in China.

At the Chung King, Darby has gained enormous respect as a manager, not only because he is well organized and works as many as 20 hours a day, but also because he is willing to take some unusual steps in meeting goals of cleanliness, courtesy, and quality. [Indeed, it might be suggested that these practices are not only unusual, but they also vary dramatically from traditional management practices that have been in use for decades in China. Gradually—actually, it might be accurately claimed, quite rapidly—many of these practices are changing within China, as the Chinese economy increasingly takes on characteristics of a market economy, including personnel and management practices.] If anyone among the hotel's staff of 600 fails to perform a task, a warning is issued; repetition brings a fine. During the first six months of Darby's tenure, he fired 52 workers, although he does not see it that way. "I do not fire people, they fire themselves. I make the rules and penalties. You knowingly break a rule, you are out." If a staff member is caught spitting in the kitchen—common practice in many places—it is reason for immediate dismissal. But if employees perform well, they earn bonuses that raise their wages well above average. In contrast, Chinese managers rarely dismiss workers, except for those who commit crimes or engage in major derelictions of duty. Some are hesitant to make demands on their subordinates.

As an example of Darby's drive for excellence, on one occasion he found a hole in a napkin on a coffee shop table. The waitress was fined five yuan ($1.35) for failing to notice it. He fined his own wife Norma three yuan ($.81) because as the coffee shop supervisor she was partly responsible.

Source: "Chinese Inn's No Holiday for U.S. Manager," THE WASHINGTON POST, August 2, 1987, p. H18. Reprinted with permission of publisher from THE WASHINGTON POST, copyright 1987. All rights reserved.

Japan

Japan has become the second largest economy in the world, behind the United States, with about one-half the population. Many authors have written (sometimes in disagreement with each other) about Japanese management and HRM practices, in attempts to explain the obvious Japanese economic success. Among these practices, three particular HRM practices (the "Three Treasures of Japan") have been focused on: lifetime employment (at least for employees in Japan's largest firms), promotion primarily based on seniority, and company-based unions (as opposed to national, craft, or industry-wide unions).

Lifetime employment was instituted after World War II during a period of great labor shortage and under pressure from labor unions as a way for the major firms to recruit and hold on to the best employees. In the Japanese island culture oriented toward group involvement (and minimizing individual competition), and in this environment of lifetime employment, then promotion based on seniority made sense. And because every firm has its own union (resulting in some 33,750 unions throughout Japan), unions tend to use short-term pressure tactics (almost all strikes in Japan are only one day in duration), and union interests are primarily focused on economic issues within their particular firms.

In major Japanese firms, compensation is based on seniority (rather than on performance)—although all employees receive bonuses generally paid at year-end, and during the summer as well many also receive profit-sharing bonuses. Compensation for managers may be modest by U.S. standards (although the data provided in Chapter 5 suggests the disparities among major countries are becoming increasingly less significant), but pay is generally paternalistic, favoring employees and managers with families over single or female employees.

Vacation allowances are generally a minimum of ten days per year which increases at a rate of one day per year to a maximum of twenty days per year after ten years of employment. Maternity leave is provided for six weeks prior to birth (at the employee's request) and for a compulsory eight weeks after birth at 60 percent of salary. Notice for termination is thirty days or pay in lieu of notice. Generally, there are few limitations because there have been few layoffs with virtually no unemployment. If a firm must terminate employees, severance pay is usually figured at one month per year of service.

Japan has the earliest average age of retirement among the industrialized countries (fifty-five years of age) along with the longest life expectancy (about eighty years of age). Because Japan does not provide a social security pension (nor do most firms provide a pension), Japan workers must save heavily for their lengthy retirements (partially explaining why Japan has one of the highest savings rates in the world). During the prolonged Japanese recession of 1992 to 1994, businesses and the government began to question whether or not this low retirement age ought to be raised.

Increasingly, however, Japanese firms are beginning to feel the pressures of global competition, resulting in more attention to staffing (with some firms, for the first time, having to lay off employees) and other employee-related cost issues, such as reexamining their lump-sum retirement payments, which are getting increasingly costly as their workforces get older and increasing numbers of employees approach retirement.

Asian tigers

These four countries of East Asia (South Korea, Hong Kong, Taiwan, and Singapore) have become major players in the global economy. All have thriving economies and all are common locations for activity by MNEs (their own and those from other countries). The following is only a short introduction to some of the HR issues in two of these countries.

SOUTH KOREA.   Only a few Koreans speak English (or other foreign languages), so having local sponsors and relationships with local firms is often important. Since World War II, unions have played an important role in South Korea, but laws passed in the 1980s encouraged the use of labor-management committees, which have lessened the importance and role of labor unions. Even so, unions in major industries continue to wield significant power, as evidenced by the strikes against Hyundai during the summer of 1993, which resulted in a major reduction in Korean exports and thus involved government intervention to mediate a settlement.

HONG KONG.   Hong Kong has been one of the amazing success stories of the post–World War II world. Hong Kong is a British protectorate, although Britain has agreed to transfer Hong Kong sovereignty back to the People's Republic of China on July 1, 1997. This has created a high degree of emigration of professionals and managers, although many of these people, after acquiring a second passport, are returning to Hong Kong and its opportunities for high income.

The Hong Kong economy is, in fact, so vibrant, that it has essentially no unemployment. Hong Kong developed initially because it provided basically a low-wage labor force for the assembly and manufacture of products to be exported to the rest of the world. Now Hong Kong's labor force is highly skilled and predominantly nonunion and operates in a highly entrepreneurial and laissez-faire business environment. In addition, the highly successful Hong Kong Chinese are now becoming major investors in other areas of Asia, particularly China (but also Malaysia, Indonesia, and Thailand).

Other Asian countries

There are a number of other major countries (including Indonesia, the Philippines, Thailand, Malaysia, India, and Vietnam) in Asia that are providing important new opportunities for multinational firms. All are in varying stages of development and in terms of HRM reflect that reality. IHR managers operating in these countries—or contemplating such a move—must be prepared for the need to investigate widely varying practices and regulations.

Africa

Most countries in Africa are still struggling to develop modern economies, with multiple political and cultural barriers to overcome. Even so, it cannot be assumed that Africa comprises a broadly uniform context.[7] The 50-odd countries of Africa represent approximately 2,000 different ethnocultural communities. The countries reflect great diversity in terms of population size, level and sophistication of economic development, resource endowment, and political structures and ideological orientations. Nevertheless, the broad historic-cultural and politico-economic similarities, at least in sub-Saharan Africa, probably permit cautious generalizing.[8]

In larger firms and MNE subsidiaries (as well as in smaller, local firms), HR practices tend to be highly politicized and subject to pressures other than efficiency, merit, performance, and cost-effectiveness.[9] For example, hiring, placement, and promotion decisions are typically more likely to be made with reference to a person's family, tribe, or contacts, than on the basis of the person's merit or qualifications. However, it is becoming increasingly necessary for all organizations in Africa to pay closer attention to their human resources as African economies become more complex, as they face increasing pressures from foreign competitors, and as their workforces intensify the pressures on their employers for better compensation, benefits, work environments, and performance management.

SUMMARY

This chapter provided a short overview of HRM practices in a number of countries and regions of the world. It began with a comparison of the size of the civilian labor forces for a number of countries as well as their varying labor force participation rates. These are important issues for MNEs as they plan in which countries to develop subsidiaries (considering the size and make-up of the local labor forces). The remainder of the chapter described HRM practices in the various regions and countries of the world.

The variety and complexity of those practices greatly compound the difficulties with which international HR managers must cope. Consequently, IHR managers need to understand these practices in every country in which their firms operate.

ENDNOTES

1. Much of this information is derived from Brewster, C., and S. Tyson, eds., *International Comparisons in Human Resource Management* (London: Pitman Publishing, 1991); Johnson, T., and M. O'Culachain, eds., *Employment Law in Europe: A Country by Country Guide for Employers* (Coopers & Lybrand, Aldershot, England: Gower Publishing, 1992); Losey, M., *International Comparative Human Resource Practices*, a workshop presented at the annual meeting of the Institute for International Human Resources, Society for Human Resource Management, New Orleans, March 28, 1993; and Pieper, R., ed., *Human Resource Management: An International Comparison* (Berlin: Walter de Gruyter, 1990).

2. Briscoe, D. R., and G. Gazda, "Human Resource Management and the Single European Market 1994: An Update," *Proceedings,* Fourth Conference on International Human Resource Management, Goldcoast, Australia, July 5–8, 1994.

3. "European Court Ruling Bars Gender Bias in Pension Plans," *The Wyatt Compensation and Benefits File,* 6(7), July 1990, 1.

4. Much of this section is based on the information contained in Price Waterhouse's *Doing Business in the United Kingdom,* 1991, one of a series published by Price Waterhouse World Firm Limited. Price Waterhouse publishes guides on doing business in over fifty different countries.

5. Briscoe, D. R., C. Pavett, and G. Whitney, "Human Resource Management in Central and Eastern Europe: A Capsule Summary," *Proceedings,* Fourth Conference on International Human Resource Management, Goldcoast, Australia, July 5–8, 1994.

6. Much of this discussion is adapted from Jarvis, S. S., "Preparing Employees to Work South of the Border," *Personnel,* June 1990, pp. 59–63.

7. Kamoche, K., "Towards a Model of HRM in Africa," *Proceedings,* Third Conference in International Personnel and Human Resource Management, Ashridge, England, July 2–4, 1992.

8. Ibid.

9. Blunt, P., and O. Popoola, *Personnel Management in Africa* (London: Longman, 1985); and Akinnusi, D. M., "Personnel Management in Africa: A Comparative Analysis of Ghana, Kenya, and Nigeria," in *International Comparisons in Human Resource Management,* eds. C. Brewster and S. Tyson (London: Pitman Publishing, 1991).

9

The Future of International Human Resource Management

In many ways, the future of IHRM is now. This is a new field. It is in its developmental stages now. Most of this book has been written in an attempt to understand what is happening in this constantly developing area of management responsibility. Some aspects of IHRM appear to be supported by considerable research and experience, such as various aspects of dealing with expatriates—their selection, preparation, compensation, and repatriation (even if many firms do not yet use what is known about how to improve the likelihood of success when using expatriates). But many other aspects of IHRM have yet to receive the attention of firms or researchers to the extent that the process of expatriation and repatriation has. This chapter, therefore, provides one author's perspective and speculations on the issues that are likely to confront IHR managers in the near future, as this discipline further develops in its attempts to be a major participant in the management of at least the human resource aspects of the ever-exploding activity of international commerce.

For purposes of description, this chapter has been divided into three sections. These include (1) organizational concerns in the advancement of IHRM; (2) the further professionalization of IHRM; and (3) the development of IHR managers.

ORGANIZATIONAL ADVANCEMENT OF IHRM

Increased global business activity is, by necessity, creating increased organizational problems of coordination and integration. Not only do MNEs of all types now operate with traditional subsidiaries in ever increasing numbers of countries and regions of the world, but they also increasingly use alliances, joint ventures, consortia, and other forms of business linkages to conduct their international business and to gain access to global resources.

The result is that multinational and global firms are becoming incredibly complex organizations. Large domestic businesses are difficult enough to manage. Add in problems of cross-border, multilanguage, and multiculture (organizational and national) issues, and the complexity often seems beyond the abilities of "mere" people to manage. The numbers of cross-border mergers and acquisitions, joint ventures, and alliances of every conceivable type continue to expand as does, of course, traditional direct investment through turn-key start-ups and technology transfers.

Achieving desirable results from these international activities will require MNEs to pay increasing attention to more than the merger of international operations, research and development, sales forces, and accounting systems. Increasingly, top-level attention will have to be paid to the merger of workforces and individual employees who represent multiple corporate and national cultures, speak multiple languages, and have widely varying perspectives on customer, product, and business issues. In addition, the MNEs will find increasingly difficult the development of IHRM systems that deal effectively with global human resource problems, such as pension and health-care systems, management development, employee and management recruitment, compensation systems, and the like.

In the end, this merger of the cultural aspects of international businesses boils down to finding ways for individuals with varying backgrounds and perspectives to work together; that is, finding ways to develop a corporate "glue" that will hold the organization effectively together.[1] ABB provides a recent good example.[2] The Swedish-Swiss power and transportation conglomerate wasn't sure how to digest its 1990 acquisition of Stamford, Connecticut–based Combustion Engineering, Inc. (CE). Initially, ABB benefited from a couple of transatlantic personnel moves. It hired an American, General Electric Co. veteran Craig S. Tedmon Jr., to head the firm's Zurich-based worldwide R&D efforts. And it installed an Austrian who holds an American Ph.D., Gernot H. Gessinger, to run CE's Windsor (Connecticut) combustion lab.

People who transfer from research labs in one country to those in another often experience considerable culture shock. Gessinger found the Connecticut lab dirty, stuffed with unneeded equipment, and unfocused. He ordered a cleanup and canceled dangling projects. And he uncovered distrust. The pragmatic engineers in Connecticut feared intrusions by ABB's combustion theoreticians in Baden, Switzerland. The Swiss doubted the Yanks' credentials. Gessinger built trust by having Windsor help perfect a gas-fired boiler that Baden developed. Other forms of task-force interaction, as well, have led to the hoped-for interaction that has encouraged a synergistic sharing of ideas and innovations.

This type of organizational glue—effective cross-national task forces and work teams—will need to be increasingly used to pull together employees from disparate country and corporate cultures. IHR managers should be able to provide the firm with the human resource expertise to help design and implement such strategies.

Given the many human resource problems in conducting business on a global scale, MNEs in the future will need to encourage the following agenda for their IHR executives:[3]

- Ensure IHR involvement as an integral partner in formulating the global strategy for the firm.
- Develop the necessary competence among the senior IHR staff so that they can be contributing partners in the strategic management of the global firm.
- Take the lead in developing processes and concepts for top management as they develop the global strategy. These might include developing capacities for information scanning about HR issues throughout the world, for decision making, particularly related to global HR concerns, or for the learning processes that the firm needs to adapt to new global requirements.
- Develop a framework to help top management fully understand the (increasingly complex) organizational structure and people implications of globalization.
- Facilitate the implementation of the global strategy by identifying the key skills that will be required by management, assessing current global competencies in IHRM and the rest of the management team, and developing strategies for locating outside talent that may be required (either through consulting or hiring). Table 9.1 illustrates the types of skills that competent global managers will need in the future to ensure the implementation of global strategies by transnational firms. These perspectives and abilities clearly create an agenda for IHRM and its MNEs for change that will not be easy but is certainly necessary.

Table 9.1 Transnationally Competent Managers

TRANSNATIONAL SKILLS	TRANSNATIONALLY COMPETENT MANAGERS	TRADITIONAL INTERNATIONAL MANAGERS
Global Perspective	Understand worldwide business environment from a global perspective	Focus on a single foreign country and on managing relationships between headquarters and that country
Local Responsiveness	Learn about many cultures	Become an expert on one culture
Synergistic Learning	Work with and learn from people from many cultures simultaneously	Work with and coach people in each foreign culture separately or sequentially
	Create a culturally synergistic organizational environment	Integrate foreigners into the headquarters' national organization culture
Transition and Adaptation	Adapt to living in many foreign cultures	Adapt to living in a foreign culture
Cross-cultural Interaction	Use cross-cultural interaction skills on a daily basis throughout one's career	Use cross-cultural interaction skills primarily on foreign assignments
Collaboration	Interact with foreign colleagues as equals	Interact within clearly defined hierarchies of structural and cultural dominance
Foreign Experience	Transpatriation for career and organization development	Expatriation or inpatriation primarily to get the job done

Source: Adler, N.J., "Managing Globally Competent People," Academy of Management EXECUTIVE, 6:3, 1992, 54. Reprinted with permission of Academy of Management. All rights reserved.

PROFESSIONALIZATION OF IHRM

In order to achieve the above agenda, IHRM as a management function will need to professionalize. Organizations that will operate in the highly competitive global economy of the future and that will want (indeed, they will *need*) to develop world-class IHRM functions and departments will need to examine at least each of these six areas:[4]

Importance of the IHR Function

IHRM will need to be seen by top executives, strategic planners, and line management as critical to the success of the business. Thus IHRM must receive high-priority attention and resources. It will be critical for managers to have experience in the IHR department (and it will be just as important for IHR managers to have experience in line management of the firm).

Distribution of the Responsibilities of the IHR Function

Increasingly (and in line with the previous point), IHR will become a shared responsibility. Line management, IHR managers, and work teams all will share in the objective of ensuring the effective hiring, development, and deployment of the global firm's human resources. This will inevitably lead to the decentralization of IHR decisions and policy making. There will be less use of headquarters' IHR departments, with IHR responsibilities delegated out to the business units of the firm. This decentralization will occur particularly in five key areas:

1. IHRM strategy development;
2. IHRM policy/program development;
3. Management of IHR programs;
4. IHRM department administration; and
5. Communication about IHRM strategies, policies, and programs.

Operation of the IHR Department

The world-class IHR department will be operated under these particular guidelines:

1. IHRM will be linked to the management of the business at strategic, managerial, and operational levels;
2. IHRM will shift from being primarily an operational activity (managing issues such as staffing, training, and compensation) to more of a strategic role in the management of the global firm; IHRM will shift from being primarily responsive to decisions made by top management to being proactive in the design of IHR programs and in the strategic management of the firm; IHRM will shift from doing IHR for line executives to assisting and counseling them on IHR matters; IHRM will shift from operating primarily with a focus on individual employees to a focus on work teams; and IHRM will shift from focusing primarily on internal problems to focusing on issues external to the firm, even to a societal focus.

Staffing the IHR Department

The IHR department, itself, in order to pursue this new role, will find it has a need for fewer specialists and more generalists; that it will need to be even more business-oriented (this means IHR managers will need more line experience and training); that individual IHR managers will need to have more experience working in teams themselves and more training in how to make teams work effectively together; and that IHR managers will need to develop internal counseling abilities (with line managers, helping them to solve people problems) and become information specialists (creating, maintaining, and using/interpreting IHR data for the rest of the firm).

Linking the IHR Department with the Business

In the global firms of the future, IHR departments will need to be more closely linked into the actual management of the business, through development of IHR philosophies (values, culture, vision), policies (guidelines for action), and programs, practices, and processes (involving line managers at every step) that fit the vision and strategy of the firm.

Demonstrating the Contributions of the IHR Department

The IHR department in the future global firm will need to learn how to demonstrate that the right things (needed by the organization to be successful) are being done right (as efficiently as possible and with positive impact on the bottom line).[5] One aspect of this will be research to determine what the best IHRM practices are around the world and to use them both to judge the quality of a particular firm's IHRM activities as well as to develop better IHRM practices.

Indicators of being world class

The following provides a short list of possible criteria to use to determine whether the IHRM practices in any particular firm are indeed among the best in the world. Some of these criteria, in fact, are being measured by the Saratoga Institute and the Society for Human Resource Management so that they can provide quality benchmarks for IHR departments.[6]

- Inclusion of IHRM in key business issues—including both their formulation and their implementation;
- IHR and organization issues being seen as critical in strategy implementation;
- Ability of IHRM to deal with events proactively;
- Alignment of IHRM policies, procedures, and practices in all businesses, including a clear and shared statement of IHR vision;
- A number of individuals wanting to have an IHR assignment;
- IHRM meeting its plans and objectives;
- IHRM having a structure, organization, and operation that services the strategic needs of the business;

- IHRM having satisfied customers within the organization;
- IHRM activities being shared and understood by all employees;
- IHRM being flexible and adaptable to new conditions;
- IHRM measuring the effectiveness of its activities;
- IHRM measuring the efficiency of its activities;
- IHRM facilitating, or being capable of facilitating, major organizational change; and
- IHRM having competent, adaptive, and flexible staff.

THE DEVELOPMENT OF IHR MANAGERS

Since the IHRM function has evolved primarily from human resource activities related to the management of expatriates, but as the above discussion suggests is rapidly evolving into many other areas of responsibility, a major issue for IHRM in the future will be one of the development of broader-gauged IHR executives. MNEs will need IHR managers who can do more than handle the selection, preparation, relocation, and compensation of expatriates. As the previous section described, MNEs need IHR managers to assist in the strategic management of their international businesses, develop IHR policies for operations located around the globe, and hire and develop highly productive workforces in multiple countries. The development of this type of strategic IHR manager will become an important focus for IHRM.

Firms can strengthen their IHRM departments and develop more competency in IHRM in a number of ways:[7]

- By assigning upwardly mobile domestic HR generalists to overseas regional staffs for two- to three-year periods. For example, Pepsi Cola has done this successfully, assigning U.S. HR managers to its regional offices in Europe, Asia, and Latin America. However, this is not yet a widespread practice. Note that, at this time, over 90 percent of IHR managers in overseas regions for American MNEs are not Americans.
- By considering assignment of one or more repatriated expatriates from any function to IHR in either an operating division or the headquarters staff. Their overseas experiences will add credibility to the IHRM function as well as a critical international perspective. In addition, experience in HR should be beneficial to their careers. (Assignment of nonperformers, i.e., individuals who had difficulty in their international assignments, should be avoided. Such a move would weaken the IHRM function.)
- By assigning several entry-level university graduates with degrees in human resources to overseas subsidiaries and regional positions. Instead of giving them typical expatriate compensation packages, pay them as locals. Indeed, these individuals might even be from the country of assignment, having attended university in the country of the parent firm.

The success of IHRM in the future will depend on the ability of companies to develop IHR executives with broad global perspectives, international experience, and strong technical skills. This can be achieved by including one or more overseas assignments in the career paths of highly skilled HR managers, introducing some of the best non-American HR talent into U.S.-based subsidiary divisions and regional headquarters staffs, assigning repatriating Americans from other functions, and providing high-potential HR practitioners with international experience early in their careers.

An IHRM function strengthened by a combination of these approaches would have the capability to develop entirely new IHRM technologies to ensure the success of globalization. Exxon and Chase Manhattan Bank have instituted one or more of these recommended approaches and have made major strides toward increasing the effectiveness of their IHRM functions. Many other firms still have a long way to go.

IBM's study of HR practitioners from around the globe identified a number of skills which will be increasingly important for IHRM in the future. These capabilities were also identified as the ones for which the widest gaps exist between current HR abilities and those which were perceived as needed in the world-class organization of the future. They included:[8]

- The ability to educate and influence line managers on IHR policies, practices, and importance;
- Being computer literate, so as to be able to use global data base for HR advice and decision making;
- Being able to anticipate internal and external changes, particularly of importance to the availability and qualification of human resources around the world;
- Exhibiting leadership for the IHRM function and within the corporation;
- Focusing on the quality of IHRM services within the corporation;
- Defining an IHRM vision of the future and communicating that to the IHR department and to the firm;
- Developing broad knowledge of many IHRM functions;
- Being willing to take appropriate risks in the development and implementation of innovative IHRM policies and practices; and
- Being able to demonstrate the financial impact of IHRM policies and practices.

SUMMARY

This last chapter provided a glimpse at the challenges that will confront IHRM in the future. These challenges will include the organizational advancement and the professionalization of IHRM. International HR managers will have to further develop their understanding of the functioning of their businesses and, as a consequence, become better integrated into the planning and strategic management of those businesses.

As these challenges are met, multinational firms will find themselves developing world class IHRM departments with these characteristics:[9]

- Responsive to a highly competitive marketplace and global business structure;
- Closely linked to business strategic plans;
- Jointly conceived and implemented by line and international HR managers in an equal partnership; and

- Focused on quality, customer service, productivity, employee involvement, teamwork, and workforce flexibility in all the firm's operations around the globe.

Only when such an integrated, responsible, and accepted IHRM is developed will IHRM reach its potential and take its rightful place in the management of today's successful global firms.

ENDNOTES

1. Evans, P. A. L., "Human Resource Management and Globalization," keynote address presented to the Third Conference on International Personnel and Human Resources Management, Ashridge Management College, Berkhamsted, Hertfordshire, U.K., July 2–4, 1992; and Evans, P., and Y. Doz, "The Dualistic Organization," in *Human Resource Management in International Firms*, eds. P. Evans, Y. Doz, and A. Laurent (London: Macmillan Press Ltd., 1989).

2. Coy, P., with J. B. Levine, J. Weber, R. Brandt, and N. Gross, "In the Labs, the Fight to Spend Less, Get More," *Business Week*, June 28, 1993, pp. 102–104.

3. Adapted from Tichy, N. M., "Setting the Global Human Resource Management Agenda for the 1990s," *Human Resource Management*, 27 (1988), 1–18.

4. Much of this section is adapted from Schuler, R. S., "World Class HR Departments: Six Critical Issues," *The Singapore Accounting and Business Review*, September 1993; and based partially on two studies conducted by Towers Perrin for IBM: "A 21st Century Vision: A Worldwide Human Resource Study" (1990) and "Priorities for Competitive Advantage" (1992).

5. Walker, J. W., and T. P. Bechet, "Defining Effectiveness and Efficiency Measures in the Context of Human Resource Strategy," HRPS Research Symposium, Newport, RI, June 1991.

6. J. Fitz-enz, *Human Value Management*, San Francisco: Jossey-Bass Publishers, 1990; and annual reports of Society for Human Resource Management/Saratoga Institute, *Human Resource Effectiveness Report* and *Human Resource Benchmarking*, Saratoga, California: Saratoga Institute.

7. Based on Reynolds, C., "Are You Ready to Make IHR a Global Function?" *HR News: International HR*, February 1992, pp. 1–3.

8. IBM/Towers Perrin, "A 21st Century Vision"; and Schuler, R., "World Class HR Departments."

9. Ibid.

Index